The People's

PLACE

SOUL FOOD RESTAURANTS AND REMINISCENCES FROM THE CIVIL RIGHTS ERA TO TODAY

DAVE HOEKSTRA

PHOTOGRAPHS BY **PAUL NATKIN**

CHICAGO
REVIEW
PRESS

Published by Chicago Review Press, Incorporated
814 North Franklin Street
Chicago, Illinois 60610

ISBN 978-1-61373-059-1

Interior design: Jonathan Hahn

Library of Congress Cataloging-in-Publication Data
Hoekstra, Dave.
 The people's place : soul food restaurants and reminiscences from the Civil Rights era to today / Dave Hoekstra ;
photographs by Paul Natkin. — First edition.
    pages cm
 Includes index.
 ISBN 978-1-61373-059-1 (cloth)
 1. African American cooking. 2. Cooking, American—Southern style. 3. Restaurants—United States. 4. African
Americans—Social life and customs. I. Title.

 TX715.2.S68H64 2015
 641.59'296073—dc23
                        2015001436

Printed in the United States of America
5 4 3 2 1

◆◆◆

I laugh when I hear that the fish in the water is thirsty.

You don't grasp the fact that what is most alive of all is inside your own house,

and so you walk from one holy city to the next with a confused look!

Kabir will tell you the truth: go wherever you like, to Calcutta or Tibet

if you can't find where your soul is hidden

for you the world will never be real.

—*"THE HIDDEN SOUL" BY KABIR, FIFTEENTH-CENTURY SUFI MASTER*

◆◆◆

FOR ALL THOSE WHO LIFTED THEIR VOICES

CONTENTS

Foreword by Chaka Khan   vii

Introduction   ix

I ◆ UP THE MISSISSIPPI RIVER

Dooky Chase's Restaurant | NEW ORLEANS, LOUISIANA   3

Mother's Restaurant | NEW ORLEANS, LOUISIANA   15

The Big Apple Inn | JACKSON, MISSISSIPPI   26

The Four Way | MEMPHIS, TENNESSEE   37

Alcenia's | MEMPHIS, TENNESSEE   48

Sweetie Pie's | ST. LOUIS, MISSOURI   58

II ◆ STORIED SOUTHERN SOUL

Odessa's Blessings | MONTGOMERY, ALABAMA   71

Paschal's Restaurant | ATLANTA, GEORGIA   79

Lassis Inn | LITTLE ROCK, ARKANSAS   94

Swett's Restaurant | NASHVILLE, TENNESSEE   105

Martha Lou's Kitchen | CHARLESTON, SOUTH CAROLINA   119

Africanne on Main | RICHMOND, VIRGINIA   130

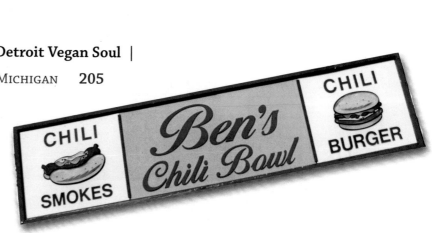

III ✦ URBAN SOUL

Marvin | WASHINGTON, DC   141

Ben's Chili Bowl | WASHINGTON, DC   149

Sylvia's Restaurant | NEW YORK, NEW YORK   161

Ruby's Restaurant | CHICAGO, ILLINOIS   171

Baker's Keyboard Lounge | DETROIT, MICHIGAN   182

New Bethel Baptist Church Kitchen | DETROIT, MICHIGAN   195

IV ✦ VEGAN SOUL

Original Soul Vegetarian & Detroit Vegan Soul |

CHICAGO, ILLINOIS & DETROIT, MICHIGAN   205

Acknowledgments   218

Index   219

Chaka Khan at the Petrillo Band Shell on June 27, 2008, in Chicago.

FOREWORD

My history with foodways goes back to when I was a teenager on the South Side of Chicago. I cofounded the Breakfast for Children program when I was president of the Calumet High School Afro Student organization. About five other people and I found this church somewhere on East Forty-Something Street. We would meet there every morning. We'd get donations from grocery stores. Lots of oatmeal. Bacon, sausage, milk. Orange juice and bread. We'd feed the kids very early at the church. We should have been more nutrition conscious with those kids but we got what we could get.

Miss Jenkins was an Afrocentric teacher at Calumet who was my role model. She helped me get the breakfast program off the ground. We staged a lot of walkouts and got a new principal instated at the school through boycotts and stuff like that. That's about the same time I joined the Black Panthers. I was wearing jeans, going barefoot, standing on the corner selling the Black Panther newspaper. I was inspired by Eldridge Cleaver's memoir *Soul on Ice* and James Baldwin's *Go Tell It on the Mountain*. I went to a lot of rallies and knew Fred Hampton [chairman of the Illinois Black Panther Party] and his brother very well. When Fred got killed [in a December 1969 FBI raid] I realized how serious this shit was. I decided to be of service in another way.

There's not a good reason for us as a people to be obese and rampant with type 2 diabetes. There can be vegan soul food. I'm now vegan six days of the week. On the seventh day I eat what I want. But there are certain things I do not eat: mushrooms, pork, any bottom feeder. I'm not a beef person. I rarely eat chicken. I make a mean pot of kale with no meat at all. I use tofu or soy-based meat products.

I've been to Sylvia's in Harlem. I love that place. I'm very good friends with Minister Louis Farrakhan and whenever I can find one of his restaurants I will go there. What does he own? Like all of Seventy-Ninth Street in Chicago. I've had dinner many times at his house. His wife, Betsy Ross, cooks the best foods, a great pumpkin soup, a brown rice dish with vegetables. It's almost Turkish in the flavoring. For dessert we have sugar-free fruitcake. It's all homemade.

My perfect meal is a large bowl of black bean soup and corn bread with salsa. My mother makes a homemade salsa that is very hearty and nutritious. I eat a lot of vegetables. I do put sugar in some things. I'll eat a piece of apple pie and frozen yogurt. That is a big treat. I used to bake my own multigrain bread. I made eggplant casseroles and lots of soups. Split pea is my favorite.

Soul is natural. Soul will always be natural.

—CHAKA KHAN, OCTOBER 2014

Chaka Khan was born Yvette Marie Stevens on March 23, 1953, in Chicago. Her blend of jazz, rock, funk, soul, disco, and pop opened the door for ten Grammy awards and twenty-two Grammy nominations. In 1999 she established the Chaka Khan Foundation, which assists children at risk through poverty or health issues like autism.

INTRODUCTION

Helen Maybell Anglin was the beloved owner of the Soul Queen Restaurant, 9031 South Stony Island in Chicago. She opened Soul Queen in 1976, although her life in Chicago soul food began in the late 1940s.

Helen fed the Rev. Jesse Jackson during the embryonic days of Operation Breadbasket, which in 1971 became Operation PUSH (People United to Save Humanity), as he worked to improve the African American economy.

Anglin died in 2009 at the age of eighty. In her nascent days as a small business owner she served civil rights marchers and invested in African American–owned businesses, including *Ebony* and *Jet* magazines. Muhammad Ali, Count Basie, and Mahalia Jackson were among the notables who dined like royalty at the Soul Queen.

In 1994 I was exploring the meaning of soul in a piece I wrote for the *Chicago Sun-Times*. Soul music is my favorite genre of American music, especially the politically charged yet sensitive Chicago soul of Jerry Butler, Curtis Mayfield, the Staple Singers, Otis Clay, and Donny Hathaway.

In a conversation over candied yams and mixed greens, Helen told me, "The soul is one of the most sensitive areas of the body. Not necessarily to be in tune, but to be sensitive and to show concern. You ask ten different people about soul and you'll get ten different answers. Soul is whatever rings your bell. But soul definitely exists within the body. It's in the mind of the observer, whether or not you can relate to that other being. It's like plugging a cord into a wall."

And food is often an overlooked cord of the civil rights movement. An unheralded number of women chefs, workers, and small business owners like Helen energized the movement.

What follows are oral histories about time and place. The conversations over food—then and now—are what construct the narrative. I chose the places for the power of their stories and for their role in the movement.

"Restaurants were very important gathering places," Rev. Jackson said over a midsummer 2014 breakfast at Ruby's (formerly Edna's) on the West Side of Chicago. "It was a water hole in the desert. You had *Jet* magazine, our bible of press relations at the time. Then you had landmark restaurants, which was more than the food. We were making $37 a week as field workers for Dr. King and Helen [Anglin] would feed us for free. Edna [Stewart] would feed us for free. We had a lot of meetings at Helen Maybell's restaurant on Fifty-Fifth Street [in Chicago].

"She would prepare eggs, grits, and sausage for Dr. King and the group. Sometimes on the side there would be pork chops! Later in the day it became potato pie. You could do so much with a potato, like George Washington Carver did. If you were without shoes and stepped on a nail or a piece of glass you could wrap your foot in the potato peelings to draw out the infection."

My template for this journey is the "Soul Food corridor," major stops that begin with the cultural blend of New Orleans and the remarkable Leah Chase, the beloved chef at Dooky Chase's restaurant. Soul food and activism migrate north from Louisiana through Jackson, Mississippi, where we meet James Meredith and the pig ear sandwich; through Memphis and St. Louis, where a former Ike and Tina Turner background singer has found new life in soul food; through Chicago and on to Aretha Franklin's church kitchen in Detroit.

Soul food cannot be ignored in the civil rights incubators of Atlanta, Montgomery, Little Rock, and the overlooked Nashville—the birthplace of the sit-in movement at diner counters. In Montgomery I did research while getting my hair cut by Dr. King's barber. I gather stories at these portals as well as the eastern borders of Washington, DC; New York City; and the slave port city of Charleston.

I look at young entrepreneurs and chefs who are redefining soul food. I taste vegan soul food. I learn about "swagger jacking" in Washington, DC.

This book is not a critical look at soul food or soul food restaurants. These are unique stories about a movement, in physical and spiritual terms.

These restaurants underscore the importance of place. Liz Williams, president of the Southern Food and Beverage Museum in New Orleans, explained, "Leah Chase's place was important because it was one of the few places you could have meetings of white and black people together. In other places you were meeting in people's homes or maybe in a church. A public place like a restaurant gave it a legitimacy—when it wasn't done in somebody's home in 'secret.'"

I tried my best to be a clarion for gallant voices. In more than 150 interviews, I heard bitterness, I saw tears, I felt anger, and I gained a deep respect for healed composure. I tried to see life through a different prism—which opens the window to greater understanding.

Throughout my writing career I have learned how food memory evokes stories. Smells, tastes, and conversation are woven into the fabric of our being. Food stirs the soul. The concept of a free country is the ability for all people to sit at a common table. Why did it take us so long?

Fifty years ago, civil rights turned a page in America. On August 10, 1965, Congress passed the Voting Rights Act of 1965, allowing southern African Americans to register to vote. Literacy tests, poll taxes, and other requirements used to restrict black voting were made illegal.

Just six weeks later—September 24, 1965—President Lyndon Johnson raised the bar, issuing Executive Order 11346, which enforced affirmative action for the first time. The law required government contractors to "take affirmative action" toward prospective minority employees in all aspects of hiring and employment.

Throughout the civil rights movement, black and white young people from the North were taking action and traveling south to work in freedom summers. Soul food and its deep roots were gaining a wider audience.

Soul food is about sense of place, for sure.

"It's interesting, sometimes as these places got bigger people wouldn't patronize them because they didn't seem to have that soulful flavor," Rev. Jackson said. "But Edna's was a real place. And a lot of these places were identified with the person who operated them: 'Edna's Place,' 'Helen Maybelle's Place.' These people were deeply involved in the community. They were members of churches and social clubs."

The term "soul food" was created in 1962 by Amiri Baraka, born in 1934 as LeRoi Jones in Newark, New Jersey. Baraka wrote a poem as a rebuttal to critics who said that African Americans had no cuisine of their own character. He insisted that hog maws, sweet potato pie, gravy and pork sausage, fried chicken, hoppin' John, hush puppies, fried fish, hoe cakes, biscuits, dumplings, and gumbo all came directly out of the South and personified top-notch African American cookery. Baraka advocated soul food as true African American cuisine. During my interviews and discussions with members of the African American community, two points were repeated to me time and again:

- Soul food is love.
- Soul food is a way to find identity within African American communities (not unlike soul music).

"Soul food" is a product of a more mobile twentieth-century society. It became a term of identification when natives left the South. "If you're southern it is *food*," said Williams of the Southern Food and Beverage Museum. "It's not *soul food*. Whether you were a redneck or poor white trash, everybody ate that food. I still eat a lot of my greens with pickled pork and pig's feet. It might have been poor people's food

but it was food. When there was a diaspora of people leaving the South and going to Chicago or Detroit the food become part of your identity. You have this food you remember on Christmas or a birthday. It becomes celebratory food. The next generation in Chicago who is not eating that food needs to have a name. Then it is called 'soul food.'"

Soul food fueled the movement, as Freedom Rider Doratha "Dodie" Smith-Simmons reminded soul food matriarch Leah Chase during one of our interviews in New Orleans. Chase, who was born in 1923, was lamenting the fact that maybe she didn't do enough for civil rights. Smith-Simmons held her hand and assured Leah that her food provided sustenance and spirit.

New Orleans Freedom Rider Doratha "Dodie" Smith-Simmons (left) with beloved nonagenarian chef Leah Chase in the kitchen of Dooky Chase's restaurant, January 2014.

Rev. Jackson said, "Cooking was a mission. I was down at Dooky Chase [in July 2014]. Leah is ninety-one. She's still in the kitchen on one cane. Dooky is eighty-six and he's there. They're in that hot kitchen every day but they love cooking and serving. Some places like Dooky Chase and Sylvia's [in Harlem] have grown to become an institution with a white and international constituency. Sometimes it is difficult for blacks to get into Sylvia's on Sunday."

Myles Horton was cofounder of the Highlander Folk School in rural Monteagle, Tennessee. The school was an incubator for the civil rights movement. In July 1955 Rosa Parks attended a two-week summer workshop on public school desegregation at Highlander. Dr. Martin Luther King Jr., Pete Seeger, and Julian Bond attended Highlander.

As early as 1934 Dr. J. Herman Daves and his wife became the first African Americans at Highlander to violate Jim Crow school laws prohibiting African Americans and whites from eating together and staying under the same roof. Many doors soon would be opened from the rural kitchen table.

As the civil rights movement developed in the late 1950s and '60s, soul food restaurants became logical meeting places. Al Bell is a record producer, songwriter, and former co-owner of the rhythm and blues Stax Records in Memphis. Bell wrote and produced the 1972 Staple Singers civil rights clarion "I'll Take You There." Bell, born in 1940 as Alvertis Isbell in Brinkley, Arkansas, has lived in North Little Rock almost all his life.

"When you look at the African American community during segregation and even after that, it's been the church, the soul food restaurants, the barber shop, and the beauty salon that have been the key institutions," he said in a June 2014 interview. "As we developed the [soul food] restaurants, we had an opportunity to do some strategizing. You could freely release yourself. You could only do so much in church. Your children were with you and you could only talk so much. This freedom was true in soul food restaurants across the country."

We talk to other artists like Bobby Rush, the "King of the Chitlin' Circuit"; Gene

Aretha Franklin, the Queen of Soul. Her father, the Rev. C. L. Franklin, was a heavenly spark for the civil rights movement.

Barge, the Operation Breadbasket band leader and Chess Records session leader; Chicago soul legend and former soul food restaurateur Syl Johnson; jazz pianist Ramsey Lewis; and Marvell Thomas, the Stax Records session player who, on the day Dr. Martin Luther King Jr. was assassinated, was picking up a soul food order in Memphis, just a few blocks from the Lorraine Motel where the civil rights leader was gunned down.

How can one write a book involving soul and not call on Aretha Franklin, "Lady Soul"?

We go to Aretha's church, the New Bethel Baptist Church on the west side of Detroit. Her late father, C. L. Franklin, was the pastor at New Bethel between 1946 and 1984. Rev. Franklin organized the 1963 "Walk Toward Freedom" with Dr. King. Aretha still hosts charity dinners at the church, replete with tableware and fine china.

The challenges of mom-and-pop minority ownership is a theme that emerged through my conversations. It reminded me of writing about baseball's Negro Leagues. Kansas City Monarchs' first baseman and manager Buck O'Neil (1911–2006) told me not to feel sorry for him. The leagues were self-sufficient because African Americans owned their own teams, hotels, and restaurants. Make no mistake, Branch Rickey integrated baseball with Jackie Robinson because he saw the green of dollar bills.

Those who know soul food the best do not think of it in terms of color.

Anglin told me: "I always try to see past what I think I see. I'm not looking to find something. We're not born equal, but we're all created equal. Everybody has soul. It's just that it doesn't always come forth. If it hits you and gets to you, you're going to respond."

Barge said many observers put African Americans "all in one boat." He elaborated, "And it is not true because we are all culturally different. The islands on the coast of the Carolinas and around Savannah they call African American geechees [or "Gullah," Sea Island Creole; descendants of African slaves]. They eat a lot of rice. African Americans who come from south Louisiana are very mixed blooded; Spanish, French, and their version of soul food is entirely different. They eat more seafood."

The future of soul food is strong, according to Amy C. Evans, lead oral historian for the Southern Foodways Alliance, an affiliated institute of the Center for the Study of Southern Culture at the University of Mississippi. "Soul food ties people to place, home, and family," she told me in the spring of 2014. "No matter what trend is happening it is something people will always hold to. When you're talking about soul food you're talking about southern food in general."

Indeed, soul food carries evocative memories. Biamani Obadek is one of Barge's compatriots who meet weekly in "The Round Table" discussion of current events and foodways at Pearl's Place, a fine soul food restaurant on the South Side of Chicago. "My family came up through Jackson, Mississippi," he said over a catfish dinner at Pearl's. "My great-grandmother Helen Thompson was the first family to move into Robert Taylor [housing projects]."

The now-demolished Chicago Housing Authority projects were built in 1962 in the Bronzeville neighborhood just a few blocks from Pearl's Place. Baseball star Kirby Puckett and basketball great Maurice Cheeks grew up in Robert Taylor. Obadek said, "The bottom line is I remember the days of the hoe cakes. You could smell them throughout the whole project. People would come knocking at my great-grand-mother's door. These were biscuits she made with Carnation powdered milk, flour, butter, and Alaga [named for Alabama-Georgia] syrup. We were poor but we didn't know that because everybody wanted to eat what you were eating."

These oral histories stir the spirit of this book.

Rev. Jackson has strong food memories of Dr. King. He was on the balcony of Room 306 at the Lorraine Motel in Memphis on April 4, 1968, the night that Dr. King was assassinated. Dr. King and Rev. Jackson often ate at the adjacent Lorraine Coffee Shop (now closed) and ordered "well-seasoned" food for room service. But that evening Dr. King had requested soul food, cooked up by Gwen Kyles and members of her husband Rev. Samuel "Billy" Kyles's Monumental Baptist Church.

Rev. Jackson and the Operation Breadbasket Band from Chicago were invited to the dinner that would have included ham hocks, chitlins, spaghetti, corn bread, ice cream, and more. "We had the mood set where they could just relax," Gwen Kyles said in the 1990 Joan Turner Beifuss book *At the River I Stand*, an account of Rev.

(Left) Room 306 at the Lorraine Motel. Dr. King was standing on the balcony of this room when he was assassinated on the evening of April 4, 1968. The King entourage booked rooms 306 and 307. The rooms are now part of the National Civil Rights Museum. (Right) The National Civil Rights Museum at the Lorraine Motel in Memphis, Tennessee, on Dr. Martin Luther King Jr.'s birthday, 2014.

King's final trip to Memphis. Relaxation was a key tonic in civil rights soul food gatherings.

The group never ate their meal.

"The Lorraine Motel and restaurant were a healing place," Rev. Jackson said. "People don't realize that Mrs. [Loree] Bailey, who ran the restaurant, had a heart attack [other reports say she had a stroke] and died after Dr. King was shot." Loree Bailey was the wife of hotel owner Walter Bailey. He named the hotel after his wife in a nod to the hit song "Sweet Lorraine."

President Bill Clinton evoked soul in his hefty 2004 memoir *My Life*. During segregation in Hope, Arkansas, his grandfather ran a grocery store that catered to an integrated clientele. In the winter of 1969 while studying at Oxford University in England, President Clinton read Black Panther Party leader Eldridge Cleaver's *Soul on Ice* to get his head around the meaning of soul.

"Soul is a word I use often enough to be Black," Clinton wrote, before pondering Cleaver's definition—"'The soul: I know what it is—it is where I feel things; it's what moves me; it's what makes me a man, and when I put it out of commission, I know soon enough I will die if I do not retrieve it.'"—and concluding, "I was afraid then I was losing it."

Everyone can gather around the kitchen table and talk about soul. Take your time. A camaraderie develops. Honor yesterday and digest tomorrow's ideas. Pearl's Place round table veteran Rudolph Brown said, "The food was the magnet for the mettle. We asked, 'Why can't we do better?'"

Keep an open mind.

Soul will find you.

—DAVE HOEKSTRA, AUGUST 2014

Part 1

Up the Mississippi River

DOOKY CHASE'S RESTAURANT

◆◆◆

2301 Orleans Avenue, New Orleans, Louisiana
(504) 821-0600 • www.dookychaserestaurant.com

LEAH CHASE WAS BORN IN RURAL LOUISIANA IN 1923. She is the oldest of eleven children. Before "Mrs. Chase"—as she is known to locals—was a world-famous chef she was a boxing manager. On a warm afternoon in January 2014, Mrs. Chase smiles at the fading glimpse of that memory.

"Joe Louis came to my school, St. Mary's Academy [in New Orleans]," she says while sitting at a table in the kitchen of Dooky Chase's restaurant in the Fifth Ward. "He was boxing's world champion. He showed that you could do anything. I managed a couple of lightweights in the early 1940s. I studied all the [boxing] books I could find. You look at the shoulder, you got to sweat them out."

Mrs. Chase gets by in a walker, but it doesn't prevent her from preparing her famous gumbo and gravy on a daily basis at the most famous gathering place of civil rights leaders in New Orleans.

Mrs. Chase places her curled left index finger on the empty kitchen table.

She slowly shifts her finger along an imaginary checkerboard. She deals a satisfied smile. "When I was coming up you had to find your own way," she says. Her finger is frail but fast as it traces the past. "You go here, but that's not going to work," she says. "But don't move your finger off because if you move your finger off, someone is going to jump you. Then you go to the next one. And the next one."

Heavyweight boxing champion Joe Louis was an early hero of Leah Chase. Louis (second from left) is promoting his beverage with Edgar Dooky Chase Sr. (second from right) at the restaurant. *Courtesy of Dooky Chase's*

Dooky Chase's circa 1940s.

Courtesy of Dooky Chase's

She is always moving forward.

Mrs. Chase grew up in a black-and-white world but has made New Orleans a better place because of her understanding of colors. Dooky Chase's opened in 1939 as a bar at the corner of Orleans and Miro Streets in a neighborhood of African Americans, Italian Americans, and some Chinese Americans. In 1941 it moved to its present location.

Riverfront workers and longshoremen began eating po'boys, set up with Scotch and 7-Up. Sometimes Dooky Chase Sr. gambled with the workers in the back of the bar. Because of a segregated banking system the workers would also cash their checks at Dooky Chase's.

Mrs. Chase's gumbo has been the great common denominator.

"It is the gumbo that Creoles of color made," she says. "You go into any local home and you're going to have that same taste. You're going to have the shrimp, the crabs, sausage, chicken. And ham and veal stew. You had to make it hearty enough to be a main meal. The veal stew gave it no flavor, but picked up the flavors from the other things. It is soul food with all your heart. It's not the food, it is what you put into it.

"When I'm fixing this food I'm thinking of who is going to be happy."

She scolded Barack Obama for putting Tabasco sauce on her gumbo. In August 2006 the future president was the commencement speaker at Xavier University. He stopped at Dooky Chase's for lunch. "We told him you don't use Tabasco, uh-uh," she says. "George W. [Bush], what a kind man he was. Not a good president, but a kind man. Every time he came to New Orleans he sent security for me. We had dinner at Commander's Palace. They had me sit right next to him. After dinner he asked me to fix breakfast. I didn't want to do it, but how do you turn down a president? So I fixed breakfast here [in April 2008]. He brought the president of Mexico [Felipe Calderon] and the prime minister of Canada [Stephen Harper]. I gave President Bush shrimp and baked cheese grits, which he never had before. He loved it."

Mrs. Chase is also an avid art collector and dozens of paintings adorn the restaurant that is accented with white tablecloths and smooth Victorian chairs.

The elegance of Dooky Chase's: The restaurant bounced back after Hurricane Katrina with the help of volunteers from all over America.

Chef Leah Chase is one of the most avid collectors of African American art in the south. The Main Dining Room and Victorian Room of Dooky Chase's showcase her collection.

"Karl Rove [former White House deputy chief of staff] came in a couple months ago," she says. "He said, 'You know your friend [President Bush] is painting now.' I said, 'Can't tell by me. I don't see a thing by George W. on my walls.' [hearty laugh] All the presidents are well and good but they come and go. But it is the everyday person that never forgets you.

"That is what has given me the energy and courage to go on."

Doratha "Dodie" Smith-Simmons is sitting next to Chase in the kitchen. Smith-Simmons was a task force member of the Congress of Racial Equality (CORE), a test rider for the 1961 Freedom Rides, and a youth member of the NAACP. The Freedom Riders came from all over the United States on interstate buses to protest segregation, poor housing, and other shackled measures in the South. Smith-Simmons and Mrs. Chase are sisters of the soul. "Dooky Chase was the only restaurant that allowed blacks and whites," she says. "When I was arrested in 1961 for picketing at the police station our lawyers came here for food [fried chicken and shrimp po'boys]. We didn't eat jail food. The third time I was arrested was over Easter; Mrs. Chase sent baked ham, potato salad, green peas, everything. So I enjoyed going to jail!"

Mrs. Chase considers the not-so-distant past for a few quiet moments.

Then she says, "Deep down, I feel in some ways this restaurant really changed the course of America. This was a safe haven for all of us. We fed everybody. We had an upstairs dining room where people met. The Republic of New Afrika came upstairs and I said, 'Look, take your chip off your shoulder. I'm going to feed you, you're going to abide by my rules, and I'm going to respect you.' And there was no trouble with the Republic of New Afrika [a favorite target of the FBI]. Big Daddy King [Dr. King's father] always came here. Dr. Sam Cook [president of Dillard University, 1975–1997] used to bring in all the people and Big Daddy King. He was a stickler for introducing these people to his young students. Big Daddy King was fun. He'd say, 'Sister, I want you to come and cook for me.' I had a better relationship with him than his son.

"Dr. King was like a prophet. He didn't come to eat or drink. He came for special things. He would sit down with Judge Augustine, Dr. Mitchell, and Dooky at night. Thurgood Marshall would come and eat his gumbo and crawfish on the floor. Dr. King wasn't like that. It's like he was always on a mission."

Judge Marshall was a compatriot of civil rights attorney Ernest "Dutch" Morial, the first African American mayor of New Orleans. In 1954 Morial was the first African American graduate of the Louisiana State University School of Law. Morial and A. P. Turlow had offices in a former French hospital down the street from the restaurant. In the upstairs room of Dooky Chase's, Marshall and Turlow planned integration strategies in the Crescent City, with schools being the first target. The community became empowered when Morial became mayor.

James Baldwin wrote in the corner of the bar. James Meredith ate at Dooky Chase's.

"I'm here every day," she says. "I stay in the kitchen. I do all my own basic cooking. I get help because I can't carry the pots like I used to."

She stops and considers a secret. "I love the *White Trash Cooking* cookbook," she says. "It's a bad name, but those recipes are what they are. What the heck? I have *Cracker Cookin'* out of Florida. But I don't look at the foods as much as I look at the pictures of the people. You look at life the same way.

"You might not like what you see the first time, but look again and you're going to see something different."

Leah Chase was born in Madisonville, Louisiana, about fifty miles across Lake Pontchartrain. Charles and Hortensia Lange had thirteen children, but Mrs. Chase's older sister Claudia died at about eighteen months. And younger sibling Myra died at nine months.

"It was tough and then here comes the Great Depression in '29," she says. "So we had nothing but what my daddy could grow. He was a caulker in the shipyards. But his big thing was farming and planting. He loved the soil."

Charles Lange was proud of how even his rows of crops were. He told his children to plant every onion twelve inches apart. "That way the onions could grow real big," she says. "Food came to our table like that. You raised a hog primarily for the lard. If we got the hog to three hundred pounds, we knew you were going to get one hundred pounds of lard off of that. We preserved the pork by cooking it and preserving it in its own lard.

"I remember purslane grass. My daddy's crops were low and he didn't have hardly anything. So they had this wild grass. My mother would say, 'Go pick it, but don't let the neighbors see you doing that because they'll know we're so poor, we're eating this wild grass.' It cooked like spinach, really. So when I get up in the world and go to Citi's restaurant in California, I order the liver, twenty-five dollars a plate or whatever—here's purslane on my plate! Doggone it, I've been eating it free all my life."

The entire kitchen staff laughs.

"It's been a good life for me," says Mrs. Chase, who at age twenty-four lost the top half of her right index finger in a bout with rheumatic fever. "My daddy taught us to never worry and never cry in public. I remember when my mother died. He got home and went in the bathroom and cried. He told us three things: you pray, you work, and you do for others. Now, my mother was different. She was what old people called 'sassy.' She gave all us girls plaques, 'How to Be a Woman.' First, you had to look like a girl. You had to act like a lady. You had to think like a man—don't try to be like that man. And work like a dog! Those are the rules I have tried to live by, but I had a lot of help.

"Nobody can grow by themselves."

In the mid-1940s Mrs. Chase was attending a concert by the Dooky Chase (II) Jazz Orchestra. The trumpet player Dooky Chase (II) spotted her in the audience.

They married in 1946 and she began working in her father-in-law's kitchen in 1950. She was serving up the right food at the dawn of the civil rights movement.

Mrs. Chase reflects, "Even our own people would say, 'You're nothing but a cook.' They don't realize I'm feeding a lot of people so they can do what they have to do. I can energize them with my food and that is my contribution to their work. But we took it all for granted. You have to make a difference.

"And that is what I'm still fighting today."

And she is ninety-one years old on this day.

Mrs. Chase's work resonated across America. Her contributions are not lost on someone like Minnijean Brown, a Congressional Gold Medal winner and one of the bold Little Rock Nine who integrated Little Rock Central High School in 1957. "Her persistence is a form of activism," Brown says from her home outside Vancouver, Canada. "It is hard to do that over time. And she did it. Everybody can't march and do all the things that are thought of in activism. But people do things under horrible circumstances. I've eaten there. I have her cookbook. I have great admiration for this person."

Mrs. Chase says, "Martin Luther King died for me to work. He died for me to be part of a community. He died for me to get a good salary. Well, I don't get a good salary. But you make a difference." She nods to Smith-Simmons, who is listening from her right-hand side. Mrs. Chase says, "I will go to my grave admiring them [Freedom Riders]. I don't know how they did what they did. It energizes me. I just keep going. I can't give up."

Mrs. Chase was an early member of the NAACP. In 2011 the American Civil Liberties Union of Louisiana presented Mrs. Chase with its highest honor for her lifetime of work promoting racial equality.

A catalyst for the political activity at Dooky Chase's was "the

Leah Chase in her kitchen, January 2014.

Freedom House," operated by Oretha Castle Haley at 917 N. Tonti, two blocks from the restaurant. The Freedom Riders would stay at the house because they were in safe quarters. James Baldwin and Stokely Carmichael stayed at the house. They would meet at Dooky Chase's to mobilize college students. Smith-Simmons and Mrs. Chase believe a historic marker should be placed in front of the house.

"You met people who accepted you for what you are as long as they are good things. You don't change yourself. Dooky worked for the NAACP, he believed in that. But he didn't want to offend anybody. Ben Smith organized the ACLU here," Mrs. Chase says.

Dooky Chase's weathered the storm. The worst physical transgression against the restaurant was when someone in a passing car threw a pipe bomb through a front window. "They used to send us ugly things in the mail," Mrs. Chase says. "Such terrible things. This was at the beginning of the movement. We didn't have black policemen. My mother and father-in-law were popular. They didn't bother us much because they knew us."

A majestic picture of Dooky Chase II hangs in the bar. Every Mardi Gras day his band would perform in the bar. The doors would be wide open and people danced in the street. "When you think about how jazz moves your body and makes you want to dance, a good meal makes you want to dance and your body feels good about eating," Edgar Dooky Chase III says during a conversation in the restaurant's bar. "Soul food and soul music is the same thing."

Ray Charles referenced Dooky Chase's in his 1952 hit "Early in the Morning." The waitress he sang about was Virgi Castle of the Freedom House. "She worked the night shift at the bar," Chase III says. "And she had a way of keeping men in their place."

"Virgi was one of the strongest women I ever came across," Mrs. Chase declares. "They were very quiet at what they did [at the Freedom House]. I did take a stand as I do now for what I believe in and shout out when I don't like something."

Music could be a bonding force. The restaurant also sold concert tickets to the African American community. Chase III recalls, "In the 1950s and '60s before there was a Ticketmaster, if you wanted to buy a ticket for anything in the African American community you had to purchase your ticket at Dooky's. James Brown would come here and eat. We almost operated twenty-four hours a day. We opened at 10:30 in the morning and on the weekends we didn't close until 5:30 in the morning."

It took time for change to come to Dooky Chase's. "Even after the Civil Rights Act of 1964 things were still not integrated," Chase III says. "It gave us kind of a monopolistic market. Dizzy Gillespie, Duke Ellington, civil rights leaders would come. Poor people. NAACP people. Black ministers came here and became a political powerhouse because they believed they could organize voters through the pulpit. We went into every ward of the city and tried to register people to vote.

"Civil rights should be every man's right."

Smith-Simmons says, "The first time I was arrested in 1961 we had a sit-in at the police station and started singing. They said, 'Stop the singing.' And we sang louder and louder. So they brought the police dogs out. And we started [and she sings] 'Ain't gonna let no police dogs turn us 'round, 'round.' They took the dogs away and arrested us. That goes back to slavery days. Singing was like a prayer."

Mrs. Chase understands the sacrifices Smith-Simmons and other Freedom Riders made. She says, "Who wants to see your daughter going to jail? But they did what they had to do to move on and get the work done. We didn't support them like we should have. I fed them every day, but we should have given moral support. We didn't want our children going to jail. But they went to jail for us."

Smith-Simmons counters, "Our parents were the real heroes of the civil rights movement. If my mother had said, 'You're not going down there to picket,' Dodie would have been home. But they supported us. Dooky Chase's was the first first-class restaurant for blacks. The first Freedom Ride was supposed to end here on May 17 [1961]. We had a banquet scheduled for Dooky Chase's and this is where all the Freedom Riders were going to come. We had to feed them and that's where Mrs. Chase came in."

Mrs. Chase comes in and says, "I'm an old George Patton fan. He was tough."

Edgar Dooky Chase III was born on May 10, 1949. He grew up as a waiter in the restaurant.

"I first worked the bar but I was never good at the bar because I don't drink much," he says. "Most of the customers at that time were people who worked on the river. ILA [International Longshoremen's Association] workers. I thought you had to put ice in everything. I'd put ice in their beer and they'd say, 'What's with this young man?' so my dad said I couldn't work the bar.

"But the bar was a very big thing. The bar doesn't look the way it looks now, but people would be lined up about six deep." Chase III is wearing a sharp green tie that would put him at home at Pat O'Brien's in the French Quarter. His tie matches the green walls of the bar. "I love the color green," he says. "It has nothing to do with money or the Irish."

Frank Maselli walks into the bar from the other room.

"We went to high school together," Chase III says with a nod to Maselli. "He's older than me by one year."

Maselli is chairman of the New Orleans American-Italian Cultural Center and is on the board of the Chicago-based National Italian American Sports Hall of Fame. Maselli has just finished lunch with Deana Martin, daughter of Dean Martin, and former NFL quarterbacks Vince Ferragamo and Daryle Lamonica, who are in town for a cultural center charity event. "The best chicken in the whole world," Lamonica says. "The okra was great in the gumbo. You can't eat this food in California. I have good memories of playing in New Orleans. We always beat the Saints, but they were just getting started."

Martin is in town to accept the Louis Prima Award for comic Joe Piscopo. She says, "This is like Italian food, with family and love."

This kind of cross culture continues to define Dooky Chase's even today. Mrs. Chase loves spaghetti and meatballs.

"My mother serves that every Wednesday," Chase III says. "We spice up the meatballs [Creole style with garlic, onions, and black pepper]. She likes to eat her own food

Edgar Dooky Chase III grew up as a waiter in Dooky Chase's. He loves his mother's spicy spaghetti and meatballs.

so that's great for her. If you asked her what kind of food she would want on her own birthday, it would be meatballs and spaghetti."

While holding Deana Martin's new LP in one hand, Maselli reflects, "In the early 1940s the French Quarter was called 'Little Palermo.' The Palermo family is quality people, which is the same here. It is all about doing good for others."

Now a predominantly African American neighborhood, the Fifth Ward was multicultural when Chase III was growing up. "Sheriff Harry Lee, who is now deceased, was Chinese American," he recalls. "They operated laundries and bars further down on Clairborne Avenue. Sheriff Lee would gauge his business off our business. His father would tell him, 'Harry, it's slow down here. Go see what Dooky's is doing down on Orleans and Miro. If Dooky's is slow, we know it's just a slow period.' The point was that the mixture of cultures was so influential in New Orleans, all ethnic groups felt welcome."

Like the rest of the city, life changed at Dooky Chase's after Hurricane Katrina hit on August 28, 2005. The restaurant did not reopen until April 2007. Volunteers from across America and many fundraisers helped the flooded landmark get back on its feet. The entire two-hundred-seat restaurant was redone, from carpeting to ceiling. "The city used to be open twenty-four hours a day," Chase III says. "All the time we would close at four in the morning. Now we don't open for dinner except for Friday. We're trying to do better but the city is more structured right now. For example, my family and I used to eat our dinner at eleven o'clock or midnight. Now we eat dinner at seven or eight.

"Spiritually, Katrina cleansed our soul. It made us open to the world because we saw people all over the world helping us. You can't but love people who help you.

"Soul is something spiritual," he says. "Soul transcends your body. It hovers over you. That sense of soul is a sense of permanency. It's the *me* with food or music. No force can destroy it."

Creole Sausage Stuffed Tomatoes

My mother, Leah, loves a Sunday Brunch. The restaurant used to be open seven days a week; especially on the weekends, the restaurant was always booming. As my mother has aged, she is aware that to do all that she used to do is not practical. Since Katrina, the restaurant hours have been cut back, although the restaurant is still booming with business when it opens from Tuesday through Fridays. Still, mother dreams of having her Sunday Brunch. She loves seeing women dressed to the nines after noon religious services on Sundays in New Orleans. Fortunately, her grandson, Dooky IV (Dook, as we all call him), may give his grandmother her dream as he takes over (just on Sundays that is) as the head chef for Sunday Brunch on Dooky's. At the very least, this may be the case on the first Sunday of every month. Chef Dook is a Le Cordon Bleu Paris trained chef. He can bring this recipe and deliver Sunday Brunch at Dooky's to his grandmother's complete satisfaction. Now that gift of love would put another smile on Leah's face. —Dooky Chase III

(Serves 6)

Ingredients

6 tomatoes
1 tablespoon butter
½ pound pork sausage
½ pound Creole hot sausage (Chaurice)
¼ cup chopped onions
2 tablespoons chopped bell pepper

2 tablespoons chopped celery
1 clove garlic (mashed and chopped)
2 teaspoons salt
1 tablespoon chopped parsley
½ teaspoon ground thyme
¼ teaspoon cayenne pepper
½ cup bread crumbs

Directions

Preheat oven to 375°F. Cut top from tomatoes and remove pulp. Place pulp in a bowl. In a skillet, place a tablespoon of butter; add pork and creole sausage. Mix meats together well while cooking (5 minutes). Add onions, bell pepper, celery, garlic, salt, parsley, thyme, and cayenne pepper to the tomato pulp. Mix the ingredients and let cook for 10 to 15 minutes. Tighten the mixture with the bread crumbs. Stuff tomatoes with sausage stuffing and sprinkle tops with remaining bread crumbs and dot with butter. Bake for about 10 minutes. Do not overcook or tomatoes will fall.

MOTHER'S RESTAURANT

◆◆◆

401 Poydras Street, New Orleans, Louisiana
(504) 523-9656 • www.mothersrestaurant.net

THE WINDOW INTO SOUL IS OPENED WITH YOUR HEART.
Patricia Ellzey has done everything in her decades at the historic Mother's Restaurant in the Central Business District of New Orleans. She has seen it all.

Ellzey started at Mother's in 1989 as a dishwasher and has since made sandwiches, been a greeter, done deliveries, worked behind the bar, and served New Jersey governor Chris Christie—by her account a nice guy who loved the Ferdi po'boy (baked ham, roast beef, debris, and gravy).

"Some of them come in with a complaint," Ellzey says on a warm afternoon in January 2014. "After I get done talking to them they say, 'I'll be back tomorrow.' You have to try something in life. Say they want Mae's omelet. I explain that Mae's [named after Mother's beloved chef] consists of black ham, green onion, and mushroom. We are famous for the ham. They dice up the black ham with vegetables and put it into an omelet. With grits and biscuits."

Ellzey describes the famous po'boy to a well-dressed tourist. The original po'boy was a sandwich made from hot gravy and scraps of roast beef ladled onto French bread and sold to "poor boys" from the back doors of restaurants during a railroad strike.

She smiles.

Born on June 2, 1954, Ellzey grew up with her mother, Alberta, and six siblings in the since-razed Desire housing projects in the Lower Ninth Ward. Soul singer Barbara George, who had a nationwide 1961 hit "I Know (You Don't Love Me No More)," spent her youth in Desire. Musicians cut their chops at the Desire Community Center.

Patricia Ellzey's most precious gift is her un-bending spirit.

The projects consisted of two floors, and 260 buildings were simply labeled as A, B, C, and D. Residents called the entire projects "the Dirty D."

"Soul food is from the heart," Ellzey says during a lunch break. "So when you're fixing food for other people you are going to fix it with love as if you are fixing it for yourself. I grew up in Desire and I had a lot of trials and tribulations. It taught me a lot. It taught me to accept what I have and not try to get more than what I want. Smile, keep on going, and keep your head up."

"At Desire they had a [food] truck named Mama Quill. They sold snowballs. People sold food out of their house: chicken, stuffed bell pepper, baked macaroons, potato salad, cake. I was twelve."

Ellzey was enamored with food. She started attending cooking school at St. Maurice Parochial School in a "step-up" program designed to help young women move forward in life. On a job research assignment she interviewed Mother's owner Jerry Amato.

Amato hired Ellzey the next morning.

In his collection of essays *What Are People For?* regionalist Wendell Berry wrote, "A human community, if it is to last long, must exert a sort of centripetal force, holding local soil and memory in place. Practically speaking, human society has no work more important than this."

And this is Mother's.

In 1938 Simon and Mary Landry opened Mother's in a former diner at 401 Poydras. The cafeteria became a gathering place for African Americans. The corner of Poydras and Tchoupitoulas Streets was a working-class neighborhood with banana wharfs, spice companies, and meat-packing plants.

When Mother's opened there were no hotels around the restaurant like there are today. Regular customers included longshoremen and newspaper people from the *Times-Picayune* down the street. The Debris sandwich was named after retired *Times-Picayune* advertising rep Larry DeBuys. He told Simon Landry not to forget

Mother's has been a meeting place for charity and soul since 1938. *Courtesy of Mother's*

the roast beef remnants that fell into the gravy in the pan while the meat was being sliced.

Mary Landry treated her regulars in motherly fashion.

Mother's moved one building over in 1965 to its current location, a brick shipping and receiving building built in the 1850s. An adjacent dining room is in an 1850s-era tobacco warehouse and visitors can still see the old tobacco elevator shaft. The latest addition, simply known as "the Third Room," is in a turn-of-the-twentieth-century power utility station with exposed brick and a skylight. President George W. Bush dined in the Third Room. Mother's fed President Bush and his party a family-style menu of étouffée, gumbo, jambalaya, and red beans and rice at a U-shaped table they'd requested.

"The only special food request I had was that [daughter] Barbara Bush wanted a salad," says Jerry Amato, who was born in 1950. "So they all got salads. I was in

Creole-Italian jambalaya with Creole tomato and herbs sauce.

the kitchen and they sent somebody out to watch me cook. We did not talk politics. I was honored to have a sitting president come to the restaurant, as much of a screw-up as Hurricane Katrina was. That will always be with me. About an hour after they left, [actor] Rob Lowe came in and sat down. I talked with him for about an hour. He was a regular guy with his wife and kids. But there's a continuous scene here. It's always been in the middle of the Central Business District. It's across the street from the federal courthouse. It appeals to everybody. It's not dressy. It's home-cooked food.

"People come here to shoot the fat."

Today you will find a mix of working-class local African Americans and tourists frequenting Mother's, a rumble of mayhem and merriment known for its po'boys and the "World's Best Baked Ham." The sandwich makers used to take orders directly. When Mother's switched to cashiers who took orders, their shtick was to yell at customers to move along their orders. There are lines out the door even on a January weekday. Locals like to say Mother's is a local restaurant that has been discovered by tourists. On a good Saturday, three thousand people will roll through Mother's.

If you want to touch the rugged heart of New Orleans, this is the place.

Jerry Amato, a second-generation Sicilian, bought the restaurant from the Landrys in 1986. One of the first things the chef-proprietor introduced to the menu was a Creole-Italian jambalaya with Creole tomato and herbs sauce instead of the Cajun spicy and brown sauce. Louisianans like to debate which came first, red or brown sauce.

Italian Americans can get lost in the discussion of New Orleans cuisine. By the late 1800s a large number of Sicilians had settled in New Orleans, and in 1906 Salvatore Lupo opened the Central Grocery in the French Quarter. The section of the quarter became known as "Little Palermo."

Jerry's nephew, John Dennis "Denny" Amato Jr., is the general manager of Mother's. Denny Amato understands the diversity of the menu, which captures the sounds of Louis Prima, the Neville Brothers, and Louis Armstrong.

John Dennis "Denny" Amato, Jr. is the general manager of Mother's. He is the nephew of owner Jerry Amato, a second-generation Sicilian in New Orleans.

"One of my first memories is the smell of Central Grocery," says Denny, who grew up in the early 1970s in Old Metairie, outside of the city. "We would go down there every Saturday as a family. What I've learned at least in my lifetime, in this city the music and food, the cultures, blend together. Our food is part Italian, part Creole, part soul. Now we're introducing a Spanish component to the city we haven't seen and it will be interesting to see where that evolution goes. Post-Katrina we've seen the influx of Hondurans, Guatemalans, Mexicans, and Spanish-speaking people in general. One of my chefs has made me a Honduran hot sauce which is absolutely fabulous."

Popular tamale po'boy stands have popped up in Metairie and other ports outside of New Orleans where new immigrants have settled, serving spicy beef encased in cornmeal served on a traditional po'boy roll.

But some traditions remain firm at Mother's. Denny says, "The [shrimp or crawfish] étouffée is Jerry's recipe, the [seafood] gumbo is his recipe." Mother's serves gulf shrimp; in the 1950s shrimp came from the Mississippi River. Denny adds, "Before they did fried seafood only on Fridays. They served seafood until they ran out then they shut the doors at 1:30 in the afternoon. We do it every day. We're a 7 AM to 10 PM business now."

Ironically, Mother's is closed on Mother's Day, as well as Easter and Thanksgiving.

In a year Mother's cooks more than 136,000 pounds of ham. The baked ham is succulent and sweet with a glaze that creates a crispy, caramelized black ham. "The glaze came with the restaurant," Jerry says. "I am the only one that knows the recipe. And it is an old family recipe we will never give out. All the recipes were Mrs. Landry's: the baked spaghetti pie, the black-eyed peas and rice. I might have seasoned them a little more. They were never written down. I just watched the Landry's great-aunt. I made the glaze for twenty-seven years."

The Amatos no longer use lard but still use ham scraps and trimmings for seasoning.

Beyoncé and Jay Z visited Mother's in February 2013 when they were in town for Super Bowl XLVII. Beyoncé ordered catfish with double grits. Jay Z had fried calamari, and they each enjoyed crawfish étouffée. Beyoncé tweeted a photo of herself at the cafeteria—after that got out the restaurant was mobbed. Over the next couple days actor Neil Patrick Harris showed up as did many Baltimore Ravens players.

"We had the Rev. Jesse Jackson and Martha Stewart in here at the same time in the same room," Danny Amato says. "But they didn't sit together." Crosby, Stills, and Nash and Aerosmith's Steven Tyler have enjoyed meals at Mother's.

The most popular item on the Mother's menu is the Ferdi po'boy. The sandwich is named after the late Ferdinand "Ferdi" Stern, who owned the Interstate Electric Company. He was a member of the Stern family, who owned WDSU-TV (NBC) in New Orleans. One day over lunch he asked Simon Landry to add a little roast beef on his ham sandwich.

Landry named the sandwich "the Ferdi." Jerry explains, "So then his nephew Ralph comes in and says, 'Mr. Landry, why don't you put some cheese on that sandwich?' So they called the Ferdi with cheese 'the Ralph.' Those were the first two hits and they are still on the menu. It is the same sandwich it was fifty years ago."

Denny Amato says, "The crawfish étouffée is an outstanding dish, one I enjoy better. The seafood gumbo is interesting. Brandon [Estrada], one of my managers, comes from some of the fine dining restaurants in this city. He said, 'You realize you are the only restaurant that starts and makes its own crab stock, you start with the hard shells and go through this effort.' He said that's what drew him to our restaurant. We do everything old school. We're not buying crab stock, we buy crabs. We waste a lot in the process but it is the way it was originally done."

In 1938 the Landrys hired cook Mae "Odie Mae" Peters, originally from Columbia, Mississippi. Odie Mae worked at Mother's for nearly fifty years. She trained nieces and cousins who currently work in the kitchen, including chef Pat Santiago. "My aunt taught me when I was six years old," she says. "They would put us on a little bench and we would stir the pots. We would watch to see what ingredients they put in the pots. The recipes were in their mind. They never measured anything. My aunt made an awesome tea cake. They cut it up like a patty.

"A lot of people don't know anything about my aunt. She worked in the fields before she came to New Orleans. We farmed, we did peas, cotton, tomatoes. We dug the sweet potatoes out of the ground. I did that when I was a little girl. We don't know how my aunt found Mother's. She worked for the Landrys at first.

"But when she found Mother's, we found Mother's."

Santiago's sister Betty Hamilton also cooks at the restaurant. Hamilton earned the nickname "Rambo" by frantically moving around the hot kitchen with a towel around her head. She started at Mother's in 1988 and has also done a little bit of everything. "Our jobs are a family thing, just like Mother's," says Hamilton, born in 1954.

Server Janet Grant delivers the signature Ferdi sandwich, a po'boy packed with baked ham, roast beef, debris, and original au jus gravy. Debris is the roast beef that falls into the au jus gravy while baking in the oven.

Family is the heartbeat of Mother's. Late sons Eddie and Jack Landry were marines who came home from World War II and ran the restaurant with their parents.

"It's a beautiful business," the sons told the *Times-Picayune* in February 1979. They recalled that Mother's was a small Greek sandwich shop in 1938 and their father bought it "mainly to give our mother something to do."

Simon Landry was an ambulance driver in World War I. Eddie and Jack's sister, Frances Landry, was the first female marine in the state of Louisiana.

The marine command used to be in the neighborhood and Mother's became a destination point for the military. A wall on the kitchen side of the restaurant features twenty-eight photos of military brass who have visited Mother's, including the Times Square kissing couple that appeared on the famous 1945 V-J Day cover of *Life* magazine. Kissing sailor Glenn McDuffie autographed the Mother's photo and left a card that says his image is "forensically verified" since several men have claimed to be the sailor in the mother of all V-J Day photographs.

The wall on the river side of the restaurant has another fifty-eight photographs. Because New Orleans is situated on a bend in the Mississippi River, the city is curved, which is how it got its Crescent City name. As a result, terms like "west" and "south" are rarely used. Locals say "river side," "lake side," "uptown," or "downtown." For example, the Amato's beloved Central Grocery is downriver from Mother's.

Mother's is a designated TUN Tavern, named after the Philadelphia tavern where the marines were organized in the 1700s. Jerry Amato is designated honorary sergeant major in the Marine Corps.

Mardi Gras is the busiest time of the year at Mother's. Denny Amato says, "This is home-cooked food just about the food. The ambiance is glued together over the years. As long you serve a good product consistently people will come back."

Mother's closed for six weeks after Hurricane Katrina. Jerry Amato arranged to provide thirteen FEMA trailers for staff. They were placed in the parking lot. He handled all the paperwork.

Denny says, "We didn't have any water problem; we had a little roof damage. Our big issue was food rot. We gave away as much as we could as long as we could. Our last manager before we closed heard gunshots, then ran. He ended up with ten thousand, twelve thousand pounds' worth of raw product in a walk-in cooler on the third floor. The firemen were taking the food, the hotels were trying to feed who they could. It was the worst thing I have seen in my life."

How hard was it for the family to get through Katrina and its aftereffects?

"For me it turned into a very exciting time," Denny answers. "I know that sounds terrible. But I ended up feeding city hall for a month and a half, using other restaurants. The city's food contractor didn't show up. I'm a lucky man, my house didn't flood. My parents' did. But I'm a bad example of what really happened in the city. It was a giant fishing camp. There was nothing but men running around, playing cards and drinking. We were trying our best to put things back together. If nothing else it brought us closer as a family inside this restaurant. I call them lifers."

In the winter of 2014, there were eighteen staff members left of the ninety-nine who had worked at Mother's for more than twenty years. Denny Amato says, "These people are going to be with me and my family until the day we pass."

Jerry's Jambalaya

Please note that the recipe calls for a Creole tomato sauce (recipe follows). You will need to make that first. This is considered a Creole-Italian jambalaya because it includes tomatoes and Italian herbs. To the north and west of New Orleans, in Cajun country, one would not see those ingredients included—Cajun jambalaya is always brown and typically includes spicier ingredients. This is a source of endless and contentious debate in Louisiana . . . which version is authentic?

(Serves 6)

Ingredients

2 ounces butter

1 cup diced onions, divided into two half-cups

3/4 cup white rice

2 cups chicken stock (divided into two separate cups)

3 bay leaves

8 ounces smoked sausage, sliced

8 ounces chicken, diced in large chunks

1/2 cup diced celery

½ cup diced green bell pepper

1½ tablespoons finely minced garlic

1 teaspoon chopped fresh thyme

1 teaspoon chopped fresh basil

1 teaspoon chopped fresh oregano

1/4 teaspoon white pepper

1/4 teaspoon cayenne pepper (or to taste)

1½ tablespoons flour

6 ounces Creole tomato sauce *(see recipe)*

1/2 cup chopped green onion tops

Salt and pepper to taste

Directions

Preheat the oven to 450°F. In a medium saucepan (use a pan with a handle that can go into the oven safely), melt the butter, add 1 half-cup diced onions, and sauté until clear. Add the rice, 1 cup chicken stock, and 1 bay leaf. Bring to a boil, then remove from the stove and place in a 450°F oven for 5 to 7 minutes. Remove from the oven and hold. Rice should be approximately half (par) cooked.

In a heavy pot, cook and render the fat out of the sausage. Remove the sausage from the pot and sauté the chicken in the rendered fat. Sauté the rest of the onions with the celery, green peppers, garlic, and seasonings (thyme, basil, oregano, white pepper, cayenne pepper) in the same pot. Sprinkle the flour on top of the vegetables to thicken and flavor and cook for 5 minutes. Add the remaining cup of chicken stock, cook 2 minutes, add the sausage and chicken, par-cooked rice, Creole tomato sauce, green onions, and remaining 2 bay leaves. Simmer for up to 30 minutes until done but not too dry (add a little more Creole tomato sauce if necessary).

Add salt and pepper to taste.

Creole Tomato Sauce

The following recipe is a basic tomato sauce that is difficult to make in small quantities. Make the whole amount and freeze the remainder for other uses, such as pasta dishes (toss with grilled or sautéed seafood, etc.).

(Yields 5 cups)

Ingredients

5 pounds ripe Creole tomatoes (or any beefsteak tomato)
1/4 cup olive oil
3/4 cup diced shallots
6 medium cloves garlic, diced
1 teaspoon chopped fresh thyme

1 teaspoon chopped fresh oregano
4 teaspoons chopped fresh basil
2 teaspoons white pepper
1/4 cup red wine
1 teaspoon sugar
Salt and pepper to taste

Directions

Set a pot of water on the stove and bring to a gentle boil.

Using a sharp paring knife, score a large *X* across the bottom of each tomato (the opposite side from the stem end). One by one, insert a fork into the stem end and plunge the whole tomato into the boiling water. Remove from the water once the skin starts to peel off easily (15–30 seconds). Cool (an ice bath will speed this) until safe to handle, then remove the rest of the skin.

Cut each tomato in half, remove the seeds, and dice (you should end up with roughly 7 cups). Heat the olive oil in a medium saucepan, add the shallots, and cook for 2 minutes. Add the garlic, thyme, oregano, basil, and white pepper. Sauté the shallots until clear. Add the diced tomatoes, bring the mixture to a boil, then add the red wine and sugar. Reduce heat and simmer for 45 minutes to 1 hour, until the tomatoes begin to break up.

Add salt and pepper to taste, then purée in a blender or food processor.

THE BIG APPLE INN

◆◆

509 N. Farish Street, Jackson, Mississippi
(601) 354-4549

FARISH STREET FALLS LIKE A TEARDROP FROM THE FACE OF DOWNTOWN JACKSON.

From 1900 until the 1950s the five-block strip within a block of the Mississippi state capitol housed African American nightclubs, restaurants, doctor's offices, and a bank. Farish Street was a thriving African American community with the same self-reliance of Beale Street in Memphis and East Forty-Third Street in Chicago.

Civil rights leaders met in the 1950s and '60s in Farish Street offices and restaurants. Medgar Evers and Stokely Carmichael held court on North Farish Street. In 1954 Evers had become the first state field secretary of the NAACP in Mississippi. In 1963 he was assassinated in the driveway of his Jackson home by Byron De La Beckwith, a member of the White Citizens' Council (later the Ku Klux Klan). Evers was thirty-seven years old.

The Big Apple Inn is one of the most important restaurants in Mississippi. It is a blessed haven.

On a sunny afternoon in the winter of 2014, the Big Apple Inn is the only place open on Farish Street. About fifteen people are in the small café, equal numbers of working-class African American regulars and a table of young white hipsters who say they saw the Big Apple on the Food Network.

The Big Apple Inn debuted across the street from its present location in 1939. The present-day Big Apple was built in 1952. Medgar Evers's office was upstairs in the two-story brown brick building. So was blues harmonica player Sonny Boy Williamson's apartment. Blues guitarist Elmore James was a regular visitor to the Big Apple.

The Big Apple is known for its pig ear sandwich, which is exactly what it sounds like. Many have called the pig ear sandwich "the world's most unusual sandwich." It tastes like bologna. The only item more popular is the smoked sausage sandwich.

The present-day Big Apple Inn, built in 1952.

"We've always cooked five different types of sandwiches and tamales," fourth-generation owner Geno Lee Jr. says during a lunchtime conversation at the Big Apple.

"The pig ear is a pig ear," he declares. "It's not some name. Pigs' ears are very big. They come about four to five inches long. So you cut one ear up into threes and make three sandwiches off of one pig ear. When my great-grandfather opened in 1939 he used to boil them two or three days to get them tender enough to eat. Now we pressure cook them in sauce and they get done in two hours.

"Think about bacon. Not too salty. Still kind of soft, but the middle part is kind of like an al dente lasagna noodle. That is the gristle part of the pig ear. A piece of soft bacon, a piece of lasagna—and you have your pig ear. We serve it with [watered down] mustard sauce, red cabbage, but what makes it a kicker is the hot sauce. The main ingredient in our hot sauce is actually bread, which is a thickening agent. It almost looks like chili. We put in cayenne pepper, a few other spices, and the meat we use for our hot tamales. We put that sauce on each sandwich."

In 1939 the Big Apple got its meat from a Lebanese butcher shop that was next door. Lee's great-grandfather was Juan Mora, an immigrant from Mexico City who ran with Pancho Villa. He jumped a train from Chicago to land in Jackson. Mora found a job at the downtown King Edward Hotel (built in 1923, now a Hilton Garden Inn). On the side Mora cooked and sold hot tamales from an open tin drum on Farish Street. He used his mother's recipe, which is the same recipe the Big Apple uses today. It is not written down.

"My wife and I sat down with my grandfather and grandmother and they taught the recipes to us before my great-grandfather died," Lee says. "It was 'grab this much of this,' and they would reach into a bucket of salt and grab a handful of salt. They

Geno Lee Jr. is the fourth-generation owner of the Big Apple Inn.

called my great-grandfather 'Big John.' The butcher next door always gave him pig ears for free because he was going to throw them away. My great-grandfather figured out a way to cook them up and make money off of it."

Big John was something of a bon vivant. He decided to name his restaurant the Big Apple Inn because he was an accomplished dancer of the Big Apple, the popular 1930s African American zoot-suit dance that originated in South Carolina.

When I visited, all Big Apple sandwiches were only $1.25. The sandwiches were ten cents in 1939. They are served on small and warm White Castle–style buns.

Today's meat is purveyed from Polk's Meats in Magee, Mississippi. After the neighbor butcher closed his doors, the Jackson Packing Company bought his recipe for the sausage used at the Big Apple.

"Jackson Packing existed until the mid-1980s," Lee says. "We got worried when they went out of business. There was only one place we could buy our sausages. Ours was very inexpensive but it has a certain flavor. It is red roast sausage. People did not like the other sausages we were using and we almost had to close our doors. Polk's now has the recipe. They don't ship out of the state. I did a food show in New York a couple years ago and asked them to send thirty cases of meat there. They don't do that. I had to carry thirty cases of sausage with me on the plane."

But the Big Apple offers so much more than food.

Geno Lee Jr. was born in October 1965 when Otis Redding's "Respect" was climbing the charts. He is proud of the Big Apple's legacy. Sometimes he looks around the restaurant and wonders at his place in this unique slice of America.

"When I was born my mother [Mary] and father [Geno] said the first thing they were going to do was move out of the state of Mississippi," he says. "Mom had been arrested. Dad had been harassed because of this business. So we moved to Kansas City, Missouri. My grandfather [Harold Lee Sr.] continued to run the restaurant."

Geno Lee Sr. became principal of a high school in Kansas City. Mary Lee found work as an elementary school teacher. The family found a modest home for sale. "The realtor told them, 'I'm so sorry, the neighborhood isn't integrated yet,'" Lee says. "Dad got fed up and applied for a job in Germany. So we moved and I didn't come back to Jackson until I was a junior in high school. We had summers off. So for three months in the summers we'd tour different countries: Spain, France, Holland. I had no idea what racial tension was until I got back to Mississippi."

Lee says he came into the family business by accident. He was studying to be a priest. "I was going to minister full time," he explains. "Then I changed my mind and ended up in the stock market somehow and did that for a living. My uncle [Harold Lee Jr.] got sick. Dad quit his job, I quit my job, and we came to take care of the restaurant. I've been down here about twenty-five years. I consider this my ministry.

"God had a way of bringing me back to Farish Street to experience this, to learn about my heritage and about the importance food plays in civil rights and the nurturing of African American families. Food is the bottom line of the political movement."

Lee remembers his father telling him stories of how apartment tenant Sonny Boy Williamson II took him fishing along the nearby Pearl River. The Mississippi-born blues harmonica player cooked the fish he caught. Williamson recorded at Lillian McMurry's Trumpet Records, which was headquartered on Farish Street from 1950 to 1956.

"This area got started in the late 1800s by Walter Farish, who was a freed slave," Lee says. "He settled here after he was freed and he had family and friends who followed him here. Every building you see on Farish Street was built by freed slave labor. No architectural degrees. No school degrees. They just put bricks together and built buildings. They formed a community. Not just a housing community, but an economic district. There was ownership. Integration killed Farish Street. Not meaning integration is bad, but that's what killed Farish Street."

During its heyday Farish Street was called "Little Harlem."

Lee says, "The apartments were changed into offices. Charles Evers says one reason his brother [Medgar] had an office here was because it was an African American hub. And the rent was cheap here. Between the 1920s up until the mid-'70s this was the mecca of African American commerce in the state of Mississippi. To this day it is the largest intact historical African American district in the United States. It's on the ten most endangered historic areas list [according to the nonprofit National Trust for Historic Preservation]."

Lee looks around. An old mop leans on a broken jukebox. No one hears the blues.

"Even this is a hole-in-the-wall," he says. "The place is falling apart. We can't remodel because the grease in the wall holds it together. [laughs] I'm not really a preservationist, but I want to preserve as much as I can. There's a lot of history down here in the buildings alone.

"Each building tells a story."

The Big Apple is across the street from the Farish Street Baptist Church, built in 1909. The Alamo Theatre opened in 1949 and still features an occasional soul or rhythm and blues concert. During the 1940s and '50s acts like Nat "King" Cole, Cab Calloway, and Elmore James performed at the Alamo. The site is honored with a marker from the Mississippi Blues Commission.

On this day the forsaken buildings of Farish Street are being used as a set for the James Brown biopic *Get On Up*. Lee glances out the small restaurant window and says, "There's been an effort for the last thirty years to bring something back here. It is very sad. No one is willing to put up money to get it done. Very seldom does someone from downtown or the state capitol come here. That's my complaint. We are one block from the state capitol building. Right now there is no reason to stop in the city of Jackson unless you are going to stop and get a Coke on the way to Memphis, Atlanta, or New Orleans. We need a draw to Jackson, and Farish Street could be that draw."

James Meredith received national attention in October 1962 when he became the first African American student admitted to the segregated University of Mississippi. US Attorney General Robert F. Kennedy called in five hundred US marshals to calm rioting on the Oxford campus. More than 200 people were injured, including 160 marshals.

In the winter of 2014 Meredith walks into the Big Apple accompanied by his granddaughter. Born in 1933, Meredith moves slowly, but he sees sparks in the eyes of his granddaughter Jamaria, born in 2005. She says he helps her with her homework. He tells her she needs to learn "both sides." She is amused that years ago he removed the radio from his car.

Meredith wears a red Ole Miss baseball cap. He smiles as much as his soul will allow. He doesn't smile a lot.

James Meredith with granddaughter Jamaria.

Meredith slowly eases his right hand into a shirt pocket. He removes a small piece of typed paper and gives it to me. One side of the paper features the Ten Commandments. The other side contains the Lord's Prayer, signed "It takes a village to raise a child," Prophet James Meredith. He says, "God told me to give this to you. It is between you and Him what you do with it."

In 1960, according to US census figures, 40 percent of the 150,000 people who lived in Jackson were African American. He continues, "I first came to the Big Apple Inn in 1960, and it hasn't changed. They've been talking about bringing this neighborhood back for at least thirty years. The whole program was about one thing and it is just about accomplished. It was about running out all the blacks within three miles of the capitol. It's just about done."

Rage simmers in his soft eyes.

"I was at war," he says. "I'm still at war."

Meredith moved to New York in the late 1960s where he ran as a Republican against Adam Clayton Powell Jr. in an election for the congressional seat in Harlem, but he withdrew. He returned to Mississippi in 1972. Why did he come back to Jackson?

"Because Mississippi is mine," he answers. "This is the most beautiful state in the world [which he wrote in his 1966 memoir *Three Years in Mississippi*]. My mission has always been to take it back. In eighty plus years I've won one battle. Otherwise they have been kicking my butt."

For example, when Meredith walked into the school cafeteria as a student for lunch, the other students would turn their backs.

Where did Meredith get his Ole Miss baseball cap?

"They gave me enough caps to last three lifetimes," he answers. "I go back to Ole Miss three or four times a year."

A life-size bronze statue of Meredith is on the campus. (Less than a month after the conversation at the Big Apple three fraternity freshmen put a noose and an old Georgia state flag on the statue.) "The statue is an insult," he says. "Don't you understand what that is about? That is about a black graduating from Ole Miss. And they have treated every one of them like a nigger. But as long as they can say, 'Look at James Meredith,' they can't complain. Who is that singer [Bill Withers] that said, 'Use me, use me up'?"

And James Meredith's crooked laugh echoes around the Big Apple.

In 1968 Flonzie Brown-Wright stepped forward in her own way. She was the first African American woman to be elected to public office in Mississippi since Reconstruction. Wright was voted election commissioner in Canton, where she grew up. Canton is about thirty miles north of Jackson.

Flonzie Brown-Wright has been going to the Big Apple Inn and the Farish Street district since the 1960s.

"In the 1960s every shop on Farish Street had its own uniqueness," she says. "There was a movie theater. Attorneys' offices. Ice cream parlors. Shops of all kinds. Churches. African Americans could buy anything they wanted to buy here. African Americans were not welcomed down the street around the corner on the main section [of downtown] Capitol Street."

Lee says, "Meetings were always going on in this

building because of Medgar's office upstairs. As Medgar rose through popularity the Freedom Riders would meet there. His office was very small, maybe ten by ten feet. So he would come down here to have a lot of his gatherings. Sometimes when people recognized it was Medgar, it would be standing room only, people coming to hear him speak and come up a plan for the next march.

"But my grandfather had to stop that. Because for some reason all of a sudden we began failing health department inspections. We didn't pass fire marshal codes. We were getting threatened to close down."

The Big Apple is a block away from the Greyhound bus station where in the summer of 1961, 329 were people arrested for integrating public transportation facilities. Convicted on "breach of peace" and jailed, most refused bail and went to the state penitentiary in Parchman.

But their civil disobedience worked. In September 1961 the federal government mandated that segregation in interstate transportation end.

"We sent chicken and brown bags to the jail," Lee says. "Other black restaurants did, too. My mother was a Filipino who knew nothing about the civil rights movement. Her sorority friend said, 'Come on, we're going to have a sit-in at the bus station.' They just sat in the white waiting room. Within five minutes of sitting down they were snatched up, arrested, and sent to jail. My mom did say they were promised not to worry about food."

The death of Medgar Evers is what inspired Wright to become involved in civil rights activism. She thought if he gave up his life for the cause, she should pick up her pace of commitment.

"I did not know Medgar but I worked with Charles about twelve years after Medgar's assassination," says Wright, born in 1942. "I didn't know anything about segregation and racism. But I did not understand how in America a man [Evers] could be gunned down in his driveway in the presence of his wife and children for working in civil rights. I was taught to love all people. My great-grandfather was white. I could not understand this."

Wright was working at the soul food Kitty Kat Restaurant in Biloxi, Mississippi, when Evers was assassinated.

"These three guys would come in and I would serve them," she says. "But I did not know who they were. I began to listen to their conversation. They were talking about who they got out of jail. They were getting ready to integrate the beaches on the Biloxi gulf coast. They were R. Jess Brown, Carsey Hall, and Jack Young, the three black [NAACP] attorneys from Jackson." For a while Young's office was upstairs from the Big Apple.

"They always sat at the same table," Wright recalls. "One day I was serving them and Jack Young asked me my name." Young told Wright how the beaches were being integrated in Biloxi, but he had not seen the waitress at any of the meetings. Biloxi was a pivot point in Mississippi and emotion was cresting.

"I began to attend the meetings and I began to feel a fire," she says. "It is that 'soul' we talk about. You can't put your finger on it but something happened inside of me where I wanted to know more. I began singing those freedom songs: 'Ain't Gonna' Let Nobody Turn Me Around,' 'I Woke Up This Morning with My Mind.' I was hyped up. I didn't know anything about civil rights. I did not know how it was going to shape my life. I've been shot at. I've been teargassed. I've been in jail and [had] the lives of my kids threatened. That is the price you pay when the thing to do is the right thing to do."

Canton was a hot spot for the civil rights movement in Mississippi because of its high population of potential voters. "When I got back to Canton," Wright says, "there were about ten thousand potential voters in Canton with only one hundred registered. SCLC, the NAACP, SNCC [Student Nonviolent Coordinating Committee], CORE, John Lewis [SNCC chairman 1963–66], every organization was there to conduct voter registration drives. The NAACP had to go underground for a number of years because the then-president Rev. L. S. Johnson had been beaten and literally ran out of Canton. I was twenty-two years old when I was chosen to reopen the NAACP office.

"Ironically, we opened on a street called Peace."

Wright went on to introduce Dr. Martin Luther King on the steps of the courthouse where she was once denied the right to vote. "He said to me, 'I want the soul food,'" she recalls. "I called my mother and asked if she could fix some soul food. I put Dr. King in my little Nova Chevy II and took him to my mom's home [by the Mt. Zion Baptist Church in Canton]. She fixed fried chicken, peas, candied yams, corn bread, Kool-Aid, and peach cobbler.

"I still have the plate Dr. King ate out of."

"Soul propels you to acknowledge your heritage," she continues. "It is the thing that gets you up in the morning when all else seems to be falling apart. We needed to be creative with every piece of hog that we could find. That's how people in the late 1800s and early 1900s fed their families. And now chitlins are a delicacy. That's just amazing. Just like the blues. At one times blues were taboo in some communities. Now we see blues festivals and blues museums."

Wright is proud of her Mississippi Tea Cake. Several years ago she was living in Dayton, Ohio, and bequeathed a young couple her fourth-generation tea cake recipe.

"You see tea cakes don't take a lot of ingredients to make," she explains. "Flour, flavor [vanilla], butter. When you bake it, it flattens out. When the men came in from the field for their twelve o'clock dinner with their overalls on they would grab two tea cakes and put them in their overall pockets. So in the afternoon when they got exhausted and needed a sugar rush they would pull out a tea cake and eat it to carry them to supper time. The tea cake is very important to our culture. When you went to someone's home thirty, forty years ago, tea cakes were always on the stove."

Sitting across the table from Wright, Lee says, "Soul and soul food has to do with love. You know, Flonzie, you talk about soul food with such passion. Back in the 1800s when our ancestors had the scraps, they gathered around the table and ate as a family. The cotton fields were forgotten for a little while. Whippings were forgotten for a while. Segregation on the streets was forgotten for a while. And there was love around this soul-felt food.

"That's what's missing today. You don't have that love around the table any more. It's stopping at a fast-food restaurant on the way home. With the loss of gathering around a soulful cooked meal, we've lost a very important part of our family heritage."

Big Apple Inn's Pig Ear Sandwich

(Makes 10 slider-sized sandwiches)

Ingredients

5 pig ears
½ teaspoon salt
10 slider buns

Mustard
½ cup shredded cabbage
Hot sauce (bottled or homemade)

Directions

Cut each pig ear in half and place in pressure cooker with salt. When pressure builds up, cook for an additional 15 minutes. Let pressure build down (about ½ hour). While waiting for the ears to cook, shred the cabbage.

Lightly toast the slider buns and add a small amount of mustard to the top of each bun.

Place ear on bun (folded if necessary) and top with cabbage and desired amount of hot sauce.

THE FOUR WAY

◆◆

998 Mississippi Boulevard, Memphis, Tennessee
(901) 507-1519 • www.fourwaymemphis.com

THE HISTORIC FOUR WAY RESTAURANT WENT UP FOR BANK AUCTION IN 2001. Longtime Memphis life insurance salesman Willie Earl Bates heard about the sale at his Metropolitan Baptist Church. He received a higher nudge and bought the soul food diner that had opened in 1946 in the Sugar Hill neighborhood.

Bates thought of moving the Four Way out of rough South Memphis to a former Newby's restaurant on the outskirts of town. Bates was not a young man. He was born in 1940. He grew up within three blocks of the Four Way. Leaving the neighborhood could have been the easy way out for Bates and original business partner Tyrone Burroughs.

No way.

Dr. Martin Luther King loved the fried catfish and lemon icebox pie at the Four Way, originally called the Fourway Grill. Rosa Parks ate here. And Aretha Franklin. During the 1970s the Four Way was a popular carryout for musicians churning out hot buttered soul at Stax Records, just five minutes away. Booker T. and the MG's, Otis Redding, and the Staple Singers are among the Stax artists who ate at the Four Way.

History will not be moved.

"Every time I thought about moving, I'd pop myself in the head," Bates said during a lunchtime conversation at the Four Way. "And I hit myself hard, man. It would be grave mistake to

The Four Way Restaurant served Dr. Martin Luther King, Rosa Parks, and Aretha Franklin as each of them made their way through Memphis.

move from this holy ground. I didn't fall off the truck. I stepped off the truck. And I heard about it in the church. A spirit came to me. I knew I wasn't the owner. I was a steward. The Lord was the owner.

"This was my prayer."

There is a historic marker across the street from the beige brick and stucco Four Way. You stand at the marker at the four-way stop at Mississippi and Walker and look south past the restaurant. On a clear day you can see downtown Memphis.

The marker denotes the site of the People's Grocery Company. In 1892 the store was owned by three black friends of African American journalist and suffragist Ida B. Wells. People's Grocery was viewed as competition to a white-owned grocery store across the street. While Wells was out of town, a white mob invaded People's Grocery. More than thirty African Americans were arrested in what locals called "the Curve Riot." Three white men were shot and injured, while the three black owners of the grocery were arrested and jailed. A lynch mob stormed the jail and killed the three men.

These events launched Wells's life as an investigative reporter, focusing on anti-lynching campaigns. Wells moved to New York and by 1899 had settled in Chicago, where she died. Her Chicago-based grandson Donald Duster was one of the first to visit the reopened Four Way. Duster, the founder of the Ida B. Wells Memorial Foundation, died in March 2013 in Chicago. He was eighty-one. His photograph hangs on the Four Way wall of fame near his grandmother.

Roots run deep in this restaurant.

The red wagon from Bates's younger days now sits in the south patio of the restaurant. He peered out the window at his rusted wagon and said, "I would get up at four in the morning, go to the other end of Mississippi Boulevard on the other side of McLemore, load my *Memphis Commercial-Appeal* newspapers up, and come past the Four Way at four thirty in the morning. I built up muscles. I grew up here.

"The honorable Dr. Martin Luther King ate here before his [September 1962] speech at [Bates's] Metropolitan Baptist Church down the street. At the time it was the largest church in Memphis, and Memphis didn't have a large [dining] facility to accommodate him. He knew he was welcome here, he was safe here, and he had good food here. He sat here to strategize and get ready for the next battle. Martin the third ate here.

"And Don King ate here around 2011! Don King is a great promoter and a showman, but I saw a side of him that said he is a gentleman. He did not eat his entree. He bought a meal for every female in the place.

"We say we have had all the kings."

A color photograph of a smiling Don King hangs on the wall of fame.

The current dining room is the original location of the Four Way, which also had a small pool hall. The south side entrance was a barbershop. A small beauty salon and shoe store were replaced by the current outdoor garden that features plants and stones from the garden of Bates's late mother.

"I couldn't believe this restaurant was closed," Bates said. "I didn't hear any echoes of trying to continue where Dr. King ate and where Sundays were like an Easter parade. We are continuing to keep this a common safe haven where people sit down and understand one another. They don't cuss, they don't smoke. There ain't no booze. People come up to me and say, 'This man is just like me.' I'm not talking about what I dreamed about, I'm telling you the gospel truth."

On the evening of April 4, 1968, the musicians at Stax Records were winding down a tough session for the mid-tempo Shirley Walton ballad "Send Peace and Harmony Home."

The Four Way was the go-to place for carryout food. Marvell Thomas, the son of legendary Memphis soul man Rufus Thomas ("Do the Funky Chicken," "Push and Pull," etc.) was playing piano at the session. "We would pull straws to see who would get food," he said over lunch at the Four Way. "So that day was my day. I brought a big empty cardboard box."

He drove a burgundy and white 1966 Chevrolet. He was twenty-seven years old.

"I was at the counter on the front side," Thomas said as he looked at a vanished walkway. "There was a jukebox in the corner and a few café-like chairs. While I was getting ready to pay for the food a news flash came on the radio that Martin had just been shot. It got so quiet in here it was almost like being in a crypt.

"There used to be a shoe-shine parlor on the corner. Without saying a word people started walking out on the street trying to absorb this. Some guy was driving down Mississippi right here. He made the mistake of being white in the wrong neighborhood at the wrong time. He stopped at the light and people on the sidewalk beat the shit out of him. They walked away. He was lucky to get out of here alive.

"And I took the food back."

It is about a three-minute drive from the Four Way to Stax, 926 E. McLemore Ave.

Future Stax co-owner Al Bell was producing the April 4 session. Walton was a former background singer with southern soul star Joe Tex. Bell had met Dr. King in 1959 at the Southern Christian Leadership Conference (SCLC) workshops in Midway, Georgia. "I was concerned about Dr. King's welfare," Bell said in a conversation from his home in Little Rock, Arkansas. "I told him I was going to write a song for him. That was 'Send Peace and Harmony Home.' I got with Eddie Floyd and Booker T. Jones and we got the lyrics and melody. Shirley had done eight or ten cuts on it but I couldn't hear in her what I needed to hear in the song. Just as we were rolling a take [Stax songwriter] Homer Banks stuck his head through the door at the front of the studio and said, 'Dr. King just got shot and killed.' Shirley started singing that song with tears in her eyes. Then I shut down the session to try and get a grip."

Thomas lifted his hand and slowly locked two of his fingers together. He continued, "There is no way anybody who didn't live here or doesn't live here, and maybe secondarily somebody who is not black, will ever be able to get a handle on how it felt that day.

"I wanted to kill somebody."

Stax never released "Send Peace and Harmony Home." (It did appear on the 1993 nine-CD box set *Stax Soul Singles Vol. 2, 1968–71*). Bell said, "I mastered it, manufactured a few records and gave Mrs. King some copies. I gave one to Congressman Dan Kuykendall, who read it into the *Congressional Record*. I haven't told that story but once or twice, but that's exactly what was happening when Dr. King was murdered.

I went home and sat in front of the television. I was stunned and lifeless. I loved Dr. King. He still lives on in me."

What is soul food?

"Soul food is from a loving spirit," Bates answered.

"The Lord has provided whatever is in the icebox—if you want to go back to the time you had an ice pick to get the ice off the ice truck—and you put your best effort into it in the preparation of it with love," he said. "Cook it from the heart. That's soul food, whether you are talking about chicken feet or chicken meat."

Thomas listened from across the table. He was eating a lunch of pinto beans, macaroni and cheese, and catfish. He was not smiling.

He stopped eating and said, "I have not seen one [soul food] definition that makes any sense. There are so many definitions of what soul means. And ninety-nine percent of them are by white writers who haven't a fucking clue what that means. Soul food and soul music exist because they are extensions of the people who lived the culture. They've been around for a long time but nobody knew about it."

The Fourway Grill was opened in 1946 by Clint Cleaves and his wife, Irene. Cleaves was the chauffeur for Memphis mayor Edward Hull "Boss" Crump. Crump became mayor the same year Prohibition passed in Tennessee. He declared he would not enforce Prohibition and was re-elected in 1911 and 1915. In the 1930s he became a US congressman and in 1940 was voted Memphis mayor again, despite giving no speeches and not presenting a platform.

"Being the chauffeur for Boss Crump, Mr. Cleaves had the support and notoriety of the whole community," Bates said. Cleaves drove Crump around during the day and worked at the restaurant at night where Irene was in charge of the kitchen. Irene Cleaves advertised the Fourway on local radio, promoting its "rightly seasoned" food. Cleaves ran the restaurant for fifty years, until his death in 1996. Irene Cleaves died on March 17, 1998, at the age of ninety.

Bates researched the original menus. He talked to Bernice Martin, sister of the late Irene Cleaves. He interviewed former employees.

"I found a menu in storage in the back," Bates said as he nodded toward a picture of Irene Cleaves on the wall. "We basically have the same menu items from the 1960s and '70s. Good character was another common denominator of the Four Way. I tell my people if you don't want to make a person happy, don't make love to your cooking talents. I'm serious.

"Our process of yams is different. We used to cook them to serve. Now we cook them in large portions and we style them up on the back end. We do fresh greens. We don't do greens out of a can. We go to eight different marketplaces. If they don't look good, I go to the next marketplace. Cabbage is another item we use fresh."

Thomas's richest food memory is the lemon icebox pie at the Four Way. "To this very day," he said before ordering a slice. "Do you know what key lime pie is? Key lime pie was derived from lemon pie. It's essentially the same thing. It has cooked meringue. I prefer it with whipped cream, but that's me. I'd order a whole lemon icebox pie.

"Miss Cleaves made the best lemon icebox pie. What was unique about hers is that scattered throughout the filling of the pie were tiny bits of pineapple. And it was deeeeelicioous."

Thomas said, "The first time I came here I was in high school. It was like it is now. But there was a dining room in the back that you had to use a secret password to get in. [laughs] You'd ring the doorbell and somebody would come and peer out the window. If they didn't know you, you would not get in."

The back area was a private dining room with white tablecloths for fine dining. Napkins would be placed over the customers' glasses of water, a southern tradition that keeps flies away. Anyone could come through the front door for seating at the counter and carryouts.

Al Bell recalled, "In the back room the waiter would come out very first class. That is where the ministers came, and the middle class of that era. Strategies developed because you had clergies from all denominations. It was almost like a little Pentagon. All of the artists, Johnnie Taylor, Ike and Tina Turner, would head to that back room. A sharing of our culture took place in this environment."

The studded leather back door with the small window is still at the rear of the Four Way, although it is not in use. The old door now leads to the modest kitchen.

Catfish filet, fried chicken, and, oddly, roasted yet moist turkey with dressing are the top three sellers at the Four Way. Four Way regulars love the "V.I.P."—half lemonade, half sweet tea—in all four seasons.

"We reopened in October, just before Thanksgiving," Bates explained. "I thought how people just eat turkey and dressing on holidays. And here we're also talking real corn bread [dressing], no light bread or biscuit dressing. Well, turkey wouldn't be bad the entire year. I never knew it would become our number one seller. When I thought about it I went back to [Stax singer] William Bell, who sang 'Every Day Is a Holiday.' People order turkey to celebrate their birthday."

A challenge with traditional soul food restaurants, however, is to engage younger customers. Many people in their twenties and thirties are veering off the soul food train in search of healthier options. The Four Way draws ample numbers of young people who come in with their families, although it is not a hipster destination.

Students from nearby LeMoyne-Owen College celebrated their 1975 NCAA Division III basketball championship at the Four Way. Bates said the restaurant gave the LeMoyne-Owen College Magician players meal tickets throughout the season instead of relying on a dining hall. LeMoyne-Owen was formed in the 1968 merger of LeMoyne and Owen College, whose roots go back to educating slaves in the 1860s.

"Young people are always trying to separate themselves psychologically and other ways from their past," Thomas said. "Especially if the past has been unpleasant. The association with 'soul food'—and I use that term derivatively—could be that it conjures up notions of an unpleasant past. If someone wants foie gras instead of peach cobbler and chitlins, have at it. But your reasons should be more visible than that."

The Memphis nonprofit social change youth group Knowledge Quest visited the Four Way about a month before my September 2013 visit.

"They came to taste the quality of variety," Bates said. "Peach cobbler that everybody loves. Strawberry cake. Potato pie. Yams. I eat here twice a day. I weigh 187 pounds. In 1955 I weighed 160. When I played football at Tennessee State I got up to 215. So when I tell you soul food is a wonderful means of bringing people together and satisfying an appetite, I am going according to real experience."

Soul food restaurants shed light on history.

"B. B. King ate here and so did Elvis Presley," Thomas continued. "Elvis frequented the neighborhood. He'd go to church and look in the window. My church, the Pentecostal Church of Christ, was five blocks from here."

Presley and his family moved from Tupelo, Mississippi, to Memphis in 1948. Presley, who was raised in the Pentecostal church, was thirteen years old. Aretha Franklin grew up six blocks from the Four Way. Her father, the Rev. C. L. Franklin, performed the marriage ceremony for Rufus and Lorene Thomas.

Bates said, "If you go one block down and take a left you will see Elmwood Cemetery [est. 1852]. Confederates. Governors. Peasants. Mayors. Mr. Crump is there. They are all there. Ask yourself a question about this neighborhood: 'How valuable is the area I grew up in?'"

Thomas was born in 1941, three blocks from Beale Street. "My first crib was a meat box with a feather pillow in it."

Marvell's mother, Lorene Thomas, cooked meat loaf every Thursday. The only day she never cooked was Saturday. "My mother was a nurse for thirty years," he said. "She was the best dessert maker I ever knew. Sweet potato pie. Homemade ice cream, which I had to do the cranking for. Lemon icebox pie was her specialty.

"You're making me reminisce about stuff I keep back in a corner someplace. I don't drag it out that often because it is painful sometimes."

Lorene Thomas died in 2006.

"Music and my family is who I am," Thomas continued. "Growing up in the Thomas household and being the firstborn child of Rufus Thomas. My sister [Carla] strived at the possibility of winding up like my father did. Couldn't help it." The 1960 Carla Thomas ballad "Gee Whiz" was Stax's first national hit record. The song put Memphis in the national limelight as Thomas guested on the *Tonight Show*, the *Ed Sullivan Show*, and other popular television shows.

During the 1960s Carla and Marvell Thomas attended Hamilton High School in the Dixie Heights neighborhood, about five miles southeast of the Four Way. They lived across the street from the high school. "Memphis was very segregated at the time," he said. "There were three black high schools. The rest were all white."

Bates added, "The community stuck together. When there were hard times in sit-in demonstrations, people were fed from here and money would be collected to get them out of jail. I operated in the nonviolent movement. There was a service station down the street. They had a water fountain. I was eleven years old, this was before the movement."

The young Bates wanted a drink of water. The older Bates took a sip of sweet tea and continued, "I started drinking out of the fountain and a man said, 'Boy, you're not supposed to drink out of that fountain.' When I heard him talking, instead of stopping I just got a bigger mouthful of water. When I got through the boss came out, saw me, and said, 'You're a smart nigger, aren't you? Wait a minute.' He went to the door and pulled out a pistol. I saw it and said, 'You wait a minute.' I jumped. I went home and went into bed. I didn't tell my mother about it."

Bates is built long, lean, and strong like a Tennessee poplar. "When you tell me about relocating somewhere, I claim where I've been," he said. "Raised with three sisters by a single-parent mother [Magnolia Gossett Bates] exposed to all kinds of challenges that helped bring me to this point in life. So when I [voice breaks] think about the value of this and what it could mean for tourism, I am overwhelmed. It's talking about conviction and the dream of Dr. King. The echoes of the past coming forward today to encourage people to take a look and participate. So many things happened right in this area. That grocery store was right across the street . . . "

Thomas gently shook his head back and forth. He added, "All they can do is imagine."

Bates graduated from Booker T. Washington High School and earned a degree in business management from Tennessee State University. When Bates left Universal Life Insurance after thirty-seven years to help resurrect the Four Way, he used his annuity money to invest in the project. Bates and Tyrone Burroughs bought the Four Way for $70,000. The building was falling apart.

Former Memphis insurance salesman Willie Earl Bates helped save the Four Way Restaurant in 2001.

"There are people who make things happen, people who watch things happen, and people who don't know what's happening," he said. "I try to make things happen. I run the restaurant. Tyrone and I own fifty percent each of the building. We go to the same church. Tyrone wasn't interested in the restaurant. I did the construction. I did the renovation. It took me about a year. We separated investment from participation."

Bates's outdoor garden icons won't mean much to strangers, but he is deeply proud of the lush landscaping that honors his mother. Every spring he plants marigolds and petunias, his mother's favorite flowers, in the garden accented by white stones.

A Lambis No. 12 shoe-stitching machine also stands outside by the front door. The machine is from the 1940s and was used by the neighborhood shoemaker where Magnolia Gossett Bates took her family's shoes. He fixed her shoes on credit.

"It is rusting and maybe I shouldn't have put it out there," Bates said. "But that machine is an expression of appreciation for those who have helped me. That machine is a symbol to never forget to stitch together in love. I've had parents and grandparents who had children in LeBonheur Hospital [in Memphis]. This is a place of happiness and motivation. You feel it in the atmosphere. It's not just the food, it's a combination of spirit and plus plus plus.

"That's what love has to do with it."

Kathy Watson's Popular Sweet Potato Pie

Secret grandmother's recipe—Kathy grew up near Millington, outside of Memphis. The Four Way serves approximately 72 sweet potato pies a month.

(Serves 6–8, depending how the pie is sliced)

Ingredients

4 large peeled sweet potatoes
2 sticks butter
5 cups sugar
1 teaspooon ground nutmeg
1 tablespoon vanilla extract

1 teaspoon lemon juice
6 eggs
½ can evaporated milk
1 regular 9-inch pie shell

Directions

Preheat the oven to 350°F. Boil the sweet potatoes until soft. Pour out the water and add the butter. Once the butter is melted, mix well.

Then add the rest of the ingredients. Beat together well and place in pie shell.

Bake for 45 minutes to 1 hour, depending on how brown you want it. Once baked make sure the center is tight.

As dictated by Kathy Watson on January 3, 2015, her thirteenth anniversary at the Four Way.

ALCENIA'S

◆◆◆

317 N. Main Street, Memphis, Tennessee
(901) 523-0200 • www.alcenias.com

THE PYRAMID ARENA CASTS A STRANGE AND LONG SHADOW OVER ALCENIA'S RESTAURANT JUST SOUTH OF DOWNTOWN MEMPHIS. The world's sixth tallest pyramid was constructed in 1991 as the home of the NBA's Memphis Grizzlies. This pyramid sits on the banks of the Mississippi River.

When the Grizz left in 2004 for a new downtown arena, the pyramid became an empty tomb. It is now the world's largest Bass Pro Shop and alligator pond.

Betty Joyce "B. J." Chester-Tamayo opened Alcenia's in November 1997. With the Grizzlies' departure she lost a huge market share. The Pyramid held more than twenty thousand fans for a basketball game or concert.

"I've learned that nothing affects me," Betty Joyce said during a fast-talking October 2013 conversation at her restaurant. "Because there is only one soul food place in the world. And that's Alcenia's. I'm the best because I have God and love. If you have those two things you can't do nothing but win. My food is seriously cooked with love. I care about what I give a person. I've had people from Hong Kong, Mississippi, Chile, Sweden, and Harlem. Soul food is a bond. Soul food brings people together from different races. No other food on this earth does that."

Betty Joyce is known in all Memphis food circles for greeting every customer with a hug. "It's just family," she explained. "I did it the first day I opened. It never dawned on me. After sixteen years, I'm serious, I've not had more than ten rejections. A couple months ago a guy got offended. OK, that's your problem. Other people say, 'I think she thinks she knows me.' The responses are funny, but it's amazing how receptive people are."

Alcenia's is designed in green and purple Mardi Gras colors, but Betty Joyce is

The Pyramid Arena (right) was built in 1991 as the home of the NBA's Memphis Grizzlies. Alcenia's (left) flourishes through its own homespun majesty.

from Meridian, Mississippi, the birthplace of country yodeler Jimmie Rodgers. "I just love colors," she said. "I'm here to feed your heart, your head, and then your stomach. If I can make your heart and head feel better, I automatically got your stomach." Her colors are accented by beaded curtains and white lace that hangs from the ceiling. It is clear that blue moods are checked at the door.

Her restaurant is named after her mother, Alcenia, who was born in 1921. A large portrait of Alcenia hangs on the south wall of the fifty-seat restaurant.

"My mother has been cooking since she was nine," Betty Joyce said. "I can call her right now. I don't use any recipes but hers. My mom never measured [recipes]. Everything is in her head. And I don't measure. My mom was such an excellent cook and I didn't want her recipes to pass with her. So many times in the African American community we have great cooks and we never know what they did and how they did it."

The Memphis pyramid is taller than the Statue of Liberty and Alcenia's is in the historic Pinch District, a landing point for immigrants and the first commercial area of Memphis. The hilly neighborhood was first named Pinch-Gut for the malnourished look of many new residents.

And now Betty Joyce is here to serve you.

"Soul food is about feeling," said Betty Joyce, born in 1954. "Back in slavery time soul food was [made from foods] that people thought were nothing and they took and made into something. That's the same thing I do. I was an only child, but I didn't cook. If I can cook, anybody can cook. I didn't start cooking until I opened my restaurant. You can't cook soul food unless you have soul.

"I make up my own seasonings. I use nine to ten seasons and when I make my cha-cha [sauce with jalapenos, orange habanero, red chili pepper, three heads of cabbage, two green tomatoes, etc.] most people say it is like the food from Trinidad. Or the cabbage is close to the way they do it in Africa. That's what makes me different from any other soul food. It's the seasoning I use and I make everything from scratch. I use my mother's bread pudding recipe and have never seen any recipe like it. I can't tell you what is in it. Do you think Paul Newman gave away the recipe to his salad dressing?"

Locals love to guess what is going on with Betty Joyce's "Ghetto-Aid" drink. Her concoction is one package cherry-flavored Kool-Aid, one package tropical punch–flavored Kool-Aid, one package grape-flavored Kool-Aid, and four cups of sugar (to taste). Don't use anything else but Kool-Aid! Fill a container with water (to taste); a lemon is optional. And serve over ice.

The Pinch District still retains this sense of discovery.

Almella Emoja grew up about ten miles from the Pinch Distict neighborhood. She has been coming to Alcenia's since 1998. On one afternoon in January 2014, she brought her friend Bishop Bettye Alston of New Beginning Ministries in Memphis. Born in 1938, Alston had lived in Memphis all her life but she had never been to

Alcenia's owner Betty Joyce Chester-Tamayo's chicken and waffles and salmon crouquettes are customer favorites, made with a Technicolor blend of spices and herbs.

Alcenia's. "I love soul food and I like places that cook soul food for vegetarians," she said. "That's hard to find. This is family style and B.J. is so very friendly."

Both women see empowerment in African American–owned small businesses. "Civil rights is important in the discussion of soul food," said Emoja, born in 1952. "The Lorraine Motel [where Dr. King was assassinated in Memphis] had its own soul food restaurant. Fried chicken and gravy with mashed potatoes. Pork chops. All the civil rights people who stayed there ate there.

Betty Joyce "B. J." Chester-Tamayo in front of a portrait of her mother and mentor, Alcenia Clark-Chester, a domestic worker.

"There was a franchise in Memphis known as the Harlem House. It was a soul food Burger King or McDonald's. It was owned by the Toddle House but blacks were not allowed in the Toddle House so the company operated a separate franchise for blacks, the Harlem House. There was one located in each of the main black communities. And just like soul food restaurants, the hamburgers were cooked the way they were cooked at home. The signature dish at the Harlem House was the hot dog special' [with fries, salad, and toast]."

Delta blues artists like B. B. King, Bobby "Blue" Bland, and Ma Rainey were regulars at the Harlem House, according to an April 17, 2008, article in the *Tri-State Defender*. The Harlem House chain was founded by Joe Rogers Sr. of Waffle House fame. He was a former regional manager of Toddle House, a national chain of small brick house diners that was started in 1932 by Frederick Smith, father of Memphis-based FedEx founder Frederick W. Smith.

"The effect of civil rights was that all the Harlem Houses were closed and the Toddle House restaurants remained open. And by and large blacks never went there. The boycotts made us sensitive to the small black-owned restaurants that were here. We were more intentional about going to black-owned businesses at that time. I don't know if that intentionality is still there. It was a bonding thing," Emoja said.

Bishop Alston began her ministry under Emoja's father, who was a pastor. Bishop Alston added, "The civil rights era helped us more appreciate our African American doctors, lawyers, food, whatever it was. Because every time you read about most of our leaders they were eating here, eating there. It was always documented. I didn't know much about it so I wanted to go see. My brother took me to Paschal's [in Atlanta]. Almella pushed me to get here. You get the right people talking, you're going to bring back what you had before."

Grammy-winning blues great Charlie Musselwhite is a hardcore fan of Alcenia's. He likes the fried green tomatoes and pork chops. An autographed photo of Musselwhite hangs on a wall by the colorful checkout counter. "I've stayed open for him," Betty Joyce said. "He was going to Clarksdale [Mississippi] and called and said he was bringing the band. The first time he came here I didn't know who he was. He gave us a CD. He ended up doing the foreword for my cookbook."

In 2011 Betty Joyce self-published a 156-page autobiography and cookbook, *Alcenia Healing the Soul*. Musselwhite wrote, in part, "I grew up in Memphis and so I visit there as often as I can, and every time I'm in Memphis, I go to Alcenia's for some good home cooking just like my mom used to cook."

Just like Betty Joyce.

Betty Joyce was married at age nineteen and left Mississippi. Her ex-husband was in the military, which led to a young life of travel. "We left Mississippi in 1974 when my son was nine months old," she said. "We went to Germany. I never would have left Mississippi to move to Memphis. After Germany we went to Fort Campbell, Kentucky, and then Hawaii for three years. Then we came to Memphis in 1988 and we got a divorce."

Betty Joyce found work tracing lost packages at FedEx in Memphis. The job helped her obtain her college degree at LeMoyne-Owen College—after attending seven colleges (including Austin Peay, Jackson State, University of Memphis). "I graduated in May of 1996," she said.

"I lost my son in August of 1996."

Her twenty-two-year-old son, Will A. "Go-Go" Tamayo III, was killed in a motor-cycle accident with a US postal truck. She was devastated and began taking so many antidepressants she could not sleep. A week before his death he had told her she was going to be a grandmother. Depressed, Betty Joyce quit her job at FedEx and put her life savings into opening the restaurant in the Pinch District. "Once I lost my child I went through a hurting process," she said. "I had to figure out a way to come back."

Like the legacy of the neighborhood, she was searching for a new beginning.

"I looked at this brown and beige building and could see myself in here," she said. During the 1950s her brick building had housed the office of an African American doctor. Betty Joyce recalled, "A voice from God said, 'This is it.' I had been looking on the [downtown] square. Rent there was $2,000 a month and I would have been out of business the first month."

She opened on November 7, 1997, a little more than a year after her only son's death. Her grandchild, Alcenia Altovise Nia Tamayo, was born on March 5, 1997.

How has Memphis changed since 1997?

"Has it?" she responded with wide eyes of wonder. "Has it? This city has to under-stand tourists look not just for Beale Street, but out-of-the-way places. Until the city learns to embrace small business, I don't know. If you don't have anything good to say don't say anything at all. I tell my grandbabies if I was white I would have been a millionaire ten times because I would have had the resources to do what I need to do. That's why most soul food restaurants don't last or we end up selling out. My cus-tomers are the ones who are making me. You better be in a business that serves more than love, otherwise you will be out of business. I talk trash but I can back it up."

Betty Joyce's father, H. S. Chester, was a disabled veteran. Her mother, Alcenia Clark-Chester, was a domestic worker. Betty Joyce was an only child.

"I had so much love I didn't know I was poor," she said. "My mom cooked 365 days a year. We never had canned biscuits. My dad and I thought there was some-thing wrong with her. Homemade preserves for breakfast. Baked apples. We do a sweet potato cobbler, which is my mom's recipe. A lot of people have never had that. She told me how my grandfather would take the hull of a wagon wheel and cook on a potbelly stove. They would keep that turning and make the cake rise. Then they would put it in the oven. I grew up around this food but never in my life did I think I would own a restaurant. But I knew I wanted to manufacture."

Betty Joyce has started using the Internet to market everything from cookbooks and apple butter to pecan pie. "I just made a red velvet cake," she said. "Somebody came in this morning. They're taking it to Alabama. Yesterday a Japanese guy came in and had the pecan pie. Then he ordered one for me to ship to California. I just got through cooking that."

The Alcenia's legacy is a living testimony to the healthy aspects of soul food. "Where does this 'vegan' come from?" Betty Joyce asked as she picked up steam. "My mother is ninety-two years old. My auntie on my dad's side is ninety-four. One of my mother's church members is one hundred and three. My grandfather [Theodore Clark] lived to be ninety-three. He was a farmer who had three hundred acres of timberland and had twenty-seven kids. If you're not growing your own food you don't know what you're eating. My mom said that everything their animals ate was the same thing they ate. You got to pray and keep it moving. Don't tell me, 'We can't eat this, we can't eat that.' Come on. Be for real."

Alcenia's has been featured on *The Today Show* with Jenna Bush Hager and *Diners, Drive-Ins and Dives*. Betty Joyce said, "At first *Diners, Drive-Ins and Dives* said they weren't coming to Memphis to do soul food. They were coming for barbecue. [Stax Records communications director and Memphis writer] Tim [Sampson] told them to come to this place. And Tim said people in London told him about me. And he's in Memphis."

Betty Joyce said one reason she is diversifying her business is lack of support from the African American community. "Before civil rights African Americans could not eat at many restaurants so they had to go to the Four Way Grill [in Memphis] or Paschal's," she said. "I have more famous Caucasians that call me to come here than African Americans. Now that we can go to other places, we forget home. And the younger generation is going to be worse because they are not being taught how important it is to support. You're not supposed to take care of somebody else's family before you take care of your own family," she said.

Betty Joyce then looked at me, a white visitor in her colorful restaurant, and added, "That's not being racial, but in your community you all take care of each other. That's what we used to do. We were so strong. But when you become divided you don't understand. When you start thinking everybody else's water is colder than your own water you miss out what you truly have. In the African American community we had each other. In some kind of way we have to get back to that."

Alcenia's Sweet Potato Pudding

March was the month for "seeding" the potatoes. Papa would plow the ground and dig holes, known as a bed, in rows for planting the sprouts from the sweet potatoes. The potatoes would sprout out during the last part of April or the first part of May. Then the sprouts would be removed and planted so new sweet potato crops would be ready to be gathered out of the ground in August.

Mom said they cooked the pudding on top of the wood-burning stove. To brown the pudding, they would put it inside the stove. However, today she said to cook it inside the oven.

(Serves 5–6)

Ingredients

8–9 large sweet potatoes

2 tablespoons flour

2 cups sorghum molasses

1 teaspoon grated orange peel

1 cup sugar

4 eggs

2 teaspoons vanilla extract

2 teaspoons ground nutmeg

1 teaspoon ground cinnamon

½ cup evaporated milk

Directions

Preheat the oven to 350°F. In a large bowl, mix the potatoes, flour, and molasses. Stir well, then add the orange peel, sugar, eggs, vanilla, nutmeg, cinnamon, and milk. Mix together until smooth and thoroughly blended. Pour into casserole dish and bake for 30–40 minutes, until dark brown. Remove from oven. Let cool before serving.

Optional: Add nuts or raisins or top with whipped cream if desired.

SWEETIE PIE'S

◆◆

3643 Delmar Boulevard (central location), St. Louis, Missouri
(314) 371-0304 • www.sweetiepieskitchen.com

RHYME AND REASON GO TOGETHER LIKE MACARONI AND CHEESE AT SWEETIE PIE'S, THE MOST POPULAR CHAIN OF SOUL FOOD RESTAURANTS IN ST. LOUIS.

Sweetie Pie's was founded by Robbie Montgomery, a former background singer with Ike and Tina Turner (from 1960 through 1968), blues great Earl Hooker, and Dr. John. Montgomery learned about running a business from the way Ike Turner ran his Ikettes. Attitude lives in this food. Turner was intensely no-nonsense, and while Montgomery is a gentler soul, her focused energy commands respect.

Regulars and staff always call her "Miss Robbie" Montgomery.

"Ike Turner was a firm leader," Miss Robbie says during a conversation at her Upper Crust (Sweetie Pie's) restaurant near downtown St. Louis. "Back then we all thought he was mean. You had to rehearse. He had his rules. You couldn't have runs in your stockings, but now that I am running a business I know exactly where he was coming from."

Because of segregation, Montgomery cooked on the road for Ike and Tina Turner

and the Ikettes. She bought electric skillets for her hotel room. "You would be amazed at what you can make in an electric skillet," she says. "We fried steaks and after we'd take the steak out we'd dump in a can of macaroni. We fixed rice. We'd fry pork chops, potatoes. After you use the skillet you turn it into a boiler, put your water in there and fix your greens. You could make cornbread in there. They were all home-cooked meals.

Sweetie Pie's owner-founder Robbie Montgomery.

"If we did go out when I was with Ike and Tina, the first thing we would ask is, 'Where is the soul food restaurant?' We supported black restaurants when we got into a big town. When I was growing up black people had little confectionaries in the neighborhood. That's not happening any more because we don't have neighborhoods like we used to. People moved out of the black neighborhoods. We don't pull together like we should."

Miss Robbie sang for forty years, until she developed sarcoidosis. A biopsy was performed on her lung and it never healed. "When I sang my lung would collapse," she says. "It was 'Have surgery or quit singing.' I quit singing." She moved from Los Angeles back to her native St. Louis. In 1987 she trained to be a dialysis technician at Jewish Hospital. "I did that for ten years until they merged with Barnes [Jewish Hospital]," she says. "They put a salary cap on me. I either had to go back to school to go further or do something else."

Rules of the road at the Sweetie Pie's at the Mangrove outside of downtown St. Louis.

It was 1997. Montgomery was fifty-seven years old.

Her only son, Tim Norman, was doing a ten-year prison sentence for armed robbery. "Being a black person and knowing a lot of people who have been in prison, there's no opportunities when they come home," she explains. "My son got in trouble as a teenager [born in 1979, he was seventeen when arrested]. What was he going to do? It gave me another reason to open a restaurant. My mom was a great cook and I cooked all the time.

"When I was in California and stopped singing I hustled sandwiches out of the back of my Buick. There was a lot of pressure. I had to beat the food trucks and I didn't have a permit. So I thought I'd open my own restaurant. People were like, 'You are going to quit your job?' That didn't scare me. But nobody encouraged me. Everybody was like, 'Nobody wants no greazey food.' I became more determined. So I up and did it.

"I'd go to garage sales and restaurant auctions and every time I'd see a pan I'd buy it and put it in the garage."

Her first restaurant was Wings and Things, which in the late 1970s served hot

Sweetie Pie's at the Mangrove is on Old Route 66 (4720 Manchester) in St. Louis.

chicken wings in Ontario, California. Her first Sweetie Pie's opened in 1998 at 9841 W. Florissant in North St. Louis near the St. Louis airport.

In 2002 she opened the 150-seat Sweetie Pie's at the Mangrove, 4720 Manchester (Old Route 66) in a former ice cream parlor in the south side Mangrove neighborhood, which has regentrified with gay bars and hip boutiques. "When I moved there it was nothing but slums," she says. "No one knew why I picked that area. I picked it because that's where I found an [empty] restaurant. One of my customers found it."

In June 2011 Miss Robbie opened the $4 million Upper Crust, 3643 Delmar in the downtown Grand Central, near the historic Fox Theater. The 265-seat restaurant and adjacent 400-seat banquet room was formerly a Hallmark card envelope factory.

The largest Sweetie Pie's is adjacent to the vacant Palladium Building, which in a previous life was Club Plantation. The Club Plantation was built in 1914 as a roller rink and dance hall. Duke Ellington first heard jazz guitarist Charlie Christian in 1939 at the Club Plantation.

"But when I was a young kid blacks weren't allowed in this neighborhood," Miss Robbie says. "I grew up in the projects. All this was white."

Miss Robbie gently smiles at the outlines of her youth. She was born in Columbus, Mississippi, and raised in the Pruitt-Igoe projects, built in 1954 near downtown St. Louis. The 2,870 apartments were small and the projects had no central air-conditioning, which made intense St. Louis summers even more intense. Pruitt-Igoe was demolished in the 1970s.

"The projects were good for me," she says. "My dad [James] was a railroad man and we only had three rooms growing up." James Montgomery was a Pullman porter for the Union Pacific Railroad. "When the projects opened we had four bedrooms and a kitchen," she recalls. "We never had that. They were selective about the people they first let in there. Pruitt-Igoe was a testing ground for projects and they seemed to think it failed. But to me, it was a better way of life.

"The man who lived under us was a teacher. We all sang in the ghetto, standing on the street. That was our pastime. I sang in the church choir. I loved singing with groups. We had a singing group in the projects. I was fourteen, fifteen. Our first professional [all-girl] group was the Rhythmettes. There was five of us. Eventually we added a guy [Gene "Poo Poo" Anderson], who now sings with Parliament-Funkadelic."

When you go to Sweetie Pie's, do not miss the regal macaroni and cheese. Miss Robbie's mother, Ora, had her version of mac and cheese with one cup of cheese. Ike and Tina bass player Sam Rhodes had his version with two cups of cheese. "I put all the cheeses [cheddar, colby jack] in mine," she explains. "Some people don't use eggs. I put eggs in mine. They give it consistency."

The Upper Crust store features a buffet as long as a Union Pacific freight train. Four meats are featured daily: baked chicken, smoked pork, steak, and fried chicken wings. Oxtails are featured once a week, and buffalo catfish and whole jack salmon are featured on Friday and Saturdays.

Miss Robbie remembers the smells of fried chicken in the projects cooked up by her mother. "Today I still wonder how my mother fed us with one chicken," she says. "But that was enough. My fondest memory is waking up to the smell of coffee. My dad made coffee every morning. They let us put water over the coffee grinds and we could rebrew it so we'd have 'coffee water.' To this day if the smell of breakfast wakes me up it's just a wonderful day."

Miss Robbie has never been married. Her son Tim runs the Mangrove store. Her sister Janice manages the North St. Louis store; their other sister Linda and Janice's son, Charles, help run Upper Crust. On Monday nights sisters Robbie, Janice, and Linda go roller skating at Skate-King in St. Louis. In the spring of 2014 the family was planning to open a Sweetie Pie's on historic Beale Street in Memphis. "You find a relative that has a little sense in them and wants to work," Miss Robbie says.

The work has paid off.

In October 2011 Montgomery and her family became the stars of the reality series *Welcome to Sweetie Pie's*, which airs on the Oprah Winfrey Network. The series is mostly shot at the St. Louis area restaurants. The third season of *Welcome to Sweetie Pie's* premiered in July 2013 with the highest-rated episode of the series history.

"Even though my son made a mistake, I was supportive," Miss Robbie says. "I went to every prison in Missouri. They moved him around. I'd bring food from the restaurant. I found out most of the inmates don't have support. I figured if my son had an opportunity, he wouldn't go back. That became my desire to open a restaurant, to leave something for my family.

"So when my son came home he saw how I interact with my employees, fussin' and cussin'. He thought it was funny. I said, 'There ain't nothing funny about them f——n' up my food."

Tim networked a pilot for a series on small family-run businesses in the Midwest. The pilot was taken to the California-based reality series production company Pilgrim Films and Television, which took it to Oprah Winfrey. "It happened in two weeks," Montgomery says. "Tim called me. He was going to barbecue school in Texas and said Oprah's people were interested. At first I didn't want to do it. My son talked me into it. It's been fantastic for our business."

Miss Robbie looks at regional cuisine though a kaleidoscope. "Last week someone asked me about my favorite food in St. Louis," she says. "I love the Chinese food. They put bars up their place and pass it out through a box in the little [window] holes. I've been all over the world and this is the best. They throw some onions and juice

The Upper Crust/Sweetie Pie's buffet features four meats daily and the best macaroni and cheese in the Midwest.

on it and hand it to you. I wonder if these Chinamen fix it in St. Louis because it is Ghetto. Soul. Food."

It wasn't easy for Miss Robbie to start her own small business. She felt disrespected as a female entrepreneur. "I'm from the projects," she says. "I learned to stand my own. I'm respectful to people and I demand respect because I give it. But nobody gave me a loan. It wasn't encouraging for a black woman. I had a restaurant [Sweetie Pie's Spoonful] in Granite City [Illinois] but I had to close it. It's a white town. They were breaking in our cars and writing 'nigger' on our walls. I knew this existed, but I didn't know it was right across the [Mississippi River] bridge. It's a steel town where the steel factories closed down. I closed the restaurant even though most of my employees were white."

Miss Robbie modeled her Sweetie Pie's after the now-defunct Crown's. "It was cafeteria style," she says. "Everybody in St. Louis ate there. You went through the line just like you do here. I lived in the projects right up the street. I was so excited to go to Crown's. My mom may have given me a quarter and I would go through the line and see what I could buy. If I had a dollar I would buy more than I planned. Crown's was on one side. And Southern Kitchen was another soul food restaurant across the street. So when people come to me and say, 'Oh, Miss Robbie, there's a soul food restaurant opening across the street, aren't you scared?' I'm not scared. McDonald's and Burger King open next to each other all the time."

The Sweetie Pie's restaurants serve soul food vintage style, about twenty-five different items daily, including hard-to-find fried tripe (generally the stomach of a cow or ox). "We say from the rooty to the tooty," she declares. It's the soul-by-the-pound method that Montgomery grew up on. All the recipes came from her mother's kitchen. None of them were written down. There were no measurements. They were oral histories.

"I'm the oldest of nine kids," she says. "So she made up a lot of recipes. We'd have roast pork today. Two days later we'd have that same roast pork in rice. She would call it Suicide. If there were biscuits and there was dough left over, they would roll it out and make a dessert called a Butter Roll. I'm sure her mom did that. I'm carrying them on."

Linda (born 1949) is second in line behind Robbie in the family pecking order. She is working in the downtown kitchen during a break from working on the line. She says, "My mom did a lot of cooking, but my dad did breakfast. He always made us baked apples in the oven. He made biscuits. He did eggs sunny side up and would leave a little bread in the yolk." Her sister adds, "Soul food doesn't have to be unhealthy. You can cut back on your butter and your sugar. But soul food is known for being rich. I use a lot of butter and a lot of sugar, and in fact I keep tasting it until I can taste the butter. I say if you're trying to lose weight, don't come to Sweetie Pie's."

When I was naming the restaurant I had 'Brown Sugar,' 'Sweet Mama,' 'Hot Pickles.' If it's not sweet enough, it's not great."

Miss Robbie had another son, Andre Montgomery, with the late Art Lassiter, a member of Ike Turner's Kings of Rhythm. Andre died in 1997 at the age of thirty-six. Now Miss Robbie watches over grandson Andre Montgomery, who was born in 1995.

Lassiter booked the Rhythmettes for their first professional gig. "He was also supposed to do the vocals on [the 1960 debut hit by Ike and Tina Turner] 'A Fool in Love,'" she says. "He and Ike fell out about the money. Tina was going to be background with us. Art didn't come to the session at Premiere Studios here in St. Louis. Tina said she knew the lead and Ike put her on the lead that became a hit. I was pregnant. Tina was pregnant. We stayed and waited until we had our babies and I later joined them. I was on the road with them eight years."

After the run with the Ikettes was over Atlantic Records producer Jerry Wexler was looking for background singers for vocalist-piano player Mac Rebennack, aka Dr. John. New Orleans soul singer Teri Lynn told Wexler about Montgomery. And Miss Robbie went on to sing background with Dr. John from roughly 1969 to 1977 as he embarked on his soul-meets-psychedelic "Night Tripper" era. Her music connections have led contemporary rhythm and blues artists like Chaka Khan and Ron Isley into Sweetie Pie's.

Miss Robbie is relaxing on a March Saturday morning in the four-hundred-seat banquet room of her restaurant. After her interview she was slated to speak on being a minority business owner at a St. Louis library. She also hosts occasional concerts in the Upper Crust banquet room, including yearly two-shows-a-night appearances from chitlin' circuit legend Bobby Rush. "I don't want him without his dancers," she says.

Rush—born in 1933 in Homer, Louisiana, as Emmit Ellis Jr.—knows his chops. His first *Billboard* hit was the 1971 tune "Chicken Heads," influenced by his father who was a preacher and farmer. In 1984 he recorded the saucy "Buttermilk Kid." He is the "King of the Chitlin' Circuit."

The chitlin' circuit featured gritty rhythm and blues performers like Little Milton

Campbell, Tyrone Davis, and Rush. The circuit was a mid-twentieth-century black vaudeville that generally snaked through the South and into the East Coast. "The chitlin' circuit wasn't just a ghetto joint or a hole in the wall," Rush says during an early July 2014 drive from Louisville, Kentucky, to his home in Jackson, Mississippi. "It was a place where the musician played for the food. Up until 1948 you couldn't buy chitlins in a store. They would give it to you from the slaughter pen. The people who owned the club would get it, clean it, and cook it. They didn't have catfish either. They had buffalo fish and chitlins."

Rush has known Robbie Montgomery for forty years. "Miss Robbie has the greatest food in the world," says Rush, who had spent the previous week marching with civil rights icon James Meredith in Jackson. "Sometimes you have restaurants where the owner has someone else running it. She did her restaurants herself. I like her catfish. She has it down. I love the seasoning on her fish and barbecue. It don't make you fat but it sure makes you full. I don't consider St. Louis to be a southern state but it has that southern flavor."

A veteran background singer understands giving and humility, which Miss Robbie put into play in her restaurant career. "You have to please other people," she explains. "A song might not be what you like all the time, but if they say it is good you have to learn to shut down. That became our way of life. Once you became a background singer you realized you were always going to be a background singer. You weren't going to get out of that little clique."

Ike Turner died in December 2007 of emphysema and a cocaine overdose. He was seventy-six. "Ike came to Sweetie Pie's," Montgomery says. "Tina has never been here. As a matter of fact I still have the same fifty dollar bill he tipped me. And he signed it." Miss Robbie also still sings a song or two with Dr. John when he comes to St. Louis, and she appeared with him at the 2013 Bonnaroo Festival. The Manchester, Tennessee, outdoor festival gets its name from the 1974 Dr. John album *Desitively Bonnaroo*. She laughs and says, "He's been here. That's my guy. I've done about fourteen Mardi Gras with him. Of all my employers Mac is the top. Nothing bothers him. He just wants everybody around him to be happy. Soul comes from your heart. Your heart is your soul."

Sweetie Pie's Mac and Cheese

(Serves 6–8)

Ingredients

1 pound elbow macaroni, cooked according to package directions

1 cup whole milk

2 (12-ounce) cans evaporated milk

3 eggs

2 tablespoons sour cream

1 cup butter, cut into small pieces

½ pound colby cheese, shredded

½ pound Monterey jack cheese, shredded

½ pound sharp cheddar cheese, shredded

1 pound Velveeta cheese, cut in chunks

Salt to taste

1 teaspoon white pepper

1 tablespoon sugar

1 cup shredded American cheese or mild cheddar cheese

Directions

Preheat the oven to 350°F. Place the cooked pasta in a 9-by-13-inch baking dish and set aside. Place the milk, evaporated milk, eggs, and sour cream in a medium bowl and mix well.

Add the butter and the colby, Monterey jack, sharp cheddar, and Velveeta cheeses to the pasta. Pour the milk and egg mixture over the pasta, season with salt, pepper, and sugar, and toss well. Sprinkle with the remaining cups of American or cheddar cheese.

Bake for 45 minutes or until the top is lightly browned.

Part 2

Storied Southern Soul

ODESSA'S BLESSINGS

◆◆

726 Forest Avenue, Montgomery, Alabama
(334) 265-7726 • www.odessasblessings.com

SEVERAL MULTICOLORED MINIATURE ANGELS REST ON THE FIREPLACE MANTEL OF THE LARGE 1860S VICTORIAN-STYLE HOUSE OCCUPIED BY ODESSA'S BLESSINGS, A SOUL FOOD RESTAURANT THAT SITS BLOCKS AWAY FROM A CORNERSTONE OF THE CIVIL RIGHTS MOVEMENT.

The twelve-room house is bordered by a crisp white picket fence. Greetings are hand scrawled in the cement steps leading to the front porch: "Be Blessed." "Welcome." The eatery and meeting space is owned and operated by Calvin Dunning and his wife, Odessa. They believe in angels.

Odessa's Blessings is just eight blocks from the Dexter Parsonage, the seven-room home that Dr. Martin Luther King Jr. and his family lived in between 1954 and 1960 when he was pastor at the Dexter Avenue Baptist Church. The parsonage, in the Centennial Hill neighborhood, is now a museum.

On January 30, 1956, dynamite was thrown through the front window of Dr. King's home while his wife, Coretta, and his daughter, Yolanda ("Yoki"), were sleeping. When King returned home from a speech he retreated to the rear kitchen. A bowl of pecans was at the center of the kitchen table, harvested from trees in the backyard. *The Gold Cook Book* by Louis P. De Gouy—three-decade chef at the Waldof-Astoria Hotel—with recipes for sweetbreads and black-eyed peas rested on the counter near a white porcelain sink. Dr. King was feeling weak. He wanted to know God for himself. Dr. King bowed his head over a cup of coffee. He promised to stand up for his beliefs. On that cold Alabama night, Dr. King decided to become leader of the Montgomery Improvement Association (MIA, formed 1955), which started the Montgomery bus boycott.

Odessa's Blessings (left) is just eight blocks from the Dexter Parsonage (right).

According to the King Center in Atlanta, this moment was the launching point for his role as the leader of the civil rights movement.

Today, members of the King family eat at Odessa's Blessings.

Calvin Dunning was born on June 22, 1963, ten days after the assassination of civil rights leader Medgar Evers in Jackson, Mississippi. He grew up poor on a farm in Sumter County, Alabama. "My family traded with a white gentleman who came to the house," Calvin recalled during a conversation in Odessa's main floor meeting room. "He hunted deer. My mom also cooked for him and that created a relationship. She told him about things that needed to be changed. Even at that level food played a role in civil rights."

Odessa McCall Dunning also grew up on a small farm, in Lowndes County, Alabama. Her mother, Susie May, worked in a factory and her father, Roosevelt, did construction work. She grew up very poor and got pregnant at age sixteen.

"She swore she would never have another child until she finished high school, college, and got married," Calvin said. "And that is what she did." Calvin Jr. was born in July 1987. Calvin Jr.'s sister Calshea was born in July 1994. By 2000 Odessa had earned degrees in culinary arts and cosmetology from Trenholm Tech in Montgomery.

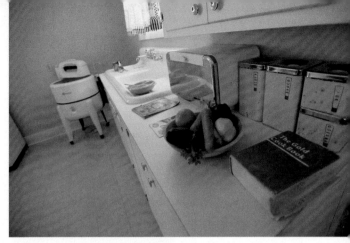

The classic 1950s-era The Gold Cook Book was a go-to resource for Coretta Scott King.

"When we were dating everyone called her 'Dessa, even though her name was Denise. Since it was an old house, we thought we'd name the restaurant Old Dessa. We thought that was too long so we made it Odessa. It is a blessing from the Lord.

"The [Montgomery] city council came to the opening and her mom was here that day. She said, 'Guess what I found?' We didn't know this until that day—"

Odessa interrupted, "On my birth certificate my name is Odessa!"

Calvin said, "They scratched through it and renamed her Denise two weeks later.

"She wanted to open her own place," Calvin continued, as he looked at his wife. "Being a man, being a husband, you try to do whatever you can do to make that come true. I started working for Capitol Filmworks, picking up leaves and cutting grass around their office. Whatever they needed."

Through that job Calvin met Sol Brinsfield, a navy lawyer and member of the Montgomery Country Club. Calvin began working at the country club while studying instrumentation electricity at Trenholm Tech. "It's changed now, but when I worked at the country club you had to be white to be a member," he said. "You couldn't be Jewish either. All the while I was there I was observing. Respect shouldn't be based on money. It should be based on customer service. Through the country club I met a lot of businessmen. And Odessa had the restaurant in her spirit."

Calvin and Odessa purchased the 3,200-square-foot house that would become Odessa's Blessing for $55,000 in 1992. It took them eight years to save enough money to open their dream restaurant. The city began taking steps to condemn the building. "The house was just sitting empty," he said. "People were taking stuff out of it. Banks wouldn't give us a loan. We used faith and credit cards. Friends helped us. We didn't realize all the work involved. The ceiling was dropped down eight feet."

Calvin and Odessa removed the faux ceiling to restore the original printed metal ceiling. They peeled off tacky carpeting to reveal the original pine floors. They painted

Odessa and Calvin Dunning spent eight years saving money to open their soul food restaurant.

the walls gold and white, colors that Calvin and Odessa believe depict life. Knick-knacks on the walls include a clock of legendary University of Alabama football coach Paul "Bear" Bryant and a picture of a young Elvis Presley. A portrait of Dr. King with John and Robert Kennedy hangs near the meeting room podium.

Word slowly got out about Odessa's. In 2008 Calvin and Odessa catered a charity golf event at the Wynlakes Country Club in Montgomery that featured Motown star Smokey Robinson, boxer Evander Holyfield, and the Rev. Jesse Jackson. The theme was to turn soul food into country club hors d'oeuvres. They prepared smoked turkey croissants with collard greens, dressing bites with green beans or peas, and sugar sweet potatoes.

In May 2014 Calvin was working a day job as an electrical technician in Montgomery. Odessa cooked and worked daily at the restaurant. She witnessed new interest in vegetables and greens. Odessa rarely uses salt on her chicken, and her turkey is smartly smoked. She doesn't use recipes or cookbooks. "I pray about it and cook," she said.

Sheyann Webb-Christburg is a regular at Odessa's. By the time she was eight she had been christened the "Smallest Freedom Fighter" by Dr. King. She would sneak out of her house to attend meetings and was the youngest participant to take part in the first Selma-to-Montgomery march that became known as Bloody Sunday.

Webb-Christburg grew up in a family of eight in the George Washington Carver projects in Selma, Alabama. The March 7, 1965, Bloody Sunday march began at Brown Chapel African Methodist Episcopal (AME) Church on the edge of the Carver projects. The march ended in violence on the far side of the Edmund Pettus Bridge over the Alabama River. Montgomery is the northernmost point on the Alabama River, which made the city a focal point for the slave trade.

"Peanut butter and jelly were popular in all our marches," Webb-Christburg said over lunch at Odessa's. "Vegetable and bean soup. We drank Kool-Aid and water. RC Cola. People didn't have a lot of money."

Webb-Christburg's parents were factory workers in Selma. Dr. King met her during a visit to the church. He told them about changes that were coming to Selma. They nodded their heads in a rhythm of acceptance and trepidation. "He asked us what we wanted," she said. "We looked at each other because we didn't know how to respond. He said, 'When I ask you again what you want, I want you to say "Freedom."'" He said to say it loud.

"Freedom! Freedom!"

"Then, he asked, 'When do you want it?' He said, 'Say "Now!" I want you to hold your hand up

Odessa's community meeting room is used for civic groups, tour groups, and wedding receptions. The former main living room of the mansion seats 115 people.
Courtesy of Calvin Dunning

and say "Now!'" That was a moment with him that I will never forget. That is when I became a disobedient eight-year-old.

"What I saw in him was he was trying to make a betterment in people's lives, not just for blacks but for all people. That jumped over big anger. I not only had courage built into me, but also character."

Webb-Christburg was eating Odessa's pork chops and pinto beans while sharing her stories. She looked at her lunch and smiled. Something in the moment took her to the past. She said, "We lived off of pinto beans when I was a child. I don't get a chance to eat them much any more. Even when we're eating in Atlanta, the King family says that no matter what they have to do in Montgomery, arrangements have to be made to come to Odessa's. I used to drive by here and see 'Odessa's Blessings' but I didn't know what it was until the Kings told me about it. Of course I loved the food, but most of all I loved Calvin and Odessa's spirit.

"It is way beyond the food and the hands."

Turning to Calvin and Odessa, Webb-Christburg said, "I've been to a lot of soul food restaurants but you are one of the most unique people because you do it from all aspects." Odessa's Blessings hosted Webb-Christburg's 2012 fish fry for her non-profit KEEP productions, a youth advocacy group. "Soul food was prevalent in the movement," she said. "Whites loved soul food. Some whites didn't want to relate to the word 'soul,' but it was derived from our black culture. We had soul music. Soul dancing. Soul food. We worked from the inside of our soul to face the turbulence we had to deal with."

Odessa's is open for lunch Tuesday through Friday. On nights and weekends the restaurant hosts large groups in search of the meaning behind soul food and civil rights. Groups from the University of Virginia, Brigham Young University, and Southern Methodist University have held meetings at Odessa's.

Stacia DeVries is a teacher and the service coordinator at Lansing (Michigan) Catholic High School. Every year her school sends a group to Montgomery on a mission trip in conjunction with Rebuilding Together (RT). The goal is to ensure that homes are warm and safe for seniors and others with limited incomes. In 2014 DeVries and her group made their twentieth trip to Montgomery.

"Calvin and Odessa are the most gracious of hosts," she said in an e-mail from Lansing. "They pray with us, they tell stories. In 2014 I had a number of seniors with our group and it would be their last chance to eat at Odessa's. Their theme was to eat enough to last a lifetime. They were so sad that they might never get to eat there again. I overheard a couple of them trying to convince Odessa to cater open houses in Lansing. I love everything there. Chicken, ham, mashed potatoes. What kind of magic and love is in their gravy? Each year we continue a tradition started the first time we ate there by taking a big group picture on the front steps. Calvin always leads that charge."

One morning in 2012 Odessa called Calvin at work. She complained that when she got out of bed her leg fell out from under her. When she made a second attempt to get out of bed she collapsed.

She had no control over her body. The couple quickly arranged for an MRI. "They said I had a tumor on my brain," Odessa said. "I told them no one in my family ever had tumors and they said that didn't matter." She obtained a second opinion that also showed a tumor. Odessa and Calvin were sent to a specialist in Birmingham, about ninety miles north of Montgomery. They talked to their pastor and prayed.

Six months later Calvin and Odessa returned to Birmingham. The tumor was gone. Calvin said, "At the same time Odessa was volunteering at the Helping Hand Seniors Citizen and Cedar Crest Nursing Home. The center residents were praying for her. From that point on every year for her birthday she said she no longer wanted a party for herself. She wanted a party where she could give out gifts and meals."

Odessa looked around the large meeting room and smiled at her husband and business partner. The angels stood tall across from the Bear Bryant wall clock. In shy tones she said, " I collect angels. Customers bring me angels. At Christmas I put up my angel tree.

"There are angels everywhere."

Odessa's Baked Chicken

(Serves 8–10)

Ingredients

chicken pieces, breasts or leg quarters
1 teaspoon onion powder
1 teaspoon garlic powder

1 tablespoon Cajun seasoning blend
1 tablespoon Old Bay seasoning
1 onion, chopped

Directions

Preheat the oven to 350°F. Fill a large 4-inch pan to a 2-inch water level. Place the chicken pieces in the pan. Mix the seasonings together in a small bowl and sprinkle over the chicken. "I'm just seasoning," Odessa says. "I don't measure. Maybe a small teaspoon of each seasoning." Top off with fresh-cut onions.

Cover and bake for 1 hour and 15 minutes. Remove the covering for the last 10 minutes to brown the chicken.

PASCHAL'S RESTAURANT

◆◆

180-B Northside Drive SW, Atlanta, Georgia
(404) 525-2023 • www.paschalsatlanta.com

THE YOUNG DREAMS OF MARSHALL SLACK INCLUDED STUDYING PHYSICAL EDUCATION AT GEORGIA TECH UNIVERSITY. Slack wanted to be a coach. Such possibilities seemed to exist under a boundless Georgia sky in the land of Coca-Cola, sweet peaches, and James Brown.

But segregation laws prohibited Slack, born in 1939, from going to Georgia Tech. Instead, he went to the University of Delaware, where he studied physical education and became an accomplished basketball player.

"In basketball you learn your spot," Slack said during an interview at the historic Paschal's restaurant in Atlanta where he is banquet manager. "Your area is what you are guaranteed of. Once we found our spot we knew how to play the game."

Few soul food restaurants embrace history with the dignity of Paschal's.

The main dining room at Paschal's has been used for an appearance by President Bill Clinton to get out the vote for State Senator Jason Carter (grandson of President Jimmy Carter) and Michelle Nunn (daughter of farmer-politican Sam Nunn), a 2014 Points of Light volunteer supper and promotional events. The 110-seat room (450 people reception style) is defined by brick walls, hardwood floors, and civil rights era pictures.

Photo by Horace Henry

The civil rights wall of fame at the present-day Paschal's restaurant. No soul food restaurant in this book displayed its political history better than Paschal's.

And Slack is the guardian of this spot.

He began working at Paschal's in 1966 at its previous location a couple miles away from the current restaurant near the campus of the all-black Morehouse College. The current Paschal's opened in 2002. The 140-seat main dining room—including a meandering thirty-one-seat bar—consists of exposed brick, a beautiful maple ceiling, and large black and white pictures from the civil rights era.

Slack has been:

- Maître d' for Paschal's restaurant, which opened in 1947
- Manager of the La Carrousel music club and lounge, which during the mid-1960s featured Aretha Franklin, Nina Simone, Ramsey Lewis, and many others

Marshall Slack has worked at Paschal's since 1966.

- Manager of the now-shuttered Paschal's Motor Hotel, where he served hot fried chicken to Dr. Martin Luther King Jr.
- A banquet manager

But his most important role is that of oral historian.

Founders James and Robert Paschal are deceased, and the original restaurant at 837 Martin Luther King Jr. Drive (formerly West Hunter Street) has been razed. But the present-day Paschal's still serves Robert Paschal's fried chicken, which was a favorite of Dr. King's.

"During the early part of the civil rights movement, Dr. King had no place to meet," Slack said. "Robert Paschal gave him space for free but he had to promise to eat his chicken. We fed them day and night. Julian Bond would be there. So would Andrew Young."

The Rev. Jesse Jackson said that meeting at Paschal's was "an everyday ritual." In a breakfast conversation at Ruby's (formerly Edna's) on the West Side of Chicago he said, "Dr. King, Rev. Abernathy, Rev. [Fred] Shuttlesworth, Andrew Young. Atlanta was such a hub of activity. You had to eat and you had to talk. Politicians had to come by and get blessed when they were running because there was such close communication."

Andrew Young was Atlanta's mayor between 1982 and 1990. He also was US ambassador to the United Nations under President Jimmy Carter. "If you wanted to know what was going on, you went to Paschal's for breakfast," Young said in an interview. "Operation Breadbasket [the precursor to Operation PUSH], which really desegregated job opportunities, met there regularly. We met in a meeting room or an upstairs suite, the meetings Dr. King called. A friend of mine at SCLC said, 'If you're going to make it in this town you have to be at Paschal's before seven thirty. Because all the decisions in this town are made before eight in the morning.' That was the breakfast room."

Young met future president Jimmy Carter for the first time in 1969 at Paschal's. "He was coming out of the kitchen," Young recalled. "He had been in the kitchen shaking hands with people."

In 2006 James Paschal self-published his memoir *Paschal: Living the Dream* with Mae Armster Kendall, the first African American professor at the University of Georgia. James Paschal wrote,

King came directly to us and asked if he could bring his team members and guests to Paschal's to eat, meet, rest, plan, and strategize. How could we refuse? We had the resources and the place. We believed we had been called to be part of the Movement.

In early 1962, we set aside a meeting room for Martin and his teams to lay fundamental groundwork and plan. Some of the work for the 1963 March on Washington took place at Paschal's. After that march, hundreds of people converged on Atlanta. So many of them gathered at Paschal's. The same was true when the Civil Rights Act was passed.

The groups later met in a large private suite at the motor hotel. Young said that James Paschal gave Coretta Scott King a suite as a retreat where she also wrote her memoirs.

Slack recalled, "When the movement leaders would travel, the students at Morehouse, Clark, and Morris Brown [College] were carrying on their work. They'd sit-in at restaurants and airports. When they got locked up, the Paschal brothers would give me and the staff some money. We'd get in the station wagon, go to the jail, pay their fine, and bring them back. We'd feed them. And Robert Paschal made sure they called their parents to let them know they were safe. It was a good feeling to be involved with the movement."

The dining room fell silent on April 4, 1968, the day Dr. King was assassinated in Memphis. "You could hear a pin drop," Slack said. "People cried. Most people stopped ordering. Most African Americans were mad. They wanted to start trouble and it

Founders Robert (left) and James Paschal at their first restaurant.

seemed like they didn't care about their own lives. But the leaders in Atlanta—black and white—believed Atlanta was too busy to hate. That was the thing.

"Atlanta was too busy with progress to hate."

Today's two-hundred-seat Paschal's upstairs banquet hall resembles a museum filled with large black and white portraits of Dr. King with his father and mother, Harry Belafonte, Rev. Jesse Jackson, and many others.

Another second-floor banquet area is named in honor of former Atlanta mayor Maynard Jackson. One photo in the Maynard Jackson room features entertainer Sammy Davis Jr. greeting Hank Aaron at home plate after Aaron hit his record-breaking 715th home run on April 8, 1974, at the since-razed Fulton County Stadium in Atlanta, not far from Paschal's.

Slack was born on the west side of Atlanta. His mother, Ruby, worked at Richard's Department Store in downtown Atlanta; his father, Jesse, was head bartender at the private Jewish Progressive Club, across the street from Georgia Tech.

Dr. Martin Luther King Jr. loved the marinated fried chicken at Paschal's.

Slack remembers going to Paschal's in 1947, not long after the brothers opened their first restaurant, where a Walmart stands today. James Paschal worked for the Pullman Company for two years after his 1943 discharge from the service. In the early 1940s Robert was executive chef at Vaughn's Cafeteria in Atlanta and later ran the fountain operations for Jacobs Pharmacies, which was across the street from the original Paschal's.

James Paschal had a keen sense of business. Robert loved the kitchen—it is his secret fried chicken recipe that is still served today. Robert learned the recipes for the uniquely marinated chicken (no longer cooked in lard), macaroni and cheese, and other staples from his mother in their native Thomson, Georgia, about two hours east of Atlanta.

The Paschal brothers were the children of sharecroppers. The brothers picked cotton in the fields, making seventy-five cents a week.

James and Robert decided to go to Atlanta for a better life.

The first Paschal's was a thirty-seat luncheonette where James and Robert served sandwiches and soda. The red brick diner did not have a stove and the brothers did not own cars. Hot food was prepared at Robert's home. His wife would deliver the meals to Paschal's by taxi.

"My dad knew the brothers," Slack said. "I'd do odd things as a kid just as something to do for the summers. Keep the plates clean, do a little sweeping and dusting. They had a kitchen, but they did not have a stove. But business continued to get huge. My first job was in the restaurant. In 1959 they went to Citizen's Trust, a black-owned bank that is still doing well today. They borrowed $100,000 and went across the street [830 Martin Luther King Jr. Drive] to open a restaurant that held about forty-five people." Rev. Jackson remembers eating fried chicken at the small Paschal's diner when he was going to school at North Carolina A&T in Greensboro.

In December 1960 the brothers expanded the operation to open the ninety-seat La Carrousel Lounge adjacent to their restaurant. James Paschal had cherished memories of the misty European nightclubs he had seen while in the service.

A circular, revolving bar featured white and brown circus horses. Entertainers performed on a raised stage. "We had pictures of clowns," Slack said. "Gentlemen were required to wear a coat and tie after five o'clock. If they didn't have a coat and tie, our job was to go out and purchase coats and ties. When they would leave we would take them back and have them dry-cleaned. James believed the way you dressed had a lot to do with the way you behaved. That's why La Carrousel was a success. James also loved jazz so we got entertainers like Lena Horne, Aretha Franklin, and Dizzy Gillespie."

Atlanta was segregated throughout the 1960s. Even the La Carrousel headliners had difficulties finding top-notch places to stay. This led to the March 1967 opening of Paschal's Motor Hotel with 120 guest rooms, banquet facilities, and a swimming pool. The hotel was above the restaurant and next door to the lounge.

"It was magnificent," Slack said. "Blacks and whites sat together, they drank together. We had the first pour license in Atlanta." Most southern clubs used the set-up style where customers had to bring their own liquor. Andrew Young added, "Ahmad Jamal, Nina Simone, everybody came through. It was the jazz hangout in the South. It would stay cool. You didn't have many opportunities to mingle racially without controversy, but La Carrousel was one of them."

Chicago-based Grammy-winning jazz-pop pianist Ramsey Lewis was in regular rotation with his trio (drummer Redd Holt, bassist Eldee Young) in the early 1960s. "There was an interracial audience at La Carrousel," Lewis said in a 2014 interview. "Everybody in Atlanta is political to this day, but more so then because of the presence of Dr. King's church [Ebenezer Baptist]. Atlanta was very sensitive to race relations.

"It was a small stage. The bar was circular. Our trio must have played there two or three times a year for a few years. The Paschal brothers not only served excellent food but they were very accommodating. It was southern comfort. I've always been a chicken, fish, vegetable guy. You have to understand we ate the same kind of food at home. There's no food in any restaurant as good as home cookin', especially soul food. But I liked their chicken. We stayed at their hotel. It worked well for each of us. We had crowds there."

North Carolina–based culinary historian Michael Twitty has called soul food "edible jazz." Lewis thought about it and said, "If the common denominator is African Americans and improvisation, we can come at it that way. African Americans had to improvise early on coming out of slavery. We didn't have money, we didn't have farms of our own, so we had to make do with leftovers. We came up with dishes that survive to this day."

Art Banks is head chef at Paschal's, having come to the restaurant in 2011 from Ted's (Turner) Montana Grill. He wouldn't dish much on Robert Paschal's secret fried chicken recipe. "We marinate our chicken overnight," said Banks, a native of Columbus, Georgia. "I can't divulge exactly what we do with it. But it is basically seasoning, salt, and pepper. The marination gives it that flavor. Fried chicken is still the number one seller. The recipe is typed out and has been passed down to the company."

Banks, born in 1970, was overwhelmed by the history when he started at Paschal's. "To know that the Paschal brothers helped bail out Dr. King and the marchers when they got arrested for marching," he said. "It is fascinating to me."

Robert Paschal died in February 1997. Atlanta had hosted the Centennial Olympic Games in 1996 and the motor hotel was sold to Clark Atlanta University. The school closed the conference center in 2003 and the historic hotel and lounge sits abandoned.

"Everything started to close when Robert died," Slack said. "James didn't want to go it alone. Ever since they were kids they did everything together. There were four brothers in all, but only two were the owners of Paschal's. The other two were like me, doing things around the restaurant and club."

Rev. Robert Smith Jr. is the pastor of the historic New Bethel Baptist Church in Detroit. He followed in the footsteps of the late Rev. C. L. Franklin (Aretha's father). New Bethel was a cornerstone of the civil rights movement.

"I would go to Paschal's from 1968 to 1978," Smith said during an interview in his Detroit office. "Robert Paschal would give me any room in the hotel as long as somebody else didn't need it. I got it for forty-eight dollars, a suite, anything. When I went back to Atlanta in 1984—the confusion of the Negro in civil rights and integration—the preacher I was preaching for wouldn't let me stay there. He had me stay at the Marriott Marquis in a room the size of my bathroom. At that time it cost him a hundred and fifty dollars a day. I could have stayed at Paschal's and it would have been much cheaper. He said, 'People wouldn't understand why I had you there, our church could afford the Marriott.' The concept was if I stayed at Paschal brothers I couldn't do any better.

"That's what happened to black business. If your son came out of the University of Alabama, he couldn't go to work for one of the five black major insurance companies at the time. He had to go to Metropolitan or New York Life. We lost so much with social integration. Let me say it like that. There's parts that were needed, of course, but you could go to Paschal's and make a name for yourself overnight. Every who's who in black America was going to be there."

Rev. Jackson said, "At the time Paschal's was the finest hotel for blacks in the country. If you came to Atlanta one of the must-see places was a black-owned hotel. After church on Sunday it was the place to go to see whomever."

Rev. Smith added, "Esmond Patterson was the WAOK [AM] radio giant at the time. He would eat breakfast there. If conversation got going and he called your name on the radio the next day, your name would be out there."

Between 1963 and 2001 Patterson hosted a morning gospel show on WAOK. He also hosted an annual live gospel concert in Atlanta that featured guests such as singer Shirley Caesar, the Mighty Clouds of Joy, and the Rev. C. L. Franklin.

Rev. Smith sighed and said, "We lost all of that."

Slack said that James Paschal was going to call it quits until he partnered with Atlanta megadeveloper Herman J. Russell in 2002 to open the present-day Paschal's. Russell was an African American entrepreneur who was born in 1930. He purchased his first Atlanta property in the Jim Crow era of 1946: an empty lot on which he built a duplex.

Paschal's is part of the upscale Castleberry Hill neighborhood, and Castleberry Inn and Suites are across the parking lot from Paschal's. It is not the same as the original space, but then, as southerner William Faulkner said, "The past is always present."

"When I was twenty-two I got hooked on the chicken from the Paschal brothers," Russell said in a phone interview from Atlanta. "It was the best-tasting chicken in the world. I own fifty percent of the land in a fifty-acre range in Castleberry Hill. In the mid-1960s that land cost me fifty cents a foot. It costs fifty dollars a foot now. I told Mr. [James] Paschal we needed a restaurant in that area. He knocked me out of my chair. He said, 'Why don't we do a Paschal together?' We made a fifty-fifty deal. We designed something that fit in the neighborhood. He didn't own the building. I made it look old. I made it look like a packing house. That area is one of the hottest art districts in Atlanta. Castleberry Hill used to have a lot of meat distributors and cotton warehouses. It was the heart of economic Atlanta."

Russell enjoyed the baked chicken and salmon at the Paschal's Sunday brunch buffet. The newer restaurant and banquet hall also features a small reincarnation of

La Carrousel. "La Carrousel was my hangout," Russell said. "Ramsey Lewis was one of the number one acts. During the heart of segregation La Carrousel was one place I could go to and feel comfortable. The police would turn their back. I could enjoy the music. I'm so proud I invested in that restaurant."

James Paschal died in 2008. Robert had a son and a daughter. The son has died and the daughter is not involved with the operation. The current operation is owned by Russell's Concessions International and Marian Johnson, the sister-in-law of James Paschal. The Paschal's at Castleberry Hill as well as the Paschal's at the Hartsfield-Jackson Atlanta airport are operated under Concessions International as well.

Andrew Young still goes to Paschal's on a regular basis. "We're so scattered now," he explained. "There were less than half a million people in Atlanta back at the other Paschal's. Almost all of the black folk lived on one side of town or the other. But you had to go past Paschal's to get to work. Now people live all over. Now the restaurant mostly attracts visitors from out of town or to the colleges. It doesn't have the same power factor—yet.

"McDonald's beat them out," Young said with chuckle.

Slack stood alone on the main floor of the restaurant. He said, "I'm the only staff person living from the Paschal days. I was with the Paschal brothers when they started, I was with them when they died. I was married twice." Slack does have a son, Shea, who is a policeman in Myrtle Beach, South Carolina. He explained, "I had to work seven days a week and it was hard for the young ladies I was with to deal with that. The Paschal brothers paid for my weddings. They finally told me to just stay single. From the man who mopped the floor to the people in the kitchen, they respected everybody who worked for them. They told young people here there are only three things in life that are important: Family comes first. Number two, your religion. And number three, Paschal's restaurant.

"Soul is a bond."

The lessons worked well. Slack is proud of his place at Paschal's. "Andrew Young still comes here," he said. "Rev. Jesse Jackson. Every time Chris Rock comes to Atlanta he eats here. He has the chicken."

Henry Aaron and his wife were Slack's next-door neighbors in 1974 when Aaron hit his historic home run to break Babe Ruth's record. They lived on West Hunter Street (now Martin Luther King Blvd.) not far from the original Paschal's. Slack still lives in the same neighborhood in a home built by his father—who lived to be one hundred.

At age seventy-five, the six-foot-one Slack no longer plays hoops, but he still swims. "There was one swimming pool in the South when I was growing up," he said in gentle tones. "All the black kids from as far as Alabama and Louisiana came to Atlanta. It was crowded. I was one of the best swimmers in the state of Georgia. I was fast. I was really fast."

Paschal's Potato Salad

(Serves 14)

Ingredients

4½ pounds Yukon Gold potatoes

2 cups mayonnaise

2 tablespoons plus 1 teaspoon sweet
pickle relish

2 tablespoons plus 1 teaspoon white
sugar

2 tablespoons plus ½ teaspoon
chopped white onion

2 tablespoons plus ½ teaspoon
prepared mustard

8 hard-boiled eggs, diced

2 tablespoons plus 3¼ teaspoons
diced celery

2¾ teaspoons diced red pepper

2¾ teaspoons diced green pepper

½ teaspoon dried parsley

½ teaspoon ground black pepper

Salt to taste

Directions

Bring a large pot of salted water to a boil. Add the potatoes and cook until tender but still firm, about 15 minutes. Drain, cool, and chop.

In a large bowl, combine the potatoes with the rest of the ingredients. Mix well, chill, and serve.

Georgia Peach Martini

(Serves 1)

Ingredients

1½ ounces Skyy Infusions Georgia
  Peach vodka

½ ounce peach schnapps

½ ounce triple sec

1 ounce orange juice

2 ounces cranberry juice

Directions

Place all ingredients in a martini shaker with crushed ice. Shake and strain into a martini glass.

LASSIS INN

◆◆

518 E. 27th Street, Little Rock, Arkansas
(501) 372-8714

A SINCERE QUEST DANGLED ON THE LINE FOR ELIHUE WASHINGTON. Washington saved the Lassis Inn, a tiny soul food roadhouse in the South End neighborhood of Little Rock. The Lassis legacy dates back to 1905. One of the oldest restaurants in Arkansas, it serves only fish: large catfish steaks, small big-boned buffalo rib, extra large big-boned buffalo rib, and more. Once you catch the dream you don't let go.

Washington was born in 1948 and raised in Portland, Arkansas. He moved to Little Rock in 1966 and found work in the city's then fledgling packing houses. He lived a block away from newspaper editor/NAACP leader Daisy L. Gatson Bates, a crusader for the Little Rock civil rights movement. Her house at 1207 West Twenty-Eighth Street is now a National Historic Landmark.

Washington bought the Lassis Inn in 1990.

The current wooden inn was erected in 1930. Joe Watson debated with his wife, Molassis, on what to name their establishment at 518 East Twenty-Seventh Street, now in the shadow of Interstate 30. They figured the derivation of Mrs. Watson's first name sounded better than the Watson Inn. "Daisy Bates and all the civil rights leaders came here," Washington said during a lunchtime conversation during which he constantly interrupted himself to attend to the kitchen. "This was the only place. People couldn't go anywhere else."

Witt's was a twenty-four-hour downtown restaurant on Seventh Street that had African American seating on one side and white seating on the other side. In the early 1960s civil rights leaders met at the now-closed Ruth's Diner on Ninth Street.

Washington's sister Annie Mae worked at Lassis Inn. She had a child with a

The Lassis Inn, built in 1930 and one of the oldest soul food restaurants in Arkansas.

nephew of the Watsons. "I used to bring her to work," Washington recalled. "The nephew was operating Lassis. He had colon cancer and passed away. During the time he was sick, his uncle would fly in from California to keep the place going. He didn't know where to find the fish."

Washington was a mixer at the Safeway bakery in downtown Little Rock. His sister told the uncle to talk to him about sourcing the fish. The easygoing Washington knew an engineer at the bakery who was a commercial fisherman.

"During that time fish were thirty-five cents a pound!" he said. "The guy from California asked me how much I would charge. I would charge him the same price I had to pay for it—thirty-five cents a pound. He asked if I would help him dress it, which I did. He even wanted to pay me for the dressing, but he was from out of town and didn't know anyone here. I wanted to help him out as much as I could.

"When he went back to California they closed the door of Lassis Inn. It was closed for about two years. He called me and said, 'You are someone I can trust because of the way you handled that deal. You could have jacked up the price on me.' He stayed on me for six months about getting involved. At the time Safeway had sold out [to Idea Bread]. I decided to give this a shot. That's how this stayed open.

"By being honest to that guy, by being true to him."

During the two years Lassis was closed the plumbing had been ripped away and copper had been stolen. Glass windows were smashed out and the air-conditioning was missing. Washington replaced all of that. He repainted the interior blue because he thought white was too bright.

The booths, which seat four, were handcrafted in 1946. They remain. All told, the inn holds about sixty people for a hot Friday night fish fry. The catfish is farm raised from Arkansas and Mississippi. "The [breaded, deep-fried] buffalo comes from White River up on Highway 70 going to Memphis," Washington said. "It is one of the best places to fish in Arkansas. Buffalo exists in moving water. They can get up to seventy-five, one hundred pounds. The only size I want is three to five pounds, because you get more fat when it is higher than that. I like clear white meat. The meat is a little coarser [like perch or crappie] than catfish. Catfish exists in any water." The fish is seasoned with a secret, fifty-year-old, "old-fashioned pepper" recipe. Catfish is more popular than buffalo at the inn.

It wasn't always that way.

"They started out selling sandwiches from a house across the street," Washington explained. "It got so popular they started driving food throughout the neighborhood in a pickup truck. There was a big demand for fish so they became more popular than the sandwiches. They did have a hot dog they called 'the Lassis Dog.' They toasted the bun. They toasted the frank. They put pickles and onions on it. It was very good.

I started selling it but I'm not doing it any more. My kitchen is so small and the large deep fryers cover half the kitchen. I had to remove the grill for burgers and franks. When I started here they were cooking in large iron pots on an old gas stove."

When Washington moved forward on the purchase of the inn, he recruited Jimmy Polite as a partner. They spent $18,000 to resurrect the restaurant. "He was very religious and he did not want to sell beer," Washington said. "I told him Lassis was known for fish and cold beer. We had to sell beer." Washington won that argument: look for forty-ounce Bud Light, Corona, and Michelob and twenty-two-ounce Miller High-Life behind the counter.

"He stayed for six months. We were doing fifty pounds of fish a week when he left me. He walked out on me and left me alone." Washington, who in 2006 married Rita Merida, hired longtime Little Rock resident Betty Jean Lewis to replace Polite. "She was elderly and started calling people, telling them to come down," he said.

The most important call she made was to longtime Little Rock disc jockey Sir Lloyd Huskey, who started plugging Lassis Inn on the air. "I went from fifty pounds of fish a week up to a hundred fifty pounds," Washington said. "From one fifty in another week to two hundred fifty pounds a week. In six months' time I was up to six hundred, seven hundred pounds of fish a week." As of this writing, the Lassis Inn was selling 350 pounds of fish a week.

"There's so many people selling fish now," said Washington, whose wife helps him serve on busy nights. "During that time there wasn't that many people selling fish. But what's most rewarding is that so many people come here and say that's where they met their spouse. [Former State Representative] Irma Hunter-Brown met her husband here seventy years ago. That's when she carved her name in a table over there."

It is not certain if Bill Clinton has been to the inn, just a few miles from his presidential library, but former Clinton aide and first female mayor of Little Rock Lottie Shackelford is a regular at Lassis. In 2014 Arkansas attorney general Dustin McDaniel was bringing his staff to Lassis every month.

Al Bell is the record producer–songwriter and former co-owner of Stax Records in Memphis. Born in 1940 as Alvertis Isbell in Brinkley, Arkansas, Bell has lived in North Little Rock almost all his life. His father, Albert Isbell, was a farmer and became a landscaping contractor. Albert did all the work for Winthrop Rockefeller, the first Republican governor of Arkansas, who became Bell's godfather.

"Lassis was the place to go during that era," Bell said in a phone interview. "We didn't have any other choices. People could release themselves and be exactly who they were at Lassis. The problems that we, as African Americans, had were discussed in that environment. After working hard and going through what they had to go through in society, some of them would get quite a bit of beer in them and talk about what they were experiencing in the white world. They would vent that. But I'm a fried fish and chicken man. If you got fried fish, you have my attention. And Lassis was the bomb, as the kids say."

The elders remind Washington of a time before his time when a hand-scrawled sign on the front door declared MINORS ENTER SIDE DOOR. A ribald jukebox has always been by the front door framed by signs that say NO DANCING. Washington said he has had to replace the floor by the front door two times because of all the dancing. His late-1990s CD jukebox contains chitlin' circuit soul legends like Patti La Belle, Bobby Rush, and the Arkansas native Billy "Soul" Bonds hit "Scat Cat, Here Kitty, Kitty."

Phyllis Brown has been coming to the Lassis Inn since the mid-1950s. Her memories are deep and as saturated as the restaurant's blue walls.

She is the baby sister of Minnijean Brown of the Little Rock Nine, the nine African American students enrolled in Little Rock Central High School in 1957. Daisy Bates encouraged African American families to enroll their children in the white high school after the historic 1957 *Brown v. Board of Education* decision that declared separate public schools for black and white students unconstitutional. At first the nine students were barred from entering the segregated school (built in 1927) by Arkansas governor Orval Faubus. They gained access after the intervention of President Dwight D. Eisenhower. The NAACP had selected the nine students because of their good grades and attendance.

Phyllis Brown breaking bread with Elihue Washington, the proud and hardworking owner of the Lassis Inn.

Eight of the Little Rock Nine were still alive in June 2014. Only two lived in Little Rock. Minnijean lived on an organic farm outside of Vancouver, Canada. All six of her children were born north of the border, a very long way from Little Rock. "I remember going to my 'colored' seat in the Central cafeteria," Minnijean recalled in a phone interview. "I was passing a table and the boys on the other side of the table were pushing the chairs and they were slamming into me. I dropped my tray where I had a bowl of chili. The principal asked me if I did it on purpose. I said 'Accidentally on purpose,' which is a form of . . . anyway, I got suspended [in December 1957]. Then I got three incidents of chili and soup thrown on me in the cafeteria.

"So chili is important food in my life because it is what my reputation is about."

Sitting straight up in a booth next to Washington, her sister said, "Minnijean went to war every day." Phyllis did not attend Little Rock Central High. "At that time there was anger," she said. "I haven't relinquished that anger. I haven't found the answer in religion. I didn't go to jail like so many other people in the movement, but I have been beaten with billy clubs. I know people who went to Parchman Prison [in Mississippi] and their hatred could be far greater than mine.

"But I haven't let it go."

Phyllis was born in 1948. Minnijean was born in 1941. The family lived in the middle class Tuxedo Court projects three blocks from the Lassis Inn. "I remember as a child walking in here and there was a front screen door," she said over catfish, hush puppies, coleslaw, and French fries. "The screen door always slammed behind you. Now he has a more modern door. [Laughs] I want to hear that screen door wail. I came here with my father. He ordered big-boned buffalo. He loved that. I brought Ruby Bridges [the first black child to attend an all-white school in the South] here."

Her other siblings were two brothers. Bobby Brown was a Little Rock civil rights activist who in the mid-1960s formed the Black United Youth (BUY), consisting of many people from the South End neighborhood. Bobby died in 2001. Dwight Brown is the youngest member of the family. He became an NBC-TV sound technician and lives in Silver Springs.

At age fifteen Phyllis volunteered to work in the Little Rock SNCC office in the historic African American Ninth Street District of Little Rock. "It's gone now because of the interstate," she said. "The interstate destroyed black business districts throughout this country." Brown worked at SNCC for three years.

After graduating from high school Brown studied radio and television broadcasting at Southern Illinois in Carbondale—the same school where Minnijean majored in journalism. "I'd like to go back to Carbondale," she said. "I loved it. But Little Rock, nor this country, was ready for a brown-skinned newscaster." Brown found work with the phone company and did freelance voiceover work.

The battles of the Little Rock Nine were the first nationally televised civil rights action. Minnijean said, "If we hadn't been on television we could have been dead in

Little Rock Central High School, built in 1927 and the site of forced desegregation in 1957.

a ditch somewhere." Phyllis said, "The world got to see what America was doing to other Americans. You need a military escort to go to school? Come on. My sister lived in this town for twelve years. Not once was she invited to speak to any of the local black colleges. People from Little Rock don't ask me to speak to them.

"I cannot answer the question why that is."

However, an ambitious visitor center was erected in 2007 across from Central High for the fiftieth anniversary commemoration of the event. In 1999 President Clinton presented the nation's highest civilian award, the Congressional Medal of Honor, to the members of the Little Rock Nine.

The high school is still functioning, and with twenty-five hundred students is one of the top academically ranked schools in the country. The school is a National Historic Site operated by the National Park Service (US Department of the Interior). Voices of the Little Rock Nine interpret events on listening stations and a gift shop includes books, DVDs, and even Central High School T-shirts and hoodies. The Magnolia (Mobile) gas station across the street from the high school is part of the historic site because news reporters gathered there to use the pay phone. National Park Service spokesperson Jodi Morris said the center attracts about one hundred thousand visitors a year from all over the world.

Phyllis Brown lives just a few blocks away from Central High. Over lunch she wore a declarative dress and gold earrings. She found ways to smile as she mined her jagged memories, presenting the poise of an urban jazz singer—or a television personality. Brown never married. Her only son died in 2012.

Her father, Willie "Bob" Brown, was a self-employed mason. "It was heart touching that we would drive through white neighborhoods—and still now—and say, 'I bet our father built that brick wall,'" she said. "Or, 'I bet our father built that driveway.'" Their mother, Imogene Dix Brown, was the first African American nurse supervisor at Arkansas Children's Hospital in Little Rock.

Imogene was from Morrilton in west Arkansas, about fifty miles from Little Rock, and this is important. "Blacks relocated to Arkansas in that area," Phyllis recalled. "The land was lush and green. The soil was black and fertile. In order for us to have a normal childhood my mother took us to Morrilton to the house she was born in. My father had a 1955 green Pontiac with the sun visor in front. The moment we drove into the driveway we jumped out of the car. The home [then occupied by her mother's brother] was a beautiful white house with a massive yard that had grape vines and walnut trees. My mother made grape jelly from those grapes. Gosh, it was so beautiful. There was a 'Back to Africa' movement that took place in that area. My father was from Rixen, about fifteen minutes away. He was born in 1900 so he saw slavery."

Minnijean added, "I now live on a small acreage and do CSA [community supported agriculture] in northern Ontario. The influence for that is from Morrilton. They had peach trees. Walnut trees. A cow. Apparently I ate butter. I got influenced by my father's sisters, who made blackberry pies and peach cobblers. I'm almost seventy-three and I'm re-creating that in my life. It was finding my preference in life, which was kind of cool. I like to be learning forever."

Where did the Brown family find their fortitude?

"We had parents who didn't tell us no," Phyllis answered. "Everybody was a participant. It was our responsibility. We experienced American apartheid in this country: state and physical laws that denied another human being to participate in the quality of life because of the color of their skin. But now we have a new Jim Crow in place. We have 'Stand Your Ground' because a young black man [Trayvon Martin] reaches into his pocket and winds up being dead."

Brown and Washington sat together in a reflective moment. Washington looks back and muses on the secrets of his success. "I never wanted to expand into barbecue or anything because the less you deal with, you can turn out better product," he said. Washington learned his focus in 1973 when he began work in the Safeway bakery. "The best paying job I ever had was Safeway," he said.

Brown told Washington, "Keep in mind that blacks would have not been employed by Safeway until my brother's [Bobby] organization wrote letters in the mid-1960s that demanded Safeway hire black folks. We have letters from Safeway that say, 'Dear Mr. Brown, per your request we are hiring one Negro man to work as a butcher, one Negro woman to work as a cashier.' That's how you got your job."

Elihue Washington nodded his head and said thank you in hushed tones. He got up and excused himself to return to the kitchen. He had more fish to fry.

Old-Fashioned Pound Cake

Ingredients

2¾ cups sugar
1 pound butter
8 ounces cream cheese
6 jumbo eggs

3 cups flour
1 teaspoon baking powder
1 teaspoon vanilla extract
1 teaspoon lemon extract

Directions

Preheat the oven to 300°F. Cream together the sugar, butter, and cream cheese. Then add 1 egg at a time to the mixture, stirring constantly. Slowly mix in the flour and baking powder. Then add the vanilla and lemon extracts.

Pour the mixture into a nonstick Bundt pan. Bake for 1 hour and 20 minutes, or until a toothpick inserted into the center comes out clean. Let cool.

Caramel Icing

Ingredients

¾ cup brown sugar
⅓ stick butter

1 12-ounce can evaporated milk
1 teaspoon vanilla extract

Directions

Over low heat (preferably in iron skillet), stir all ingredients together until the mixture thickens. Pour over the cooled cake.

SWETT'S RESTAURANT

◆◆◆

2725 Clifton Avenue, Nashville, Tennessee
(615) 329-4418 • www.swettsrestaurant.com

PATRICIA J. ARMSTRONG SITS IN A CORNER BOOTH AT SWETT'S RESTAURANT ON THE HISTORIC NORTH SIDE OF NASHVILLE. She looks straight ahead because this is what she was taught to do. It is easy to see that her brown eyes are vessels of dignity.

Armstrong was on the front line of the 1960 Nashville sit-ins, a historic nonviolent campaign to integrate local businesses. The Nashville sit-ins in downtown dining counters at Woolworth's, Walgreen's, and McClellan's took place three months before the more publicized ones in Greensboro, North Carolina.

Armstrong was part of a group of students who studied under the Rev. James Lawson. He had learned Gandhi's principles of nonviolent resistance as a missionary in India. Lawson gave his students handouts of "10 Rules of Conduct" that were composed by students John Lewis (who in 1962 was elected leader of the Student Nonviolent Coordinating Committee) and Bernard Lafayette Jr. They included:

- Do not strike back nor curse if abused.
- Do sit straight; always face the counter.
- Do not block entrances to stores outside, nor the aisles inside.

"We would order food, but they wouldn't give it to us," Armstrong says. "They would close down the counters. If someone pulled us off the counter, we had to go limp. We had spotters. The spotters would run to the First Baptist Church [Capitol Hill] and say that group one had been arrested. The second group would take their place. People would call us names. They would pour ice on our heads. We could not react."

Four hundred young people joined the Nashville sit-in demonstrations. Students were assaulted as they sat at the lunch counters. Eighty-one were arrested for disorderly conduct. Store managers closed Nashville lunch counters in response to the first demonstrators. *Photos by Bill Goodman, Nashville Banner Archives, courtesy of Nashville Public Library*

Swett's second-generation owner, David Swett, is sitting next to Armstrong. He is hearing her stories firsthand for the first time.

Armstrong was born in 1943. Swett was born in 1945. "I admire her for what she did," Swett says. "I didn't take no mess. I was asked but I couldn't do it. I was not that personality.

"You spit on me and there is going to be a fight."

Armstrong is a hero whose work paid off.

On July 2, 1964, President Lyndon B. Johnson signed the Civil Rights Act, outlawing discrimination. On July 3, 1964, Cafe Du Monde in New Orleans was serving African American customers for the first time—and without incident.

"Nashville integrated restaurants and movie theaters before any city in the South," Armstrong says. Swett chuckles and adds, "After that my people went to the West End to eat. They wanted to get over there for many years. They took off!"

Swett is direct as a root canal.

In 2002 Howard Gentry Jr. was elected as Nashville's first African American vice mayor. His father, Howard Gentry, was the longtime athletic director at Tennessee

Swett's is comfortable being part of Nashville's "meat and three" dining scene.

State University, which produced Wilma Rudolph, Oprah Winfrey, and hundreds of NFL players including Ed "Too Tall" Jones.

"I would wager we were the first city in the South to integrate restaurants and movie theaters," Gentry Jr. said in a separate interview. "Nashville was way ahead of most cities in the South in relationship to restaurants. In 1964 I would have been twelve. I could go in Elliston Place Soda Shop [opened 1939, still open]. I was able to sit at the counter there when we moved off that street when I was thirteen. Actually, when I ran for mayor I had an ice cream social there. And Swett's? I grew up on Swett's. I have four daughters and every one of them went to Swett's before they could walk."

Swett's opened September 11, 1954. The restaurant is just ten blocks from historic Fisk University. Swett's parents, Susie and Walter Swett, opened the business as a beer and sandwich tavern across the street from the current Swett's. A separate Swett's plaza/convenience store now stands in that spot. Swett also consults a Swett's restaurant at the Nashville International Airport, but he does not own the operation.

"It started off as a beer tavern, honky-tonk," he says. "Then my mother started to prepare chicken, meat loaf, green vegetables, and potatoes. We went from being a little place to a restaurant that sells meat and threes. Meat and three is a Nashville thing, but it is southern cooking. Comfort food. Soul food. It's all the same thing, cooking the food of the working-class people. Soul is a four-letter word. It means people love what they're doing and put their soul into it. You want something with garnish and prettiness about it, you go to the Gulch [nightlife district] downtown. You want a real meal, you come to Swett's or someplace similar to this."

Swett's opened in 1987 in its present location. The cafeteria-style restaurant offers beef tips, meat loaf, turkey and dressing, and other meat items with sides such as turnip greens, candied yams, and pinto beans. The linear, brown architecture resembles a heartland supper club. The main dining area seats 118; a second banquet area holds 108 people.

A wall of fame near the cafeteria features autographed photographs of Swett's fans like actor Danny Glover and soul-funkateer George Clinton. On November 12, 1994, Olympic champion Wilma Rudolph made her final public appearance at Swett's. The Tennessee-born track star was suffering from brain cancer. In 1960 she became the first American woman to win three gold medals during an Olympic game. Swett carried Rudolph's tray on her final visit. "She came here all the time," he says. "She came during her treatments. Jesse Jackson [Sr.] comes here a lot. Stokely Carmichael came to the old building and he would always talk to my dad."

David Swett is the second-generation owner of Swett's on the historic north side of Nashville.

There is no signage on the new building, which was built from scratch. Swett hand-carried the plans to the restaurant for three years before he could get the project financed. He said, "I had been to every bank in town. Ben Rogers runs a paving company in Nashville and he helped me get a loan."

During a June 9, 2014, visit a separate roadside marquee in front of the relatively new building congratulates "David and Lisa." Swett married Lisa on June 7, 2014. He was at work at his restaurant at 8 AM June 8, 2014. Swett was filling in for Ethiopian manager Kasia Haile, who had to return to her homeland. "Lisa and I have been together for years," he says. "Actually I met her in here. It's just another day."

Armstrong looks amazed and then asks Swett of his wedding, "Another day? Really?"

Swett has four children. Daughter Nikki is a dentist in Mobile, Alabama. His Nashville-based son Michael has a master's degree in mathematics and works at the Swett's store. Swett is unsure if the restaurant will remain in the family but son David Swett Jr. is helping his father expand into the real estate business in North Nashville. Patrick went to culinary school in Charleston. He learned how to cook from his parents and grandparents.

"The third generation is the toughest," Swett says. "They tend to not want to work as hard as the first and second generation. My son's opinions of that may differ. It's still a physical business. I hustle all day. I'll retire when they read my eulogy. I like what I do. I survived because we became a crossover restaurant. We welcome everyone. A lot of my business is with folks who look like you—about fifty percent of my business is Caucasian. That's not an issue for us. My lunchtime is business people from downtown. The store [across the street] is more geared to neighborhood people.

"Sundays at the restaurant are almost all African American, black, whichever you prefer to call us. I like 'colored' people more than I do black or African American people. Colored people were nice to one another when I was a child. They all took care of one another. These new people, you got to keep your eyes on. When I was colored everything was good. I'm one of the few colored people left in America."

Swett hustles to stay vital.

In 2012 he purchased a new hickory wood-fired smoker to serve barbecue pork, beef, and chicken. He found his mother's recipe for barbecue sauce in his attic. The pepper–mustard–brown sugar–garlic powder–secret spices sauce is now bottled and for sale. "People's eating habits have changed," he says. "We don't use as much oil. We don't use lard. Our green beans, squash, okra, and other items have no animal fat. They have a little margarine in them. We adjusted our menu for vegetarians. I eat a lot of our cabbage. I like the green beans. We also sell baked and grilled chicken, which is not fried."

And in a town known for "hot chicken," Swett claims to have the best in Nashville. The hot chicken movement was launched by Prince's Hot Chicken Shack in a strip mall about four miles northeast of downtown.

At Prince's, the darker the skin, the greater the cayenne pepper seasoning. Hot fried chicken is generally served on two slices of grease-stained white bread.

"Prince's does a good job," says Swett, who went to school with Prince's founder, Andre Prince. "The problem I have is when they finish frying it, it is extremely dark in color. When they use fresh grease, it doesn't taste as good as it will in four or five days after the spices get in the grease. So what we do different is that we fry our chicken regular and then fry it into an extremely hot grease for a couple of minutes. It gets real dark but infuses the chicken flavor. We also use a different [secret] pepper than the others. Most people don't even know we have hot chicken."

A mural above a row of booths honors the rural grocery store Walter Swett opened in 1942 on Twenty-Eighth Street in the North Nashville neighborhood. A red pickup truck is in the center; David is depicted as a baby.

"I found a picture of that grocery store six or seven years ago," Swett says while looking at the colorful mural. "The pictures were taken in 1947 by a photographer who lived in New York." Swett would have been two years old. The photographer was Arthur Leipzig, born 1918, who shot for the *New York Times*, *Look*, and *Parade* magazines. Swett said, "He did it for a Russian magazine to show a black family in the South in business. He went through his archives and found all the pictures of the grocery store for me."

Swett's mother, Susie, was born in Nashville. Walter was from Cheatham County, just outside of Nashville. He was a jitney driver and ran a service station before opening his grocery store and restaurant. "We were one of the few African American businesses in Nashville to survive the civil rights movement," Swett says. "For whatever reason people didn't patronize African American businesses as much after the civil rights movement."

Armstrong is wearing a creased olive suit coat and green blouse. She looks like an attorney on the winning side. She takes a sip of Coca-Cola on ice and adds, "Downtown Nashville was segregated to no end. You could not try on a dress. You had to buy it and take it home. I remember very clearly my mother having to move over on the sidewalk because a Caucasian was coming down the street. I was fifteen years old. I thought that was horrible. At seventeen I was working part-time at Baptist Hospital. I got on the bus and the front part was reserved for Caucasians. The back of the bus was for blacks. There was no place for me to sit. So I sat down in the front. The bus driver called me the n-word and told me to get in the back. I refused. He pulled up to another place, called the police, and the police took me off the bus."

While Swett was minding the store, Armstrong enrolled at Tennessee A&I (which became Tennessee State) in 1960. Students from Tennessee A&I, Fisk, American Baptist Theological Seminary, and Meharry Medical College attended workshops led by Rev. Lawson, who was attending Vanderbilt Divinity School.

The workshops were sponsored by the Nashville Christian Leadership Council (NCLC), an arm of Dr. Martin Luther King's SCLC. The Rev. Kelly Miller Smith, pastor of First Baptist Church (Capitol Hill), founded the NCLC; his church was a safe haven for the young activists.

Besides Armstrong, others who attended Rev. Lawson's workshops were future Washington mayor Marion Barry, Diane Nash, and John Lewis.

Gentry Jr. reflected, "Nashville was progressive because of the diversity in churches and education. We had so many colleges and universities we had people in Nashville from different places. At that time we had four black colleges and universities. We had Vanderbilt, Belmont. Right now we have one thousand churches in Nashville. You had a huge faith community. Our community did not push back as hard as some southern cities did. It is still that diversity that keeps Nashville moving forward. Every office that I've won [council-at-large 1999, vice mayor in 2002, and Criminal Court clerk of Davidson County in 2011] I've been the first African American to win that office. The sit-ins were the catalyst for touching the souls of the community, locally and nationally."

On February 13, 1960, Armstrong participated in the first full-scale sit-ins at segregated lunch counters at McLellan's, Kress, and Woolworth's, all along Fifth Avenue in downtown Nashville. In May 1960, Fred Harvey died (not the Fred Harvey of the Harvey House chain). Fred Harvey Jr. became the youngest independent retailer in the country when he was named president of Harvey's Department Store in Nashville. "Harvey's had a luncheonette and Fred Harvey said he would never serve a black person," Armstrong says. "We had a boycott before Easter [1960]. The boycott was so successful Fred Harvey was the first to say he was opening up his lunch counter. It is very difficult to have someone spit in your face and not react. I got a concussion in downtown Nashville."

"I was in front of W. T. Grant's store on Fifth Avenue. A man knocked me out. I don't know what he hit me with. We always got arrested for disturbing the peace, even though we were the ones who were peaceful. We were crowded into jail downtown. They would give us oatmeal and grits. And I don't eat oatmeal and grits today. At all."

How did she stay composed?

Armstrong pauses and answers, "Our training was significant. In some way Jim Lawson was able to transcend to us about being nonviolent. The principles of Gandhi and Jesus Christ were what the training was all about. I do not know how we were able to do that at our young age. A lot of us had a real commitment that we were going to make a change.

"And the things that happened in Nashville were very mild compared to what happened when we went to Alabama. Nashville was bad, but it wasn't that bad. Nobody tried to kill us. In Alabama they tried to kill us. We even had to do our wills before we left Nashville for Alabama on the Freedom Rides. When we went to Alabama we did not expect [Commissioner of Public Safety] Bull Connor. His name exemplifies what he was."

Rev. Lawson was a member of CORE, which organized the first Freedom Ride, May 4–17, 1961. By March 3, 1960—less than one month after the first successful sit-in—Vanderbilt trustees expelled Lawson for his activities. Armstrong was one of a handful of Nashville students on that ride when they were attacked by Ku Klux Klan members and local police in Montgomery, Alabama.

"I remember this so vividly," she says. "There were almost three hundred people. We got off the bus and they jumped off the roof of this flat bus station. They had

Patricia J. Armstrong was on the front line of the 1960 Nashville sit-ins.

pitchforks, garden hoses, baseball bats. They came at us, swinging at us. We had to run for our lives. Not knowing where we were, we were split up. William Barby was hit in the head and he later died from that injury. Jim Slur, who was a white gentleman who was with us, was beaten real bad. The ambulances didn't want to pick him up at first because he was with us. They finally picked him up and took him to the hospital. They wouldn't allow the black ambulances to pick up African Americans who were on the ground. At this point I realized I could die.

"The hate on people's faces was something I had never seen before."

In a subsequent meeting at Ralph Abernathy's house Armstrong was chosen to testify in court about the attack. "So the bus went on to Mississippi," she says. "There was another girl from Montgomery who testified. I did not know her."

Patricia J. Armstrong, rear at counter (circled), on February 13, 1960, during one of the first Nashville counter sit-ins. She was seventeen years old. *Courtesy of Nashville Public Library*

Armstrong removes a black and white photo from a folder. She is seventeen years old in the picture from 1961. Armstrong is wearing a white dress as she walks out of a courthouse door. A white man in a checkered suit is behind her. They are within inches of each other. He is looking down with a cigarette dangling from his lips. Armstrong looks at the photograph as if it was a broken mirror. "This is the man I testifed against," she says. "And he was found not guilty."

Armstrong is proud of her civil rights work because much of the world she grew up in no longer exists. "I'm not sure this generation recognizes the importance of what happened because everything has been given to them," she says. "They don't see the importance of voting and getting involved. There's not a lot of history about the civil rights movement.

"I also talk to kids about bullying. Yeah, I was hit, I got pulled off a diner counter, I was spit on. And look at me, I'm OK. Kids ask about that. They say, 'My mama told me if somebody hits me I better hit them back.'"

Swett listens with rapt attention. He hears words that take him to another place.

He looks at Armstrong and in blunt tones says, "What you went through is not in the history books. It is not taught in school. People in their homes don't talk about it." Armstrong continues, "Nashville is the only place in the South that does not have a monument to civil rights." However, the Civil Rights Room on the second floor of the downtown Nashville Public Library is filled with books and historic sit-in photographs. Nashville architects Tuck-Hinton anchored the room with a circular white lunch counter. The library is located on the same block of Church Street where much of the sit-in activity took place.

Swett flips open his cell phone. "Do you know who this is?" he asks. He produces a week-old photo of himself with John Seigenthaler, founding editorial director of *USA Today* and founder of the First Amendment Center at Vanderbilt University. "He got beat up," he says. "He took his whups. I always admired this man. I wasn't one of those people. He's a regular customer." Siegenthaler, who was born in Nashville in 1927, died at his home a few weeks after Swett shared his photo.

Armstrong says, "We got a lot of help from a lot of white people in this community."

Scarritt-Bennett was an all-white religious school in the heart of Nashville. As early as 1957 the college hosted Dr. Martin Luther King Jr., who spoke in Wightman Chapel. "A lot of their students acted like spotters for us," Armstrong says. "If you had a white spotter no one knew if they were ready to jeer or if they were with us. But all in all Nashville has declined to say anything about the civil rights movement."

Armstrong moved on to become an office manager for a group of doctors from 1985 until her proud retirement in 2007. She got married in 1980 and raised her husband's grandchildren. Her husband, Harry Armstrong, founded a popular Nashville appliance repair company.

She became deeply involved in church. "At first I was very angry at Caucasian people," she says. "There was a time I would never consider talking about this because it brought up too many emotions. My husband didn't even know about this for seven years until a reporter called me late one night. But by going to church and steady reading the Bible, I was able to overcome my anger. I don't have anger any more.

"You can't have soul if you hate."

When Armstrong was a little girl her mother, Jennie, and father, Andrew Jenkins, would bring the family to Swett's after church on Sunday. "There used to be a place called the Peacock on Jefferson Street near Eighteenth," she says. "My grandmother lived diagonally across the street from there and we used to go there. But after civil rights all those restaurants up and down Jefferson Street closed. Swett's was the only one that was open."

Swett says, "I don't know if they closed due to civil rights, but African American people had choices. Integration hurt African American business. People abandoned the businesses they had been going to, and when they got to going they never looked back."

Armstrong looks ahead and adds, "Yes, that is exactly what happened."

David Swett's Famous Fried Chicken

(Serves 4–6)

Ingredients

eggs

salt

pepper

granulated garlic

water

1 whole chicken

all-purpose flour

Oil for cooking

Directions

To make egg wash: crack the eggs into a mixing bowl and mix in the salt, pepper, garlic, and water. Whip ingredients together until well blended. Wash the chicken thoroughly and cut it into 8 pieces. Place the chicken pieces into the egg wash and mix thoroughly. Then coat the chicken in the seasoned flour. Take chicken out of the flour mix and let dry for a few minutes, then coat chicken a second time in the seasoned flour. Fry chicken in vegetable oil at 325°F, or at medium heat, until golden brown. Use a meat thermometer to ensure chicken is done on inside at 180°F.

(Note: Seasoned flour may be sifted and saved for the next batch of chicken.)

MARTHA LOU'S KITCHEN

◆◆◆

1068 Morrison Drive, Charleston, South Carolina
(843) 577-9583

MARTHA LOU'S KITCHEN HAS ALWAYS BEEN A PLACE TO REFRESH THE SPIRIT THAT MOVES YOU. The tiny soul food restaurant once was a 1950s gas station on Morrison Drive on the way to the Port of Charleston. Customers still walk outside to use the restaurant bathrooms. The old Atlantic Coast railroad tracks run behind the roadside diner. A folk art portrait of smiling matriarch Martha Lou Gadsden is painted on the side of the Pepto-Bismol pink building.

During a weekday lunchtime in the early summer of 2014, Martha Lou's was packed with foodies from New York, Maryland, and Georgia. Some people wore tour group name tags. A gentle warm rain fell outside. A modest line snaked out the front door into the mist. All the customers were white and under forty. A youthful impatience bounced about the twenty-five-seat restaurant even though Martha's serves the original slow food. In February 2011 Martha Lou's was mentioned in a *New York Times* article about Charleston food. In May 2011, *Saveur* magazine saluted Martha Lou's and in October 2011 the Travel Channel's *Bizarre Foods* stopped by.

So here they come.

Charleston is that kind of place.

Historians say that 40 percent of all enslaved Africans who entered North America came through the Port of Charleston. On this day, as Martha Lou's was serving fried chicken, okra soup, and juicy lima beans (the Thursday menu), civic leaders were planning for an International African American Museum to be built in downtown Charleston.

Martha Lou's Kitchen and the neighboring Bertha's Kitchen soul food restaurant are in "the Neck" area. The neighborhood is between North Charleston and the city

Martha Lou's Kitchen was reborn out of a former gas station on Morrison Drive near the Port of Charleston.

of Charleston. Down the street from Martha Lou's are the endangered Gullah (or Geechee) communities of Union Heights and Silver Hills. In the 1930s and '40s the area consisted of working-class African Americans who toiled on the railroad and in nearby oil refineries and phosphate plants. The International Longshoremen's Association still has a large office down the road from Martha Lou's.

The Gullah are African Americans who live in the coastal areas of South Carolina and Georgia, including the Sea Islands near Charleston. The Gullah are known for holding on to more of their African linguistic and cultural heritage than any other African American community in the United States. They speak in an English-based creole language. The parallel term "Geechee" comes from the Ogeechee River near Savannah, Georgia. However, it is common to hear "Geechee" in Charleston. *South Carolina: The WPA Guide to the Palmetto State*, published in 1941, captured this Charleston scene:

> From the previous night's fishing of the "mosquito fleet," owned by Negroes, the
>   vendors hawk their catch through the streets, singing an old song—
> Porgy walk
> Porgy talk
> Porgy eat wid knive and fawk
> Porgie-e-e-e-
> (Porgy is a small fish.)
> The vegetable peddlers and the flower sellers also call, in Gullah cadence, from
>   early morning until sundown . . .

"Development has taken over those communities," said Carlie Towne, director of the nonprofit Gullah/Geechee Angel Network over lunch at Martha Lou's. "They used to be one hundred percent Gullah-Geechee. Now it's maybe seventy-five percent [North Charleston population approximately 97,000 in 2014]. People lost land because of taxes. Development sees cheap property and they buy the people out. A lot of Gullah-Geechees have been pushed out of the city of Charleston back to North Charleston. I always say the city of Charleston is like Europe. North Charleston is like Africa."

Martha Lou's opened on March 15, 1983, selling only hot dogs and French fries. It has expanded into serving "meat and three" styled fare that changes daily: Monday: fried chicken, fish, turkey wings with white rice, baked macaroni, etc. Tuesday: Fish, pork chops, "mystery meat," with corn bread, bread pudding, etc.

Martha Lou Gadsden and her daughter Ruth "Butter" Gadsden command the small, steamy kitchen with the intensity of pilots on a fighter plane. Martha Lou was born in 1930 in Charleston and raised in then-rural Manning, South Carolina, about seventy-five miles from Charleston. She began her culinary journey busing tables at the Fox, an all-white downtown Charleston restaurant, in the late 1950s.

Martha Lou Gadsden (left) and daughter Ruth "Butter" Gadsden.

"I was working one night and some black people came into the Fox," Martha Lou recalled during a break in the kitchen. "The guy said, 'Martha, tell them they can't eat in here.' I said, 'You tell them. This isn't my place.' Black people had to order through the restaurant windows." In 1963 Martha Lou moved on to become the first African American waitress at the Ladson House, the first African American–owned sit-down restaurant in Charleston. She moved on to the African American–owned Dee-Dex snack bar in Charleston before finally cooking at Jessie Junior's snack bar in 1979.

"When we opened, there were soul food restaurants in Charleston, but I wanted to have something like a kitchen," she declared. "Home-cooked food. Collard greens, lima beans, neck loins, things that stick to the ribs."

The late Charleston mural artist Charles DeSaussure painted this depiction of owner Martha Lou Gadsden on her restaurant.

Martha Lou did not own her first restaurant until she was fifty-three years old. She was busy. She had nine children (one now deceased), eighteen grandchildren, and twenty-eight great-grandchildren. She knows how to cook for large groups of people. Martha Lou can stretch out flavor and ingredients.

Martha Lou wore a creased Saks Fifth Avenue apron that was given to her by one of her sons. Johnnie Taylor's southern soul ballad "Little Bluebird" played on a distant radio. Martha Lou said, "I had nine children so I had to learn how to cook. On Sunday we would have fried chicken, fish, pork chops, macaroni, corn bread, collard greens. Back then you only ate chicken on Sunday. You would kill them on Saturday. You had a good piece of chicken and you were happy." Martha Lou had happily missed the lunchtime rush of hurried tourists. She was out buying extra pork chops for her restaurant. She said she spends ten hours a day at the restaurant, including shopping.

Martha Lou's interior is accented by a black and white portrait of Coretta Scott King cut out from the pages of *Good Housekeeping* magazine and detailed murals of Charleston artist Charles DeSaussure, who died in July 2013. One mural by a dining room table features downtown Charleston adjacent to Atlantic Beach, aka "the Black Pearl," which in the 1940s through the 1960s was the only beach in South Carolina that was open to African Americans. DeSaussure, a descendent of Senegalese slaves, was born in Yemassee, South Carolina. He also painted the outside mural of Martha Lou set against the high glory of a low country landscape.

"When we moved to this area in '68, '69, it was all marsh," Ruth said during a conversation at Martha Lou's. "They cleared it off. We started cooking in the [Charleston Housing Authority] projects around the corner. We started by selling dinners to the Navy Yards. What we sell now grew from that. My mother used to cook in the kitchen every day for her boyfriend, Bertie. We called him Bertie Lou, like Martha Lou. He would always tell us, 'If you ever open a restaurant you have to name it Martha Lou's Kitchen.' In this area, every Friday, every household will have fish and red rice. And the red rice is similar to the Jollof rice [red with tomatoes] you find in West Africa. We brought those traditions over. And we continue those traditions today."

One item that appears daily on the menu is the mildly soaked lima beans. They are drenched in awesome.

"Back in the day you soaked them for a looooong time," said Ruth, who was born in 1953. "Now you just soak a short time and just start cooking. They will swell up. For an hour or two hours." In a separate interview Martha Lou said, "If you're going to do it overnight, soak them in cold water. If you're going to do it the same day, soak them in hot water for an hour or so. That makes it nice and creamy. If you're trying to cook dry lima beans you will be cooking all day."

Ruth added, "You put a little seasoning in the lima beans. We don't cook ours with the meat in it. We add our meat to it. We cook the meat on the side and season it. Recently we get a lot of people who don't eat pork. I don't understand that. Pork was the number one white meat."

The soul food restaurants in Charleston are trying to hold on to such traditions despite changing palates. Towne explained, "We say soul food, but it is actually Gullah-Geechee food. We've been cooking it since we came from the shores of Africa. Most of us came from West Africa. Gullah are enslaved Africans who were brought here to do the rice fields. Charleston has always been a port city. Just about everybody in the community was trying to get a navy man to marry. If they came in and had our red rice and the fish, we knew we had a husband."

The unassuming nature of Martha Lou's is what makes it so accessible. In recent years actor-singer Bette Midler visited Martha Lou's and signed the guest book. "She came straight from the airport," Ruth said. "She told us the word was that if you're going to Charleston, South Carolina, go to Martha Lou's, then go to your destination. She ate all her food. And she is a little woman. Her husband didn't eat all his food."

And there are other less celebrated Martha Lou's faces, like William "Bill" Saunders, who has lived on Johns Island almost all his life.

The barrier island off the coast of Charleston was a point of entry for the civil rights movement. In 1955, nearly 90 percent of the three thousand African Americans on Johns Island owned their own homes. The freedom of the sea is omnipresent. During segregation, the relative isolation somewhat protected residents from hate on the mainland. Johns Island is known for three-hundred-year-old plantation canals, dense pine forests, and the sixty-five-feet-tall Angel Oak tree, estimated to be fifteen hundred years old. Its draping limbs and far-reaching canopy resemble the wings of an angel.

Saunders, born in 1935, walks with a limp, the result of an injury in the Korean War. He wore a Korean veteran baseball cap to his lunchtime visit at Martha Lou's.

Saunders attended the Highlander School on Johns Island, an offshoot of the original Highlander Folk School in New Market, Tennessee. In 1957 Highlander opened its first citizenship education school on the island. Reading and writing were taught for voter registration, as well as governmental organization skills. Myles Horton was cofounder of the school. He would travel to Chicago to learn from Jane Addams, the founder of Hull House. She told Horton about the logical connection

American hero and civil rights leader William "Bill" Saunders has lived on Johns Island, South Carolina, almost all his life.

between food and activism. According to the book *Unearthing Seeds of Fire: The Idea of Highlander*, by Frank Adams with Horton, Addams told Horton, "To arrive at democratic decisions, you need to have a bunch of ordinary people sitting around the stove in a country house or store and contributing their own experiences and beliefs to the discussion of the subject at hand. Then you take a poll of the majority opinion of those present, regardless of who they are, and that is a democratic decision."

Saunders worked with folk singer Guy Carawan, who arrived on the island in 1959 and popularized the civil rights anthem "We Shall Overcome" at Highlander. The first time the song had been used as a protest tool was in 1945 in Charleston, when food and tobacco workers went on strike and sang the ballad on the picket line. It was the Charleston workers who took the song (born as the spiritual "I Shall Overcome") to Highlander, which opened in 1932. Dr. King and Rosa Parks were among the Highlander alumni. "People came to Highlander to learn about their legal rights, how to get organized, and how to use their economics," Carawan told me in a 1990 interview. "Music and culture were always part of that."

Saunders said, "Even on Johns Island, all the women would fix their special dish and bring it to Moving Star Hall [on River Road in Johns Island, now on the National Register]. We would bring our live chickens to the city market in Charleston. The restaurants would buy the chickens from the market. We grew our own rice. We did our own grits. We grew our sugarcane. Anything we ate came from the river, the woods, and the field. So we didn't need money to buy food. Dr. King was one of the best leaders because wherever he went, he ate those people's food. Rev. [Ralph] Abernathy was picky. My wife did the cooking for Dr. King on Johns Island. He stayed there when he saw [school cofounder Esau] Jenkins. Black leaders were afraid to have him in the city of Charleston so he stayed on Johns Island." Today about one-third of Johns Island—including the historic tree—has been annexed into the city of Charleston.

Saunders became involved in voter registration drives in Charleston and helped lead a 1969 hospital strike in Charleston that changed human rights laws in South Carolina.

What made him step up to the plate?

"I had a bad childhood," he answered. "When I was eighteen months old my mother shipped me here on a train by myself. My family lived on Johns Island. My grandfather picked me up. He died when I was seven. I caught hell. I stepped on a booby trap in Korea in 1952. I spent five months in the hospital. I'm crippled now and walk with a limp. I came back as a hero but I couldn't ride across America in the same [train] coach with the white guys I fought with. They had a special coach for black soldiers. When I got home I went into the Greyhound bus station in Columbia [South Carolina] and a cop came at me with his gun and said, 'Boy, you don't belong here.' From that day I was bitter. I was a fool. I couldn't go to the Piggie Park drive-in in Charleston. I felt so much and still do that I was fighting for freedom in Korea and my ass wasn't free here. It don't make no sense."

Drawing on his organizing skills learned from Carawan and Jenkins, Saunders moved forward with ideas of ownership. During the 1960s he published a radical newspaper called the *Lowcountry Newsletter*. In 1968, South Carolina did not pay minimum wage. African American workers at Medical-College Hospital were getting paid as low as $1.30 an hour. The hospital had no African American doctors or nurses, but African Americans were employed as nurse's aides and service workers. Saunders started organizing the workers in November 1968 not far from Martha Lou's.

They went on strike.

"Charleston was closed down for one hundred days," he said. "The National Guard came. There were curfews. We planned it for the height of tourist season." Coretta Scott King came to town in support. On Mother's Day 1969, more than ten thousand people, mostly African Americans, marched through Charleston.

"We said we'd never have a riot in Charleston," Saunders said. "We would have a war. We would bust your ass back. And nothing happened here. Nobody's house burned."

Nurse's aide Mary Moultrie contacted Saunders, who was working in a mattress factory. Her licensed practical nurse (LPN) certificate was ignored because she was African American. When Moultrie and eleven coworkers began to organize, they were fired. The hospital workers had contacted healthcare union Local 1199 in New York, which was a favorite of Dr. King's. Five of the nurses were rehired.

Once the strike was over, workers were promised to be paid above the minimum wage. African American voter registration took off. The state of South Carolina also established a Human Affairs Commission. Saunders served on the first commission. He also ran for the South Carolina senate in 1980.

Former South Carolina senator Robert Ford was organizing Bay Area voter registration for the SCLC in 1969 when he was called to Charleston. Ford saw Saunders and Moultrie on television. "At the time Martha Lou was working at Dee-Dex restaurant on Spring Street. In 1969 the peninsula of Charleston was about sixty percent black. No matter where we went, Dr. King's Southern Christian Leadership Council, we ended up at soul food restaurants. Chicago. Birmingham. Jackson. Detroit."

Ford looked around the busy Martha Lou's and said, "We were for integration, but not giving up everything we owned in the black community, which is what eventually happened. Dr. King made sure that we would eat at black restaurants, that we stayed in black motels."

On warm days most of the Martha Lou's waitstaff wear faded I HEART MLK T-shirts. Martha Lou's Kitchen or Martin Luther King? You be the judge.

Lima Beans

As told by Martha Lou Gadsden in her restaurant kitchen, Saturday afternoon July 19, 2014.

Ingredients

1 pound baby lima beans (dry). Not green. Not large.
(Martha Lou uses Hayes Star Brand lima beans.)

Salt and pepper to taste
Onion soup mix

Directions

Soak the beans in cold water overnight. Or, if used the same day, soak in hot water for approximately 1 hour.

Rinse the beans and place them in a saucepan full of water. Boil for approximately 1 hour while adding seasoning: salt, pepper, onion soup mix. *"That cuts the gas," Martha Lou said (referring to the onion soup mix).*

For meat options, precook some smoked meat, aka "pot meat," alone. Add it to the beans when the beans are almost done boiling.

Serve hot.

AFRICANNE ON MAIN

◆◆◆

200 E. Main Street, Richmond, Virginia
(804) 343-1233 • www.africannechefmamusu.com

CHEF IDA MA MUSU CROSSES A BRIDGE EVERY DAY SHE GOES TO WORK. The bridge does not traverse any water in downtown Richmond, Virginia, but the emotional tributary runs deep.

In 1980 Ma Musu fled from the civil wars of her native Monrovia, Liberia. She left her family behind. Ma Musu (*Ma*, "mother"; *Musu*, "firstborn") came to Richmond in 1986 and worked with the Red Cross for the next decade to bring her two children and her parents to the United States.

On this brisk, sunny, and promising day in late March 2014 her son Tony Hill is managing his mother's acclaimed Africanne on Main soul food restaurant, the first African restaurant in Richmond history.

Ma Musu walks through the front door of the thirty-seat eatery that is in a quaint white frame downtown building. Hill sees her from behind the counter. She wears a brown African wool head wrap. Their eyes connect like rings on a chain.

They link their past with the future of soul food.

Africanne on Main serves traditional southern, West African, Caribbean, and vegetarian cuisine by using healing herbs and spices, local farm fresh vegetables, and halal and kosher meats. Food is warmed on a traditional steam table. Customers choose what they

Africanne on Main opened in 2006 on East Main Street near downtown Richmond, Virginia.

want from the twenty items on the buffet, take their lunch in a Styrofoam container to a small scale on the counter, and pay by weight.

Ma Musu's cuisine honors her Liberian grandmother Ida, who taught her to cook at age nine. Her grandmother was a chef who operated a bakery and restaurant. Ma Musu was taught to pass it forward.

"The body is just a vessel for the soul," she says. "Soul is the essence of what a person actually is. Soul survives its origin. You can take the man out of the country, but you can't take the country out of the man. That's what soul is. I do not compromise my soul."

Ma Musu's father, Francis Ansumana, was a nurse and her mother, Catherine, was a midwife. Her father loved to eat the cassava leaf, the traditional Liberian dish boiled into a chicken or fish stew. "We would eat with our hands," she recalls, "and sit around and talk. It was a family get-together. Of course one person would get more food than the other and there would be a fuss, 'You eat too slow, you eat too fast.' My mom cooked this once a week."

Ma Musu recalls growing up under a two-class system in Liberia, where she was born in 1954. During her youth there were indigenous Liberians and the free slave Americo-Liberians, the elite colonizers with American ties. Her grandmother's side was part of the latter group. Ma Musu was raised by her grandmother.

"My grandmother chose me to live with her and work with her," Ma Musu says. "She saw I was domestically talented and trained me." Ma Musu is also a professional seamstress. Her grandmother operated a cooking school from which Ma Musu graduated.

"I had five sisters," she says. "We lost two in the [civil war]. They got killed."

Ma Musu left her homeland in 1980. She was a twenty-six-year-old studying French in the Ivory Coast, away from the war that had just broken out.

She flew into JFK Airport in New York on a one-way ticket. She brought only the clothes on her back.

Ma Musu was alone, at least in a physical sense.

"I was the only one in my family able to get out," she says. "I left everybody behind, including my children, parents, and sisters. Everybody was trapped. I worked for ten years to get everybody out. It was difficult. When I left, my daughter was a year old. I got her when she was twelve. She was home. My son was four years old. When I found him he was sixteen years old. He was in a refugee camp in Sierra Leone."

Hill had been kidnapped as a child soldier.

He had been attending a private Catholic school when rebel soldiers invaded his village. "I was thirteen years old," he recalls in a separate interview at the restaurant. "It was either be killed or 'we save your life.' I didn't have a choice. I fought for three years. I had no idea what I was fighting for."

Hill fled the countryside military camp to Sierra Leone in 1988 with his grandfather Francis Ansumana. Hill's grandfather was his mentor.

"I hiked six weeks with my grandfather from Liberia through the jungle to Sierra Leone," he says. "We had to make decisions. Do I drink this water where eight dead bodies are lying in there? Or do I keep going on for another twenty-four, forty-eight hours to find water we can drink? We strengthened each other. I had no fear. We had prayer.

"I would have rather died than have him die. I told him I would get him to safety. After that I lived in Sierra Leone for a year and came from Sierra Leone to Australia to the US. I had an AK-47 [assault rifle]. We fought back and forth. I was trained with an AK-47 at age thirteen. I got my grandfather across in 1989. I was numb when I met my mother after everything I went through. If I was excited, I didn't express it.

"Deep down inside I was mourning the lost souls I witnessed in Liberia."

"Coming to America was almost like coming to paradise, the imagination of what America is," Ma Musu says. "When I was a child in Liberia, America was like the mother country. We have the same form of government. We practice much of the American cultures."

Ma Musu's first stop in America was in the dense projects of pre-gentrified Harlem.

"The lady I stayed with had locks on all her doors," she recalls. "She went to work

Chef Ida Ma Musu and her son Tony Hill, who manages the Africanne on Main soul food restaurant.

and told me not to go outside. I started crying. 'Is this my America?' In my mind, this couldn't be." After she spent that first weekend in Harlem, a family member picked up Ma Musu and took her to their home in Queens.

Ma Musu spoke French so it was easy for her to find work at a Hilton hotel in New York City. She spent nearly three years in New York. One weekend she visited a friend in Richmond and immediately fell in love with the city.

"Richmond felt like Liberia," she said. "We have Broad Street in Liberia. We have Broad Street here. We read the same books. We speak English. In Liberia we have Lynchburg, Petersburg, all these places where the free slaves went back and tried to develop a country that was more like the South. The first president of Liberia [Joseph Jenkins Roberts, elected 1848] was born in Petersburg, Virginia [about seventy-five miles from Norfolk]. Virginia and Liberia are like direct cousins.

"Over sixty thousand slaves left Virginia in the 1800s. I didn't know that until I got to Richmond. It was unbelievable. Then it started to make sense. My grandmother was part of the free slaves who came from Reston, Virginia. It made sense why she made corn bread and sweet potato pie and collard greens. I watched her cook a lot of southern soul food in Liberia, but we added Liberian spices. When I moved to the United States I knew this was the direction I wanted to go, but I didn't know how to get there."

Ma Musu first made her mark in Richmond by opening Braids of Africa in her home on Broad Street. She lived upstairs and her store and kitchen were downstairs. People would hang out in her chairs for eight or nine hours. Ma Musu chuckles and recalls, "They would go, 'Ida, what's that smell in the kitchen?' So they started calling me and asking me to prepare food for their family, things like [Liberian] Jollof rice because they were sitting there all day getting their hair braided."

Ma Musu started a catering service from home before opening a now-defunct small carryout in 1995 in downtown Richmond.

"When I started the restaurant Virginians just kind of grabbed and held on to me," she says. "The love I have for this city," she says as her voice breaks with a smile. "I will probably be buried here. This is emotional for me. When I got to Richmond it was like a spirit was lifted because of the connections. I did research on how to operate a small restaurant and created friendships with small restaurant owners.

"I knew I had one thing that nobody could take away. And that was food, which is the heart of the restaurant."

A cheery cartoon sign near the front door declares, MA MUSU SAYS IT'S OKAY TO LICK YOUR FINGERS HERE. Kitchen chefs wear aprons that say IT'S OKAY TO LICK YOUR FINGERS HERE in yellow lettering. Food can be washed down with homemade bottled healing drinks such as the nonalcoholic ginger beer—with a boost of energy—and watermelon tea, which cleanses the kidneys.

Ma Musu prays when she cooks. She asks God to guide her with healing spices. "I sing the songs my grandmother sang to me as a child," she says. "'Lord use my hands, use my feet, use my eyes for your service.'"

People often ask Ma Musu why she doesn't serve traditional African food. "I do, but I don't have the clientele for traditional," she explains. "So I decided to make soul food healthier. I don't use salt. I don't use sodium." For example, Africanne on

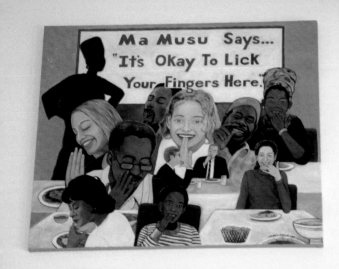

A sign near the front door and the cooks' aprons assure customers IT'S OKAY TO LICK YOUR FINGERS HERE.

Main's lean macaroni and cheese uses goat cheese instead of the usual American cheese and soy milk instead of cows' milk. The herbal fried trout uses curry powder and corn flour to batter the skinless fish. The trout comes straight from the sea. Boxes of jumbo yams are stacked in the small kitchen.

Ma Musu closed her Broad Street location in 2006 and opened her smaller 200 E. Main location. In the spring of 2014 she opened Chef Ma Musu's African and Caribbean Seasoning, a second store on the south side of Richmond. Ma Musu's younger sister, Victoria Carter, cooks at the new restaurant.

The humble Africanne on Main has been discovered by Liberian president Ellen Johnson Sirleaf, a former DC resident, and Dan Snyder, owner of the Washington Redskins football team.

In the summer of 2013 Snyder brought along his coaches, former Virginia governor George Allen (son of the late NFL coach George Allen), and the former governor's wife for lunch at Africanne on Main. In 2013 the team had moved their training camp to a new state-of-the-art facility in Richmond, about ninety minutes south of DC.

"We started setting up tables and putting up linen for them," Ma Musu recalls. "They said they didn't need any of that. They just ate and ate and ate for two hours."

The hungry football community even bought into Ma Musu's pay-by-weight program.

"Look, if you can eat three pounds for lunch that should be enough for you all day," she says. "When I started pay-by-weight the customers didn't appreciate it because they saw it was too much or too expensive or whatever. I had to explain to them even if you have a dollar, you can eat. You don't have to eat a whole pound of food. Sometimes for lunch you might want some vegetables and a piece of fish. Here, you can look and see what you want. You're not ordering off a menu. It all is there. Now everybody loves it. It is control for customers and us. We have less than one percent waste in this restaurant. On top of that it is faster. You can get your food, put it on the scale, and get out," and Ma Musu nods to a neighborhood postman picking up vegetables and chicken to go.

Sandra D. Norman is enjoying vegetables and chicken in a nearby booth. Norman is the former longtime director of the Virginia Human Rights Council. She sees Africanne on Main as a vehicle of greater understanding. "This is a place to meet," says Norman, who goes back with Ma Musu since her hair-braiding days. "I bring my board here. This is a place to reacquaint, renew, and even acknowledge. This place is unique. My girlfriend had her wedding reception at the chef's place. She now has me pack up food and have it shipped to Hawaii where she lives. I like the fact the chef educates you. Even when I'm not around her, I can still hear her."

Ma Musu's restaurants are open from 11 AM until 4 PM Monday through Friday. The boutique hours give her more time to give back to the community she loves. She operates a school teaching the fundamentals of domesticity to Richmond girls between the ages of eleven and fifteen. Classes are held in ten-week increments and conclude with hands-on cooking sessions. She began the school in 2009. She graduates fifteen girls per session. Classes are free. Ma Musu's school is sponsored by Bon Secours Richmond Health System.

"What their grandma did with soul food was not healthy," she says. "It was too heavy, too fatty. I teach grandma's flavor but healthier.

"The girls come from all parts of the city. The projects, underdeveloped areas. The girls have no eating habits when they come to me. They don't even like water. They don't know vegetables. That is the first challenge for me. I almost have to deprogram them. Every day they have to try something they have never tried before. That is hard.

"It's funny, the mom would come to the class and be furious: 'I have no money and when the kids come home they say, "We can't eat this." You're messing up my house.' I told them they can't use canned vegetables any more and they go, 'What are you talking about, I buy three for a dollar!' Then the kids started going shopping with their moms."

Ma Musu becomes frustrated when some of the children are obese when they sign up for class. She wants to teach them for more than ten weeks. She says, "My goal is to someday have a building for an after-school program to help these girls. I don't teach them basic cooking, I teach them the art of cooking. I teach them temperature control. What type of pots to use. We talk about healing spices. Parsley. Thyme. Ginger."

In 2013 the Southern Foodways Alliance awarded Ma Musu its prestigious Tabasco Guardians of the Tradition award, given to those whose work has helped keep alive southern foodways. "Chef Ma Musu being an immigrant from Liberia, her story is such a story of southern food," said Amy C. Evans, lead oral historian for the alliance, based at the University of Mississippi. "But it is such a contemporary story. She is using her restaurant for advocacy for the community and young people. It is really remarkable work."

Ma Musu concludes, "My restaurant is not for everybody. I hate to say that, but I support healthy eating. I don't cross over into burgers and fries. Even if I did sandwiches nobody would probably eat them. They'd say, 'She's from Africa, what does she know about a bologna sandwich?' So you try to stay in your box. Believe me, I've got plenty in my box to move forward. I always tell people if I died today and came back I would be doing the same thing. There isn't anything in this world I love more than cooking.

"It's not a passion for me. It *is* me, it is my soul."

Keli-Willy (Sweet Fried Plantain and Vegetable Medley)

A mouthwatering, healthy serving of Ma Musu's sweet corn bread absolutely complements this meal. However, you can also add chicken and fish to this entrée for those who enjoy meat. Bon appétit.

(Serves 5)

Ingredients

1 cup vegetable oil

2 ripe yellow plantains

1 pound fresh frozen mixed vegetables (peas, corn, carrots, etc.)

1 each yellow, green, and red bell pepper

1 onion

1 teaspoon each ground ginger, cayenne pepper, parsley, and basil

¼ teaspoon sea salt

Directions

Preheat the vegetable oil in a large skillet to 350°F. Dice the plantains and then fry until golden brown. Set aside. Steam the mixed vegetables until softened, then drain and set aside.

Dice the peppers and onion. Fry them until golden brown (soft texture). Add all remaining ingredients, including the plantains, to the skillet and stir well. Cook on low heat (250°F) for 10 minutes. Serve hot.

Part 3

Urban Soul

MARVIN

◆◆◆

2007 14th Street NW, Washington, DC
(202) 797-7171 • www.marvindc.com

MARVIN IS A BELGIAN-INFLUENCED SOUL FOOD RESTAURANT CREATED IN TRIBUTE TO DC NATIVE AND MOTOWN SOUL SINGER MARVIN GAYE. It is at the stubborn kind of corner at Fourteenth and U Street NW, center point of the 1968 riots following the assassination of Dr. Martin Luther King.

I first had dinner at Marvin while in DC for the inauguration of President Barack Obama. That seems like a very long time ago.

The ornate ninety-seat main dining room was accented with French Bistro–inspired decor and dim lighting. The room was uplifted by a wall-sized color portrait of Marvin Gaye on roller skates, made by local artists Brian Liu and Nick Pimengel.

I enjoyed steamed mussels served in a big white bowl, accented by rich, thick gumbo. About halfway through dinner Curtis Mayfield's "This Is My Country" played loudly in the background. The late Chicago native is my favorite soul songwriter. The music was not intrusive; in fact, it blended into the soul of the food and that creates magic. On the eve of the inauguration Mayfield sang:

> Shall we perish unjust or live equal as a nation
> This is my country

"I made that playlist for that week," Marvin owner Eric Hilton said during a recent conversation at Marvin. Hilton is one-half of Thievery Corporation, the electronica-soul DJ team who won a 2008 Grammy for their album *Radio Retaliation*. "That was an amazing week, especially here, which felt like ground zero," he said. "There was so much energy. Ironically Curtis Mayfield is my favorite artist. Marvin is

Eric Hilton is the owner of Marvin. He is also one-half of the Grammy-winning electronica-soul DJ team Thievery Corporation.

very close, but when I look at the body of work of Curtis Mayfield it was a bit more revolutionary. His lyrics were chilling. Marvin had that period where he made a better record than Curtis ever made (*What's Going On*, 1971), but he did it once. If we were in Chicago, maybe the restaurant would be called Curtis."

Hilton was born in 1967, a year before the King riots that tore apart the neighborhood. After the riots, DC became known as "Chocolate City," a term first popularized on the radio by politically fueled disc jockeys Petey Greene Jr., Bobby "the Mighty Burner" Bennett, and others.

The great jazz space traveler Sun Ra headlined the New School for Afro-American Thought at 2208 Fourteenth Street NW. Marvin is around the corner from the restored Lincoln Theater at 1215 U Street NW. The twelve hundred–seat theater was built in 1921 and headliners have included Duke Ellington, Billie Holiday, and Cab Calloway. The Lincoln closed after the 1968 race riots, reopened in 1994, closed again, and reopened again in 2013. During the spring of 2014, contemporary rock and pop acts Eels, Rufus Wainwright, and Wolfmother were playing the Lincoln.

Hilton said, "Now there is so much gentrification down by lower Fourteenth, and I hate that word because it sounds like white people are some sort of 'gentries.' But there is no comparison to the diversity of the crowd at Marvin. We're proud of that."

In August 2012 Marvin found itself in the center of the "swagger-jacking" phenomenon explained by Stephen A. Crockett Jr. in a *Washington Post* Root DC blog post. Crockett said that the popularity of U Street NW restaurants was framed by African American culture, even though the residents who lived that culture had to leave because of rising property values. Crockett wrote, in part, "This place was a place well before you. You didn't make Ben's [Chili Bowl], we did. This city was pig intestines after so many left and we made it into chitterlings. And these places, these fancy places with 'authentic food,' aren't homes. They're just rentals."

What set Crockett off was the opening of a restaurant called Brixton, named after the multicultural neighborhood in London that was swallowed up by gentrification in the 1990s. Crockett also called out Eatonville, Busboys and Poets (named after poet Langston Hughes's 1930s gig as a busboy), and Marvin, all within a six-block stretch of U Street NW.

"I liked it," Hilton said of the "swagger-jacking" manifest. "That article should have been written. The only reason I don't agree on is when you write something like that and blanketly call a bunch of people 'swagger jacking,' you don't know all those people individually. You don't know where they are coming from."

Hilton, who is white, paused and dished a wry smile. "A true swagger-jacker," he said, "would be somebody who has no passion behind what he is doing. There is no knowledge of the past or the place. They are doing it as a marketing ploy. But this [African American] demographic is becoming less and less and there are more places named after folks from that demographic. There is something ironic and almost eerie about that. It is worth recognizing."

Hilton sat next to Marvin manager Sheldon Scott at a table in Marvin's large second-floor private dining room. A series of black and white portraits of 1940s and '50s jazz and soul artists hung on the wall behind them. Marvin is punctuated by these pictures, many of which were given to the restaurant by an octogenarian jazz drummer who played the U Street corridor.

The walls of Marvin are adorned with photographs of artists who once performed in the neighborhood, Abbey Lincoln (top) and Marvin Gaye. They were both outspoken champions of civil rights.

The historic Ben's Chili Bowl is also around the corner from Marvin's. Ben's was a safe place during the 1968 riots that engulfed the neighborhood. Dr. Bernard Demczuk is assistant vice president in the Office of Government and Community Relations at the George Washington University and is Ben's historian. He has been dining at Ben's since 1967. "We're in a historical trend right now," he said in a separate interview. "There are three great waves of American cities. The first wave was 1840 to 1945. That's when farm boys and girls leave the farm and come to the city for a job: Chicago; Detroit; Gary, Indiana; DC; Baltimore. Cities expand. The second wave is 1945 to 1990. People leave the cities to go to the suburbs. Great highways. Everybody wants a little house with a white picket fence—except the white house, picket fence were confined to white people. Black people stayed in the city, and with the great migration, particularly from Mississippi to Chicago and through DC, these cities become primarily African American. Now, we're in the third great wave, which started in the early 1990s. Everybody loves the cities. People are tired of the traffic jams in Virginia and outside of Chicago and they're moving back to the city. It's not any conspiracy that white people are trying to take over the cities. It is basic economics. Cities have become extremely popular places."

Sheldon Scott, who is black, said, "We feel this place can pride itself on being the intersection between the new U Street and the old U Street. It is a discussion more about sharing the light than passing the torch. My relationship with soul music came from spending a lot of time at Marvin, listening to the playlists. Particularly during my generation a lot of soul music was recycled during the height of hip-hop. My growing up was Sam Cooke and Stax Records.

"Sometimes for us, soul music represents a period for black America that wasn't necessarily good."

On Valentine's Day 1981, Marvin Gaye left the United States for Ostend, Belgium, to move into the apartment of Belgian boxing and music promoter Freddy Cousaert. Gaye was trying to steer clear of drugs. He embarked on an exercise program and started attending church in Ostend.

He boxed at an Ostend gymnasium. Gaye wrote his last major hit, "Sexual Healing," in Ostend, a small seaside city on the Belgium coast. Gaye's personal attorney, Curtis Shaw, described the singer-songwriter's Ostend period as "the best thing that ever happened to Marvin." On March 23, 1982, Motown and CBS Records negotiated for Gaye to be released from Motown. The details of the contract were kept private due to Gaye's IRS debts.

On April 1, 1984, Gaye was shot to death by his father, Marvin Gay Sr., after an argument in his father's Los Angeles home. His father used a Smith & Wesson .38-caliber pistol that his son had given him for Christmas.

Marvin Gaye was forty-four years old.

Hilton said, "I started reading about Marvin Gaye and learned he went to high school right up the street. Belgian food is pretty similar to French food, and I like French food. I went to Belgium with my stepson James Claudio [the original chef at Marvin]. The first thing we got in Belgium was this big pork knuckle [the shank end of a hog's leg bone]. I thought, 'This is like southern American food.' We quickly realized these foods completely go together. Basically you're cooking classic French techniques. You can put chicken with the Belgian waffles and collard greens and it all works. Shrimp and grits with a Belgian cheese tastes really great. That was appealing to me.

"Then I called my partners about my crazy idea and said I was thinking of calling the place 'Marvin.' I'm looking out the window of my studio and the sticker for the brand of window was still on it. It was Marvin Windows. People got it. They liked the fact it brought some notoriety back to the fact Marvin Gaye is from DC. We don't claim too many musical stars from DC. There's a lot [Tori Amos, Duke Ellington, soul singer Billy Stewart], but people come and go here so often they don't invest a lot of mental energy into learning the history of the town. That is a double-edged sword. We love that people move into town and leave town, so it keeps the place feeling fresher than it would, but it also leaves the history unlearned."

Marvin Gaye's family approved of the concept and family members have dined at Marvin. Hilton never ran the idea by the family. "One day I got a call out of the blue from Jan Gaye [second wife of Marvin Gaye]," he said. "We talked for a long time. We're friends with her and she comes down for our [annual April 2 birthday tribute] Marvin Gaye Day. She's tickled somebody gave Marvin a shout-out. She understands it is a tribute. I get upset when people call it Marvin's. It is not possessive. You're not going to find his relatives behind the bar, we're not trying to market the restaurant that way. Nona Gaye [Marvin's actress-singer daughter, born 1974] and some cousins have come down. It is fun to hear old stories from them."

In 1971 Marvin Gaye broke from the formulaic pop motif of Motown Records to

Marvin opened in a former Subway sandwich shop that had been abandoned.

record the social concept album *What's Going On*. Gaye told the story from the point of view of a Vietnam veteran returning to America. Besides the title track, *What's Going On* delivered the hit singles "Mercy Mercy Me (The Ecology)" and "Inner City Blues (Makes Me Wanna Holler)." In 2009 the album placed sixth on Rolling Stone magazine's "500 Greatest Albums of All Time."

What's Going On is Hilton's favorite album, even more than anything Curtis Mayfield did. "It doesn't really change," he explained. "That record is going to be hard for someone to come along and top in terms of a popular music record. Marvin was becoming more aware at that time and it was one of the more admirable periods of his life." Motown did once have an imprint called Black Forum that released albums by Amiri Baraka, Langston Hughes, and Stokely Carmichael.

Marvin opened in a former Subway sandwich shop that had been abandoned. "The neighborhood was a bit rougher around 2007," Hilton said. "Vagrants drove the guy crazy and he closed. The building was vacant for four or five years. We have a history of opening places in vacant buildings. We gutted this building. It was a disaster. We're still very good friends with the landlord. He has a lot of properties in this area. He gave us the building at a more than reasonable price."

Marvin has become a popular stop for the music community and touring bands. The restaurant was used for a clandestine meeting scene in the 2013 Oscar-nominated documentary *Dirty Wars*, based on the book by investigative journalist Jeremy Scahill. Marvin is referenced in *Bitch Is the New Black*, the debut 2010 novel from Washington journalist Helena Andrews.

Scott grew up in South Carolina. His mom, Shirley, is a school bus driver. "Shirley could cook," he said with a smile. "She could burn. We ate rice every day. We came from rice country. My brother's name is Maurice because my Dad said my Mom wanted 'more rice' all the time. My favorite meal was rice, sweet peas, bulb onions, and fried chicken."

Hilton grew up in Rockville, Maryland, where his father, Chuck, was a home builder and his mother, Judy, was a realtor and grant writer. In 2012 Hilton opened Chez Billy, a tribute to the former Billy Simpson's House of Seafood and Steaks in the historic Petworth neighborhood just north of Howard University. Located in a building constructed in 1923, the restaurant was a meeting place for DC's African American community during the civil rights movement. The restaurant closed in the late 1970s after Simpson's death in 1975. In 2009 the restaurant was placed on the National Register of Historic Places.

Marvin manager Sheldon Scott.

"From what I've read it was the only white tablecloth African American restaurant in the city," Hilton said. "I find that hard to believe." Scott added, "It hasn't been disputed."

Hilton said the Chez Billy project was "dropped in our lap." The developer obtained the abandoned building from the city.

"That place is kind of like Marvin on steroids when it comes to fine dining," he said. "But it is just French food. It is important because in America there are so many places that are no place."

Marvin Dijon Mussels

(Serves 4)

Ingredients

1 tablespoon butter
2 tablespoons finely chopped shallots
1 teaspoon finely chopped garlic
3 quarts mussels, beards removed, cleaned and scrubbed (but you can't do this in advance!)

1 teaspoon sea salt
Freshly ground pepper, to taste
2 tablespoons chopped tarragon
¼ cup dry white wine
2 tablespoons Dijon mustard

Directions

Heat the butter in a large saucepan until melted.

Add the shallots and garlic, and cook briefly, until wilted. Do not brown.

Add the mussels, salt, pepper, and tarragon. Cover closely and bring to a boil.

Cook for about 5 minutes, shaking to redistribute the mussels. Cook until all the mussels are opened.

Using a slotted spoon, transfer the mussels to a serving bowl. Keep warm.

Continue cooking the sauce for 1 minute. Stir in the mustard with a wire whisk while heating. Do not boil.

Season sauce to taste with salt if necessary, then spoon equal portions of it over the mussels, and sprinkle with tarragon.

Serve immediately with crusty bread or frites.

BEN'S CHILI BOWL

◆◆

1213 U Street NW, Washington DC
(202) 667-0909 • www.benschilibowl.com

DURING THE DAWN OF HER MARRIAGE, VIRGINIA ALI WOULD VISIT THE PARENTS OF HER HUSBAND, BEN ALI, IN PORT OF SPAIN, TRINIDAD, WEST INDIES. The family home was along the lush Queens Park Savannah, a former horse-racing track filled with flowers and lavish saman trees.

Queens Park is the site of the country's annual calypso carnival where music, food, and smiles play on until the early morning hours.

"Queens Park is a beautiful area," Ali reminisces on a spring day at the Chili Bowl. "We'd sit on the balcony and watch the carnival parades go by. The fragrance of flowers was faint in the fresh air and often overpowered by the scent of my mother-in-law's curry cooking in the kitchen."

Ben and Virginia were married in 1958, the same year they opened Ben's Chili Bowl in what was then DC's "Black Broadway."

Ben died in October 2009. Virginia is eighty years old as she holds court in the Chili Bowl's back room on a Monday afternoon.

She still enjoys the carnival parade of U Street NW.

"When you open a restaurant the important thing is your location," she explains. "Well, this was a segregated city in 1958. And this was the heart of the African American community. There were jazz clubs. Theaters. He looked for property here."

Ben and Virginia Ali on their wedding day on October 12, 1958, when interracial marriages were illegal in the state of Virginia. Ben was Indian; Virginia is African American. *Courtesy of Virginia Ali*

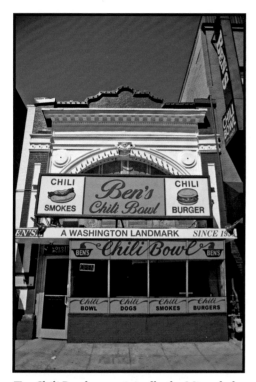
The Chili Bowl was originally the Minnehaha Theater, built in 1910.

Ben had his eye on a large pool hall that originally was the Minnehaha Theater, built in 1910. The Minnehaha was one of the first silent movie houses in America to cater to African Americans. Portions of the original facade and original copper ceiling remain at the Chili Bowl.

In December 2008 the restaurant expanded to Ben's Next Door and Gift Shop, an upscale space that features a fifty-three-foot bar and dinner seating for ninety-four at tables. It also contains a shipping department for Ben's Jumbo Lump Crab Cakes and She Crab Soup. Ben's Next Door is in the former Jungle Inn (circa 1930s) where singer Pearl Bailey was discovered. She coined the term "Black Broadway" during segregation since African Americans were not permitted to attend white downtown theaters.

The Lincoln Theater was next door, and remains as a live music venue. The Republic Theater (closed in 1976) was a block west of the Lincoln. And the Booker T. Theatre (also closed in 1976) was a block away from the Republic. "There were live shows but they were mostly [movie] theaters at that time," Virginia says. "Miles Davis and Duke Ellington came to our restaurant. They could perform downtown but they didn't dine downtown.

"We were open to all walks of life. Intellectually, economically, whatever. The music was always jumping. We always had a loud jukebox. We stayed open until four in the morning as we do today. That accommodated people who finished up at 2 AM in the nightclubs.

"Our slogan was 'Sober up with a chili dog.'"

Ben created his now-famous chili half-smoke when he opened the restaurant. The chili half-smoke (mixed pork and natural casing beef) is grilled and served on a steamed bun with mustard, onions, and a spicy chili sauce. The first thing President Barack Obama did in his January 2009 DC orientation was to eat a chili half-smoke at Ben's. Virginia and Ben missed his visit. They were on a Mediterranean cruise.

Ben's Chili Bowl circa mid-1960s. *Courtesy of Virginia Ali*

Hillary Clinton held a fundraiser at Ben's for her US Senate seat and the Chili Bowl was featured in the 1993 Denzel Washington hit film *The Pelican Brief*.

Pedestrians can see the three-foot-by-five-foot grill from Ben's large front window. One step into Ben's and you are ignited by a celebration of life: the sound of a sizzle, the steamy smell of chili and hot dogs, and on this day the Jimmy Castor Bunch's "Boom Boom" and Curtis Mayfield's "Superfly" blaring out of the Saturn II Jukebox. In August 2013 *Smithsonian* magazine named Ben's as one of the twenty best food destinations in America.

Ben conjured up almost all of the recipes, but Virginia chipped in with her family's notorious "Catch a Man Fried Chicken" (chicken, buttermilk, a tablespoon of paprika, pinch of red pepper, Tabasco sauce to taste, wheat flour, and finely chopped shallots). Ben's has used just two local, family-operated meat companies since 1958.

"I used to eat a chili dog every day," Virginia says in proud tones. "At age seventy-five the cholesterol started moving up so I had to cut back. Now I share one. At one time the half-smoke was DC's signature dish and the chili half-smoke is our most popular item. I attribute that to Bill Cosby, who has been coming here since 1959."

When he was younger, Cosby could down up to six half-smokes at a time.

"He was here for the fifty-fifth anniversary of the Chili Bowl. When he became the first African American to have a number one television show [with *The Cosby Show* in September 1985], NBC asked him to hold a press conference. The neighborhood wasn't very nice at the time but he held it here. He hosted my eightieth birthday party next door at the Lincoln Theater."

Virginia Ali grew up on a 350-acre corn and soybean farm in Loretto, Virginia, about a hundred miles from DC. She was born on December 17, 1933. Her father, Alphonso, was a Native American who delivered US mail on horseback to supplement the family income.

Alphonso and Esther Rollins had three daughters and two sons. "We raised chickens and turkeys," she says. "But we only prepared turkey on Christmas and Thanksgiving. The table could accommodate twelve people. If there were eighteen, twenty people to eat that day the table would have to be completely cleared. Sometimes I'd sit in the second group. No one took a plate and sat in the living room. No. It was around the table as a family. Ben and I mixed the cultures a little bit."

When Virginia and Mahaboob Ben Ali decided to get married in 1958, interracial marriages were illegal in Virginia. The Rollins's minister at a DC-based Christian church was a friend of the family. "He wanted to know about Ben's religious affiliation," Virginia says. "Ben was Muslim. So he would not marry me. The State of Virginia would not marry us. We didn't ask anyone else. We went to the judge's chambers and were married there in a civil ceremony." Children's voices tumble out of the Chili Bowl's front room and the jukebox music plays on.

Ben cashed in on his considerable sales skills to meet Virginia. She was a bank teller at Industrial Bank, the only minority bank in DC. It remains as one of the oldest African American banks in the country. "It is just a block and a half down the street," she says. "This guy was coming in quite often. He was working at a business in the neighborhood. One day he hung around and got in my line although the other line was shorter. He wrote a note on a quarter wrapper which said, 'Please call me.' He signed it with his phone number and Ben Ali."

Virginia pauses and looks me in the eye. This is serious. She continues, "In 1956 a lady did not call some man you didn't know. The bank closed at 2 PM. Now, Ben, being who he was, is calling me by 2:30 PM. In the conversation we realized we knew the same people. Ben had been in dental school for a little while. One of his colleagues from dental school brought him to our home and introduced us formally. He was confident. He knew where he wanted to be, where he wanted to go. He was a real charmer. A real charmer. I wasn't concerned about religion or anything else." They dated for eighteen months and were married in 1958.

Ben had left Trinidad to study at the University of Nebraska in Lincoln. He came to DC to attend dental school at Howard University.

"One day he walked onto an elevator and the floor wasn't there," Virginia says. "He fell down the shaft and severely injured his back. He was not able to complete the dental school program. He didn't have the funds to pay his way through school so he worked in restaurants from the beginning in Nebraska." Ben mopped floors and was a maître d' in DC. He drove a cab to make ends meet.

The magic of Ben's Chili Bowl has been its transparency. "When we opened there was a plate glass window in the front where you could see all the way inside," she says. "The way it was designed, you put ten people in here and it looks like it is pretty busy." The current front area seats ten people along the counter—usually regulars—and another sixteen in wide booths and tables. The fifty-two-seat back room with a traditional black-and-white tile floor was added in 2005 in a former storage area. The original twenty-two-seat middle room, aka "the Cosmopolitan Room," was spruced up in the mid-1970s with a hipster mid-century Jetson design.

Ben Ali purposely planned to debut his restaurant on the opening weekend of a 1958 Elks convention. A convention highlight was a Saturday morning parade that drew thousands of people to U Street. The visitors packed the new Chili Bowl. But in less than a decade, Ben and Virginia would witness a new America was coming down the street.

"Black Broadway" went up in flames during the riots that followed the April 4, 1968, assassination of Dr. Martin Luther King. Four days earlier Dr. King had delivered a sermon at the Washington National Cathedral. He said, "If nothing is done between now and June to raise ghetto hope, I feel this summer will not only be as bad but worse than last year."

The DC riots began one block from Ben's when a brick was tossed through the window of the People's Drug store at Fourteenth and U. It was a drugstore that prohibited African Americans from eating at the counter, according to Virginia.

One brick flying through a window became a moment of empowerment.

Dr. King had been a visitor at a satellite office of the SCLC a couple blocks away at Fourteenth and U. The Student Nonviolent Coordinating Committee had an office across the street from Ben's. SNCC leader Stokely Carmichael asked Ben to keep the restaurant open. Ben received permission to stay open during curfew periods and the restaurant fed police, firefighters, and members of SNCC.

Ben scrawled "Soul Brother" in soap on his big front window. Carmichael was also a native of Port of Spain, Trinidad.

"Stokely Carmichael was here daily," Virginia says. "Whether 'Soul Brother' saved us or not, I don't know. Stokely Carmichael provided the passes for our staff to come to work during the curfew. People needed a place to meet to try and find a way to quell the violence that was occurring in our city. There were gangs of young people roaming the streets. I remember the tear gas. But no one broke in here. This place made me feel safe."

President Lyndon Johnson had appointed Walter Washington as DC mayor. After seeing Chicago, Detroit, and Newark blow up, President Johnson understood he had a tinderbox with the large poor black community (aka Chocolate City) in DC. As a result Washington became the only mayor in America to give the order not to shoot at looters.

The neighborhood changed dramatically after the riots. There was more crime, more drug use. "The middle class moved away," Virginia says. "It became a real ghetto.

The 1968 DC riots began one block from Ben's. The restaurant became a safe haven for firefighters, police officers, and members of the Student Nonviolent Coordinating Committee. Owner Ben Ali's empathy is honored in a walkway adjacent to the Chili Bowl.

Every Sunday in the *Washington Post* there were stories of drug busts at Fourteenth and U [the site of People's Drug]. It was the center of the drug trade." The drug traffic got so bad that Ben's stopped serving homemade cakes and pies because the sugar in the desserts lured addicts to the restaurant.

"We were the poorest neighborhood in town but the last to get the subway system," Virginia says. "In the late 1980s they gave us a [Metro Green Line] subway stop. But because there were so many boarded-up properties and businesses that never reopened after the riots here, there was not a single lane of traffic on U Street. There were no streetlights. When the sun went down, we left. I only needed one employee and me to run the business at that time."

A wall of the back room is anchored by a painting made by DC artist Fasil Dawit. The painting features Ben's visitors such as Bill Cosby, Oprah Winfrey, Malcolm X, Rev. Jesse Jackson, and others. In 2008 Dawit intended to paint a portrait of Ben Ali, but when Ben's son Kamal Ali visited Dawit's studio he saw the portrait of the civil rights icons. He purchased the painting. Dawit never got around to painting Ben Ali.

In a breakfast conversation at Ruby's (formerly Edna's) on the West Side of Chicago, Rev. Jackson said, "Ben's was always good, clean, and fast. Bill Cosby has made it his hideaway. Georgetown has shifted into that area. It used to be run-down and drug-infested. When they built that new transportation line it changed everything. Ben's has been the big beneficiary of that. It has tripled in size."

Dr. Bernard Demczuk is assistant vice president in the Office of Government and Community Relations at the George Washington University in Washington, DC. He is also the official curator and historian at Ben's Chili Bowl. He often can be found working from a laptop in the restaurant's back room and sometimes waits tables.

Demczuk was born in 1948 and has been coming to Ben's since 1967. In the late 1960s he was attending the University of Maryland in College Park. Demczuk was a wide receiver for the Terrapins football team. His quarterback was future Denver Bronco Alan Pastrana.

Demczuk and his friends would take a bus to see live soul music at the Howard Theater, then have a post-concert chili dog at Ben's. He says, "We are the only restaurant in DC that has its own full-time, PhD historian. One thing I try to do here and in my courses at the university is look at the renaissance in every American city, not just DC. The preservation and protection of black history and culture is important. We preserve it and defend it, but we also celebrate it. When you hear that jukebox blasting in the morning, that is a celebration of soul food. A celebration

At age eighty, Virginia Ali maintains a regular presence at Ben's.

of soul music. We celebrate who we are. And who we are is a very proud, diverse, and historic pageantry."

Or a parade. Yes, a parade.

Virginia Ali spends most of her time at Ben's Chili Bowl. Memories come alive. "I lost my husband four years ago after fifty-one years of marriage," she says. "There's no one home. So I come here. I meet wonderful people from across the world. And I get to spend time with my kids. It's good. And I love being with the public."

Haidar "Sage" Ben Ali (born in 1960) is married to Vida Ali. Kamal Ben Ali (born 1962) is married to Sonya Ali. And Nizam Ben Ali (born 1970) is married to Jyotika Vazirani. Nizam runs Ben's on U Street in DC with Kamal. Ben's Chili Bowl is a true family operation.

Cosby views the family as role models. In the foreword for *Ben's Chili Bowl: Fifty Years of a Washington, D.C. Landmark* he wrote, "Ben's sons Nizam and Kamal represent something that is sorely needed in our culture. It is very simple: children continuing in the paths of their parents. A mother and father start a family business in a lower economic area. The sons marry, and then wife, husband, and children all take care of the business and face the change of the social environment, balancing economics and community."

Virginia converted to the Muslim faith when Haidar was born. Did the diversity in her home life give Virginia insight on how to deal with the Chili Bowl's diverse customers? Demczuk estimates that about 60 percent of those who come to Ben's are tourists.

"People are simply people," Virginia says. "It doesn't matter where you come from. I know that people treat you the way you treat them."

Demcuzuk adds, "This is a place of not just memory, but identity. People identify with their Black Broadway. Their black community. Their city of Washington, DC. It is also a place of comfort. Place is home. Home is place."

The place around the place has changed. There are now million-dollar condos and upscale apartment buildings. One newer upscale U Street apartment complex is called the Ellington—as in the same Duke who once was boxed out of downtown DC.

Virginia and her family update the menu to stay current with contemporary eating habits. In recent years they added vegan chili, vegetarian hot dogs, and salad bowls topped with tomatoes, onions, shredded cheddar cheese, and choice of veggie or chili con carne. Newer popular desserts include pineapple-coconut cake.

Virginia calls Ben's Chili Bowl "a sacred place." She recalls, "My youngest son said, 'We should celebrate you being here forty years [1998]. OK, fine, or whatever. My husband and I went on to Trinidad." Nizam called his parents a couple days before the event and told them to come home early. The Chili Bowl anniversary was gaining steam.

"Well, not just the politicians were here," Virginia says. "CNN was here. But what was profound for me was to see a line of people a block long on a hot August day waiting to buy a chili dog. We weren't giving away anything. It was then that I felt that we meant something to this community."

The street in front of the restaurant is named Ben Ali Way. And the walkway next

All of the children of Ben and Virginia Ali work at the Bowl. Kamal Ali steps up to the plate on a busy weekday shift.

to the restaurant is Virginia Ali Way, which was dedicated on her eightieth birthday, December 15, 2013. There is a Ben Ali Drive in Trinidad and a street named for Ben Ali in Ghana.

On February 26, 2014, a second Ben's opened in Arlington, Virginia, in the shadow of Arlington National Cemetery. There is also a Ben's stand at Nationals Park, the home of baseball's Washington Nationals. Bill Cosby helped Virginia cut the ribbon in Virginia, and during the ceremony the US Navy veteran said in part, "I want my body buried not far, so my ghost can get up, make the trip here instead of flying over to U Street. So when you all are here after midnight and you see a bag leaving but nobody with it . . ." Indeed, Cosby brought an insulated bag to the ceremony to take two dozen half-smokes for his staff.

In the spring of 2014 Virginia Ali was still ambling up the back room spiral staircase ten times a day to her small office. "I don't know how much longer I can do that," she says, but then you know she will—as long as she is uplifted by the spirit of Ben's Chili Bowl.

Coleslaw

(Serves 10)

Ingredients

1 medium head fresh green cabbage
1 fresh carrot
½ cup white vinegar

1 cup mayonnaise
¾ cup sugar

Directions

Finely shred the green cabbage and the carrot and combine in a large bowl.

In a separate bowl, whip together the vinegar, mayonnaise, and sugar until smooth and creamy. Add the dressing to the cabbage and carrot mixture and stir thoroughly. Refrigerate for at least 2 hours before serving.

SYLVIA'S RESTAURANT

◆◆

328 Malcolm X Boulevard, New York, New York
(212) 966-0660 • www.sylviasrestaurant.com

PILGRIMS OF SOUL COME FROM ALL OVER THE WORLD TO CENTRAL HARLEM FOR AN AUTHENTIC SUNDAY GOSPEL BRUNCH AT SYLVIA'S. Live gospel music floats from the restaurant out to Lenox Avenue. A kaleidoscopic landscape is peppered with regulars along the counter and ladies adorned in churchgoing crowns.

Sylvia Woods was the "Queen of Soul Food," and Sylvia's is the best-known soul food restaurant in America.

With the rhythm of the James Brown camel walk, buses come and go in front of Sylvia's. Left and right. North and south. Sylvia's is part of a gentrified block that includes celebrity chef Marcus Samuelsson's popular Red Rooster soul food nightspot and the Corner Social, an upscale bar and restaurant that opened in 2012 across the street from Sylvia's.

Every Sunday the Simpsons, a family gospel group, commutes one hour and fifteen minutes from New Jersey to the Harlem neighborhood of Manhattan to sing high praises at the brunch. They are also pilgrims.

You sit in the background at Sylvia's long, swerving white counter with waffles and crispy-skinned fried chicken, adding a shot of Sylvia's Triple Strength Hot Sauce (with aged cayenne pepper and distilled vinegar) for rebirth. There is a hurried air about the room except for the relaxed manner of old men dining alone at the counter.

For most of the other guests this is New York City and there are more places to see. The tour buses will soon leave the world's kitchen, but it is a detour off a train that uplifted the neighborhood. The ride wasn't on Duke Ellington's "A" train.

Malcolm Little was a porter on a Pullman train car. He was born in 1925 in Omaha, Nebraska, and grew up in Lansing, Michigan, where he grew peas and raised chickens on the family's garden plot. In 1941 Little was working on a Boston to Washington, DC, run. He disembarked at Pennsylvania Station and took a cab to Harlem. He had heard important things about Harlem.

Little settled in Harlem around 1943. In 1946, at age twenty, he went to prison for breaking and entering. While in prison he became a member of the Nation of Islam and was released on parole as El-Hajj Malik El-Shabazz in 1952.

Malcolm X birthed the Black Power Movement. And Lenox Avenue would become known as Malcolm X Boulevard.

In February 1967 Malcolm X was assassinated in New York City by three members of the Nation of Islam. His landmark *Autobiography of Malcolm X*, based on interviews with journalist Alex Haley, was released shortly after his death. In it he explained that *X* represented the authentic African family name that was lost.

He also recalled how his father spoke of Harlem with pride: "And every time Joe Louis won a fight against a white opponent, big front-page pictures in the Negro newspapers such as the *Chicago Defender*, the *Pittsburgh Courier*, showed a sea of Harlem negroes cheering and waving and the Brown Bomber waving back at them from the balcony of Harlem's Theresa Hotel. Everything I'd ever heard about New York City was exciting."

At last. A world that made sense.

This was not lost on Sylvia Woods, who found her way to Harlem from Hemingway, South Carolina. She opened a six-booth, fifteen-stool soul food restaurant in 1962 at Lenox at 127th Street. During the 1950s she worked at Johnson's Luncheonette in Harlem. She told people that working at Johnson's was the first time she had been in a restaurant because of her poor upbringing in rural South Carolina. Woods died in July 2012 at the age of eighty-six.

The restaurant has remained in the family. All four children of Sylvia and the late Herbert Woods are involved on a daily basis:

Sylvia Woods opened the first Sylvia's, a six-booth, fifteen-stool soul food restaurant, in 1962 in Harlem.

Kenneth is president and CEO. Crizette is comptroller and head of human resources. Bedelia is head of catering, and Van is head of business development. Granddaughter Tren'ness Woods-Black is Sylvia's vice president of communications. Her baby sister, Kendra, also manages the restaurant with Crizette's daughter Zaqura. Another sister, Sabeanna, takes care of the tour groups with Woods-Black's cousin Richard. They are a protective and proud group.

Members of the "Sylvia's family."

"But it's a family business and everyone fills in wherever needed," Woods-Black said during a Sunday brunch break conversation. "My grandparents worked hard to build this business. My grandmother learned from her mother, who was an entrepreneur. She was a midwife and a farmer. And her mother's mother was a midwife and a farmer who was born into slavery but died owning so much property that she was able to give property to all her children. They did not have to sharecrop.

"I'm a fifth-generation entrepreneur, which is really unheard of in African American culture."

Woods-Black was born in 1972 and her memories are as rich as Sylvia's soul food. "We go back to our roots," she said. "Soul food is the most artisanal form of cooking that exists. We have over one hundred employees and that is because of our artisanal approach. I consider the restaurant not to be a place, but almost a family member.

"Soul is energy, soul is movement."

Tamika Mallory is a young community activist. A Sylvia's regular, she was born in 1980 and raised in the Manhattanville Houses public housing project in West Harlem. Her family moved to Co-Op City in the Bronx when she was fourteen. Her father, Stanley, is a retired corrections officer. Her mother, Voncile, worked for the city's taxi and limousine commission.

Between 2009 and 2013 Mallory was executive director of Rev. Al Sharpton's National Action Network (NAN). Her parents were two of the first members of

Tamika Mallory is a Sylvia's regular.

NAN, a nonprofit organization formed in the early 1990s. At age eleven Mallory joined NAN's youth group to learn about civil rights history.

Mallory has been on the front line of civil rights issues such as the Trayvon Martin case, the Troy Davis (Georgia execution) case, and the 2012 killing of four-year-old Lloyd Morgan Jr. in the South Bronx. She is known around Manhattan for her "new look" to activism, often marching the streets in heels and business attire. She walks the walk and talks the talk. Her son Tarique was born in 1999. Her son's father, Jason Ryans, was fatally shot in 2001.

By 2013 Mallory was serving on Vice President Joe Biden's gun-control task force. President Barack Obama's senior advisor Valerie Jarrett called Mallory a "leader of tomorrow."

And tomorrow concerns Mallory.

"A lot of younger people think we are post-racial," Malloy explained. "Post-racial means we are beyond the days of racial discrimination. The issues we deal with today are not because of race, but because of circumstance. But there's no way to look at circumstance without looking at the racial issues that cause certain things. People five years younger than me are in a harsh-reality place. We have to re-educate them. Our rights are being rolled back, like the stand-your-ground law and stop-and-frisk in New York City. Discrimination in general, you realize we're going back to a very dangerous time in the history of black people in America.

"Harlem was on fire in the 1960s. Literally. We were struggling with landlords leaving. Buildings abandoned. Drugs being imported into the community. Throughout the country the civil rights movement was going heavy, and pride and culture were very strong. People were trying to figure out what that was going to feel like and look like. Sylvia's was doing this thing called 'soul food.' And 'soul' was the term that was being called. That culture—the movement, the music, the food—that was the foundation of something great."

Woods-Black added, "You had Malcolm X walking down the street. Our restaurant was in the middle of all the action that was happening, whether it be happy or sad. Even when you go back to slavery days we found a way to make food the centerpiece of happiness, no matter what.

It's the same thing here. Black businesses and black churches have always been a place that people could go to have private conversations about how to continue the struggle. We can't have a meeting in the oppressor's office to talk about how to challenge him."

New York Democratic congressman Charles B. Rangel was an early advocate for political action at Sylvia's. The Harlem native was Sylvia's attorney. In the summer of 2014 Rangel, at age eighty-four, was elected to what he said will be his final term for New York's Thirteenth District in Congress. The Harlem native has represented the district since 1971.

"From the beginning Sylvia's has always provided an opportunity for people to get together and be free to talk about how to be free.

"This is more than a restaurant."

Esteemed New York food critic Gael Greene spilled the beans on Sylvia's in a March 1979 piece for *New York* magazine. In part she wrote that "Sylvia's worn homeyness is welcoming. . . . The counter is ancient. . . . Christ on a slab of wood. Martin Luther King on a plate . . ."

Since then Muhammad Ali, Robert F. Kennedy, Diana Ross, and Winnie Mandela have dined at Sylvia's. The Apollo Theater, 125th Street, is two blocks west of Sylvia's. Almost every Apollo headliner has come to Sylvia's, including James Brown and the Temptations. "Chris Rock has been a great supporter of our business and put us in one of his movies [2013's *Madly Madagascar*]," Woods-Black said. "His character had Sylvia's candied yams for Christmas."

Spike Lee wove Sylvia's into his 1991 smash film *Jungle Fever*.

Between 2001 and 2011 the nonprofit (President William) Clinton Foundation had an office on West 125th Street, across the street from Sylvia's. In 2009 President

Sylvia's soul food gospel brunch is one of the biggest international tourist attractions in Harlem.

Clinton helped launch the first Zagat Guide to Harlem. The president, who had an office in Harlem, was a regular at Sylvia's restaurant for her chicken and waffles. He offered a eulogy at Sylvia's funeral.

President Clinton sat in with the Simpsons gospel group to cover the Edwin Hawkins Singers 1969 crossover hit "Oh Happy Day" in an August 2001 "Welcome to Harlem" private luncheon in his honor at Sylvia's. "They had us roped off in the corner with the Secret Service," singer Ruth Simpson recalled. "He said, 'Move that rope, I have to get up with the Simpsons.' He had a pretty good voice and he was very down to earth. He was with Congressman Rangel and [former] Mayor David Dinkins."

The Simpsons have been singing regularly at Sylvia's since 1995. The Simpsons' sets are based in the large Red Room, adorned with red walls. The Red Room opened in 1983 in the former Uptown Bar. But Ruth wanders through the entire complex singing through a wireless microphone.

Ruth was born in 1957 in Harlem Hospital. Her parents, Woodrow and Lena Story, were evangelists. "Harlem has changed a great deal," she said. "The brownstones are rebuilt. There's more nationalities. You used to hear the stories, 'Don't go to Harlem.' Now you should go to Harlem." Ruth and Clinton are also evangelists and their empathy helps them understand their diverse audience. "We try to do a lot of universal songs," said Ruth, who lives with her husband in South Plainfield, New Jersey, where they have raised four children. "People always request 'Oh Happy Day' [which they do as a medley with "This Little Light of Mine" and "Amazing Grace"]. And we've seen people from all over the world.''

Food critic Greene has not eaten in Sylvia's for many years. "When Sylvia's went from being a tiny luncheonette to three or four stores in a row, of course it changed," Greene said in a phone conversation. "But I haven't tasted the food recently so I can't describe it. Harlem has been invaded by white people. Many black people have left and gone south. President Clinton having his office in Harlem was the beginning of the great renaissance. Some love the fact that it has become extremely mixed. Marcus Samuelsson is next door to Sylvia's. Stores that would never have opened in Harlem now are open in Harlem."

Another change in Harlem is a continent of commercial fast-food joints between Sylvia's and the Apollo. Woods-Black adopted M.S. P.S. 7, a heavily Latino school at 125th and Lexington in East Harlem, for a "Wellness in the Schools" program. "I go in quarterly and speak with the kids about what they are deciding to eat in the cafeteria that day," she said. "I also work with the cafeteria workers on healthy recipes. Last week I brought some roasted sweet potatoes into the school. We used our secret seasoning, which is our herb blend of soft greens, a little bit of garlic, and a little bit of pepper. We're trying to help them make conscious decisions about portion control. And to be open about eating different items."

Woods-Black was destined to work at Sylvia's. She began her career at the age of thirteen as a bus girl. "I was so excited to get my apron," she said. "We would fold the menus because we had new menus for special holidays." After being a bus girl, Woods-Black was promoted to server. Her grandmother quickly transferred her to hostess. Woods-Black was upset. She said, "I felt like I was being punished. My grandmother said, 'You talk at your tables too long, they're not turning over. Let's take your personality and put it to where you're going to excel.' She put you in position to succeed and not to fail." Sylvia Woods was blessed with a sense of business acumen.

Woods-Black also learned the importance of ownership.

"That was one of the best traits my grandmother acquired from her mother," Woods-Black said. "To own everything. She got her first credit card late in life. We still have our washer and dryer downstairs. Our laundry woman for many years sat in that basement and washed all of the linens, aprons, and chef uniforms. That provided another job. There was a famous African American designer who fell down on her luck. She needed to make some money and no one knew she was our laundry lady for a while. She worked here until she was able to get her business back up."

The present-day Sylvia's is a block away from the original location, which was

gutted in a 1967 fire. Over the years the family has acquired eight properties, which are scrabbled together on a city block, with the exception of a church on the corner. The current thirty-five-seat counter area with booths and counter stools is the oldest portion of Sylvia's. "The short-order cook was in the back, visible to everybody," Woods-Black recalled. "Left Hand Sally. She was popular. People loved watching her cook with her left hand. We started out with thirty-five seats. We are now close to four hundred fifty seats."

Sylvia's continues to expand its brand. Soul food fans can buy Sylvia's sauces, Sylvia's dessert mixes, Sylvia's canned vegetables, and Sylvia's gravy mixes. In November 2013, a 150-seat Sylvia's Queen of Soul opened in the Manhattan Casino building in St. Petersburg, Florida.

Does expansion water down the original spirit?

Woods-Black declined to talk about the Florida project during my visit. Amy C. Evans, lead oral historian for the Southern Foodways Alliance, said, "Different markets have different tastes. You see that with barbecue. It dilutes

The present-day Sylvia's is a block away from the original location.

the core of the business or the soul of the family with the nature of the food. I saw that with Golden Rule barbecue out of Irondale, Alabama. The longest continuous operation in the state of Alabama. They opened in the nineteenth century [1891] and they franchised. They were trying to take Alabama barbecue to North Carolina and you just can't do that. That applies a little bit to soul food. You are one degree removed from the original. Then you get two degrees removed from the original. But with soul food, what really changes is that the physical space does not translate. Especially when you're talking about the civil rights movement."

Soul food is about sense of place. Church, restaurants, and hotels took on profound meaning during the segregation of the mid-twentieth century. In 1959, Malcolm X had dinner with Fidel Castro at the Hotel Theresa, aka "the Waldorf of Harlem." A year later Castro returned to stay at the hotel with an entourage of eighty people. Poets Allen Ginsberg and Langston Hughes visited Castro at the Hotel Theresa.

Longtime Chicago musician and civil rights activist Gene Barge traveled to New York for gigs in the early 1960s. "During the movement civil rights ideas were hatched at the lunch counter of the Theresa," said Barge, who is the saxophonist on the 1961 Gary "U.S." Bonds smash "Quarter to Three." "Blacks couldn't go downtown. And that's in New York. But they were selling soul food, even though Castro was cooking chickens in his hotel room." In 1960 Castro was in town to address the United Nations. Castro and his entourage initially stayed at the Shelburne Hotel at Lexington Avenue and Thirty-Seventh Street, but moved to the Hotel Theresa when they were asked to pony up $10,000 for alleged damage that included cooking chickens in their room.

Mallory said, "When you go into Harlem you have a very strong sense of culture although there are lots of people moving into the community who may not be as connected to the history. It certainly is a balancing act. The main questions people ask me when they visit Harlem are the names of the different boulevards: Adam Clayton Powell. Malcolm X. Who are these folks? People come to Harlem to eat at Sylvia's, to look at the pictures on the wall and learn about the history of Harlem.

"Sylvia's is still the center of all that."

Salmon Croquettes

Croquettes for breakfast? They're a favorite of the breakfast crowd at Sylvia's. These croquettes can be made entirely ahead of time and pan-fried at the last minute. Serve them with fried eggs and grits and pass a basket of warm biscuits.

(Serves 6)

Ingredients

1 15½-ounce can pink salmon
1 medium onion, diced
1 medium green bell pepper, cored, seeded, and diced
2 large eggs

½ cup flour
1 teaspoon salt
¼ teaspoon freshly ground black pepper
Vegetable oil for cooking

Directions

Drain the can of salmon and place the salmon in a large mixing bowl. Add the remaining ingredients and mix thoroughly. The croquette mix should be moist and not too chunky.

Grease one or two large heavy skillets (a seasoned cast-iron skillet is perfect) lightly with the oil and heat over medium heat. Use about ¼ cup of the croquette mixture to form patties 3 inches across and about ½ inch thick. Cook the croquettes, turning them once, until golden brown on both sides, about 4 minutes. Serve hot.

(Note: You may have to cook the croquettes in batches. Keep the cooked ones hot on a baking sheet in a preheated 250°F oven while cooking the rest.)

RUBY'S RESTAURANT

◆◆

3175 W. Madison Street, Chicago, Illinois
(773) 638-5875

RUBY'S RESTAURANT IS AT THE CORNER OF WEST MADISON STREET AND KEDZIE AVENUE IN A ROUGH STRETCH OF THE CITY. A new drugstore is across West Madison Street but several empty buildings surround each corner of Ruby's. Like the last leaf on an autumn tree, Ruby's hangs on.

More historic soul food restaurants have closed in Chicago than in any other major American city. Gone are the Soul Queen, Soul Eatery, and Army and Lou's, where I once shared a mountain of loving croquettes with soul singer Barry White.

Chicago cannot contain its soul food legacy for two main reasons: an exodus of middle-class blacks from the city, and the shifting culinary tastes of younger African Americans. According to a 2011 *USA Today* article, fifty-five thousand African Americans have left Chicago since 2000.

Ruby's is as essential to local civil rights history as old Comiskey Park was to Negro League baseball. Formerly known as Edna's, the sixty-five-seat restaurant feeds the city's complex personality. Cardboard signs in the window plead PUT DOWN THE GUNS. A larger sign above the large plate glass windows promises THE FINEST SOUL FOOD ON EARTH. On a clear day you can look east and see the United Center, the home of athletes and rock stars.

Edna Stewart was the daughter of sharecroppers in Covington, Tennessee. She opened her restaurant with her father, Samuel Mitchell Sr., in 1966 in the far West Side Austin neighborhood. She then moved to a bowling alley and dance hall at 9 S. Kedzie, around the corner from the current location. Madison Street is the dividing line between Chicago's North and South Sides. Edna's moved to 3175 W. Madison in 1986.

The original Edna's was a meeting place for Dr. Martin Luther King Jr. and a young Rev. Jesse Jackson as they mapped out strategies to combat housing discrimination. They ate for free. Edna wouldn't have it any other way. Longtime Chicago alderman and current congressman Danny Davis has his office down the street, and almost every modern-day Chicago mayoral candidate campaigned at Edna's.

Rev. Jackson was eating oatmeal diced with Alaga (Alabama-Georgia) cane syrup on an early morning in July 2014 at Ruby's. On the previous morning he had addressed the July 4 shootings in Chicago that made national news with fourteen people killed and eighty-two shot. People who leave some neighborhoods are the fortunate souls.

"There was block busting here," Rev. Jackson said as he looked around an empty dining area. "Whites moved out as blacks moved in. Then you had landlords who lived in Florida and didn't keep up the buildings. The community was drained. By the time Dr. King moved in here in [January] 1966 he lived on Hamlin. Landlords were panicking that the blacks were coming. Slum areas were intolerable."

Dr. King and his wife, Coretta, lived on the top floor of a three-floor slum apartment building at 1550 S. Hamlin. They paid ninety dollars a month in rent. Dr. King said, "You can't really get close to the poor without living and being here with them." The Chicago stay-over is regarded as the first major civil rights action in the North.

The Rev. Jesse Jackson after a summer 2014 breakfast at the last historic soul food restaurant on the West Side of Chicago.

Henry Henderson, the Chicago produce supplier who saved a soul food landmark.

"The original Edna's wasn't very big," Rev. Jackson said. "It's interesting, sometimes as these places got bigger people wouldn't patronize them because they didn't seem to have that soulful flavor. Edna's was a real place. And a lot of these places were identified with the person who operated them—'Edna's Place.' These people were deeply involved in the community. They were members of churches and social clubs."

Ownership was the pathway to success. During the early 1970s the Stewart family owned a West Side barbecue stand, pizza restaurant, and laundromat. In October 2008 Stewart was diagnosed with ovarian cancer. She died in June 2010 at the age of seventy-two. Edna's closed in August 2011.

Suddenly, with the beat of a willing heart, Henry Henderson stepped up to the plate. Henderson was born in 1951 in Clarksdale, Mississippi, and migrated to

Chicago in 1970. He was Stewart's produce supplier for twenty-two years. Henderson had never been in the restaurant business when he purchased Edna's with his wife, Gloria.

Gloria and Henry reopened the restaurant in December 2011 as Ruby's, named for Henderson's mother. They changed the name in respect for the Stewart family.

"I could not let this die," Henry Henderson said during a lunch conversation at Ruby's. "I did not look at this as a financial investment. I looked at it as a legacy that nobody wanted. Edna was a friend of mine. We talked a lot. I'd come here sometimes on Saturday and Sunday and worked for her. I worked hard."

Things have not been easy. The economy tanked. Gloria died in March 2013. In 2014 Henderson was still working as produce supplier at Navilio Produce in the South Water Market, while also running the restaurant. He began at Navilio in 1989.

"I didn't learn about the history here until I started delivering vegetables," Henderson said. He clasped his large hands on a dining room table. He continued, "I'd see Mayor [Richard M.] Daley several times. Governor [Pat] Quinn. Just about every alderman from the West Side. Cook County Commissioner [Robert] Shaw is here seven days a week. Actors like Robert Townsend and Danny Glover. Robert Townsend's mother came here when Edna was here. We get a handful of white people. I treat everybody the same. I wouldn't have it any other way."

They come for the camaraderie and timeless Edna's classics like crunchy fried chicken, collard greens, and the biscuits, which were Edna's staple. On the day of her passing, Gov. Quinn issued the statement, "I join the people of Illinois in mourning the loss of Edna Stewart, who was renowned nationwide for her legendary soul food cooking and landmark restaurant."

In the early 2000s Stewart began hiring felons who had been released from prison. Local schoolchildren ate at Edna's as she told them about the cultural significance of her restaurant. Rev. Jackson said, "No homeless people ever went hungry. They weren't put out because they couldn't afford to eat. They didn't advertise that but it was obvious that if you were hungry and desperate and came to Edna's, Helen Maybell's, or Gladys, you were going to eat."

Edna's had only been open for two years when the West Side of Chicago went

In 1986 Edna's moved around the corner to this location, 3175 W. Madison Street.

down in flames, never to be the same. Riots broke out on April 5, 1968, the day after Dr. King was killed, and lasted through April 6. Television sets and clothing were taken from predominantly white-owned businesses at the corner of Kedzie and Madison. More than three thousand Illinois National Guard and police were called in. An estimated nine to eleven people died during the rioting. Mayor Richard J. Daley, the father of Edna's regular Richard M. Daley, said he ordered police to "shoot and kill any arsonist or anyone with a Molotov cocktail in his hand" and to "shoot and maim or cripple anyone looting any stores in our city." While the order made national news, Daley made the statement a week after the riots and not directly to the police.

According to an April 5, 1968, *Chicago Tribune* report, 162 buildings were destroyed by arson, leaving behind scores of vacant lots.

Even the three-flat where Dr. King lived was torched in the riots and eventually demolished. (In 2010 the new, affordable Dr. King Legacy Apartments opened on the site.) Edna's survived through the years. She was the conscience of the community. A street sign has been erected at the corner of Madison and Kedzie. It reads HONORARY EDNA L. STEWART WAY.

Henry Henderson was delivered to Chicago from a different world. "When I got to Chicago I was totally disappointed," he said. "I came to the [post-King riot] ghettos. It was bad."

Henderson was raised on a farm and lived on the Balo Plantation northeast of Clarksdale, about thirteen miles from the Hopson Plantation, now a big tourist destination with blues fans.

"I have twenty-three sisters and brothers," Henderson said. "It took a toll on my mother. In the wintertime there would be a lot of rain. There was no way we could get out. We had to can everything. When we went to school we had to walk in the mud to get to the bus line. There was nothing for Mom and Dad to do in the winter. So they had 'fun.' Every year there was another kid. At the time in Mississippi, there was no [birth] control. My folks and I worked for $2.50 a day. From six in the morning until six at night. We had one hour for lunch. We had to leave the field at eleven in the morning and be back in the field at noon. It didn't give us too much time to eat. I was nineteen years old when I left Mississippi."

The hardscrabble ethic shaped Henderson's character. He sold produce to Edna for twenty-two years. "For the first ten years Edna was tough," Henderson said with a smile framed by cropped muttonchops. "Every day had to be perfect. I had to rotate the old merchandise every day. The next twelve years she never told me one thing, unless she wanted something extra. I knew what she wanted. How she wanted it. When she wanted it."

"I have seven kids to take care of. Edna was the first restaurant I approached. It

Ruby's assistant manager, Christopher Garnett, and waitress Cheryl Spencer, both Chicago residents.

was May of 1989. I had heard so much about Edna's but I never met her. It was the first time I had set foot in this restaurant." At the time Henry and Gloria lived at 1105 S. Michigan, about seven blocks from the Lawndale restaurant.

Henderson also learned he attended the same church as Marguerite Banks, Edna's daughter. By the time Edna became ill Banks had relocated to Virginia. She was not interested in running a Chicago restaurant. None of Edna's brothers or sisters wanted the business. "I got a call two months after Edna passed away from Dr. [Lucy] Shapiro, who ran the [upstairs] Bobby E. Wright Comprehensive Behavioral Health Center," he said. "She asked if I was interested in the place downstairs." The Wright Center is Henderson's landlord.

Legendary Chicago soul singer Syl Johnson was a fan of Edna's and during the 1980s he operated his own chain of soul food restaurants in Chicago.

Henderson was quizzed on the nuances of running a restaurant. He had never operated a business before, but he passed the test. "I called my wife and said, 'Glo, guess what? We got the restaurant!' She said, 'What restaurant?' Bless her soul. She just died. She had ovarian cancer just like Edna. We were married almost sixteen years.

"But it's life and it goes on."

The Hendersons upgraded Edna's kitchen and opened up the dining area. They removed most of the historic pictures and a sign that declared Edna's had THE BEST BISCUITS ON EARTH. One black and white photo of Dr. King and Malcolm X remains by the front window. "We kept the menu but added things like jerk chicken," Henderson said. "We have a Friday night fish fry with catfish and buffalo steak. Our best seller is the beef short ribs. Guess what's number two? The catfish steak. People's eating habits are changing. We added a salad bar. The jerk chicken raised our business twenty-five percent. If I had to depend on soul food alone, we wouldn't survive.

"Of course people still come for the biscuits. People have the biscuits at four in the afternoon. It's Edna's secret recipe that goes back forty years, but I'm not going to tell you." The "best biscuits on Earth" were drenched in butter.

"She gave me tips in the kitchen," Henderson said. "Not about recipes, but about orderliness. It has to be a certain way. If you didn't do it her way, you couldn't work for her. She didn't care who you were. She'd bawl you out in front of everybody. But it only would make you better. Learning about who to trust and who not to trust was the toughest thing for me. My mentors were my regular customers. My wife was the business person. She worked in the public aid system for thirty-two years. She said she didn't retire after thirty-two years to go into the restaurant business. It was a tug of war."

Now, alone with his customers, Henderson spends seven days a week at Ruby's. He pulls a fifteen-hour Monday shift. He is still unearthing history in his basement. During the summer of 2014 Henderson found a box of postcards that revealed that his current Ruby's was once Little Jack's, a 1950s Italian restaurant.

Henderson still supplies the produce to his own restaurant. Edna's longtime chef and manager, Lillie Joiner, helped Henderson get off the ground, but he said she no longer comes around. "It's not easy," he said. "My youngest son, Lawrence [born in 1978], helps out. My heart is soft. Soul is defined by what is good inside you. In 2012 I made $265,000. I spent out $295,000. Each year I go into the hole. I have spent $113,000 of my own money. That's what kept me afloat. That is nobody's fault but mine. I did not know how to run the business, which is why I brought my son in."

The neighborhood remains very rough. "I'd say five to ten people a day come here looking for a job," Henderson said. His staff includes eight to twelve part-time people. "We had a meeting at Alderman Davis's office with the commander of the Twenty-Fifth District. Some of the business people wanted to know how they can keep kids away from their stores because they were blocking their business. I didn't hear one say, 'What can we do to help these young men standing out there?' I raised that question. If we put our resources together we can't get them all. But if we get two percent I'd be happy. What does pushing them away do? Pull them in, give them four hours a week. Every business can do that."

All the other historic soul food businesses in Chicago are gone: Army and Lou's,

Gladys Luncheonette, the late Helen Maybell Anglin's H and H Café, and the Soul Queen restaurants. Neighborhood culture was more connected in the 1960s.

Also gone is a small chain of Chicago soul food restaurants called Solomon's Fisheries, opened in the 1980s by Chicago-based soul and blues legend Syl Johnson. Like Henderson, Johnson migrated from Mississippi to Chicago. Johnson arrived from Holly Springs on a City of New Orleans train in 1950. He was sixteen years old. He cut his chops at West Side clubs like the Wagon Wheel at Madison and California, within walking distance of Edna's. His evocative jazz-blues anthem "Is It Because I'm Black" was recorded in 1969 and was the title track for the first African American concept album, preceding Marvin Gaye's *What's Going On* by two years.

At the time he was one of the first African American restaurant owners in the downtown Chicago Loop. He used a Mississippi family recipe with fish baked in onion, vegetable oil, lots of garlic, and with liberal amounts of whole wheat flour and meal. Oprah Winfrey once requested he cater an event at her West Loop studio.

On this summer day Johnson picked up his electric guitar in the living room of his South Side home. He held it up in a vertical position.

"Listen," he said with an autographed picture of Oprah hanging on the kitchen wall behind him. "If you pull a tree out of the ground, you look at the limbs and the branches, then you look at the roots. They look the same, don't they? The roots grow just like the branches.

"You cut the branches, the tree blossoms out beautiful again. But you cut the roots? You have a dead tree."

And as long as Ruby's is cooking, history will continue to blossom within her beloved walls.

Ruby's Bread Pudding

This legacy recipe from Edna's was born in African American homes. Biscuits were often used because many homemakers could not afford white bread.

(Serves 15 to 20)

Ingredients

1 1/2 loaves of white bread *or* 1 full
  pan of biscuits
3 cups sugar
3 cups raisins

3 teaspoons nutmeg
3 teaspoons cinnamon
3 teaspoons vanilla flavor

Directions

Preheat the oven to 350°F. Cut the bread or biscuits into small pieces. Mix all the ingredients in a medium-sized baking pan. Bake at 350°F for 45 minutes.

BAKER'S KEYBOARD LOUNGE

◆◆

20510 Livernois Street, Detroit, Michigan
(313) 345-6300 • theofficialbakerskeyboardlounge.com

LIKE THE SOUND OF A DISTANT TRUMPET, THE LUSTER WAS FADING AWAY FROM THE MOTOR CITY IN 1972. Detroit was still recovering from the 1968 riots, and in 1972 Motown Records left for sunnier skies in Los Angeles. So it was a big deal the night Miles Davis walked into Baker's Keyboard Lounge unannounced.

Baker's is a soul food restaurant and jazz club that opened in 1934—the longest-running jazz club in the world.

In 1972 Eric Whitaker had made the forty-five-minute drive from his home in Flint to see the house band at Baker's. He was behind the wheel of a pink 1964 Buick Wildcat, searching to make his mark on something. Whitaker was seventeen years old with a passion for jazz.

"I was drinking lemonade in the corner of the bar," Whitaker said on a snowy winter afternoon conversation at Baker's, of which he is now a co-owner. "I didn't have a lot of time, I had to get home. There were just a few people sitting around. And in walked Miles. He had his trench coat on and he had his trumpet in his hand. He looked at the band, the band looked at him. He politely walked up to the stage. The guys kept playing. He put his coat down and took his horn out. He got up on the stage with them and started playing. It was fantastic. I fell in love with this place."

Established in 1934, Baker's is the longest running jazz club–soul food restaurant in the world.

Seeing Miles changed his life.

When a forsaken Baker's went up for auction in 2011, Whitaker and his business partner, Hugh Smith, stepped in and saved the historic restaurant and music room. Whitaker does not call himself an owner. He said he is a steward for this soul. "Baker's is rooted not only in Detroit history or US history, but world history," Whitaker explained.

Chris and Fannie Baker opened their establishment in 1933 as a sandwich deli at 20510 Livernois Street, about eight miles from downtown on the city's former "Avenue of Fashion." The one-mile corridor between 7 and 8 Mile Roads was one of the premier Detroit shopping districts before the birth of shopping malls. Motown soul singer Marvin Gaye lived in the neighborhood. Baker's was at the top of the strip, which is why it was such a popular deli. "There's always been food here," Whitaker said. "Clarence Baker asked his father if he could bring in musicians to add to the deli. He brought in some classical piano players and it evolved into jazz music."

Indeed. In the late 1950s Dave Brubeck and Gerry Mulligan played at Baker's. An up-and-coming Barbra Streisand sang at the ninety-nine-seat club in 1961. Charles Mingus mounted his 1969 comeback in a series of shows at Baker's. They loved food and they loved to play at Baker's. "Musicians would stop here even if they had a layover," Whitaker said. "We redid the stage. It was a lot smaller than what we have now." Sound resonates from original Italian ceiling tiles. Smith generally operates the sound board from a former coat check closet in the adjacent bar.

Chicago-based jazz pianist Ramsey Lewis played Baker's many times in the late 1950s and early 1960s. "When you played there it was like playing the Blue Note in New York," the three-time Grammy winner said in a 2014 conversation. "It was the place for trios to perform. It was nicely lit, the stage was nice, the room was slick and sophisticated. Clarence Baker was quite the gentleman. The crowd was well dressed."

In 1953 Clarence Baker commissioned a Steinway piano for Art Tatum, considered the greatest jazz pianist ever. The black piano was delivered to the restaurant–jazz club and still sits on Baker's stage. The final gig of Tatum's life was in April 1956 at Baker's. A tilted mirror above the small stage enables the audience to see the pianist's hands. Soul contains ghosts.

Music lore says that in 1954 Miles kicked his heroin addiction after playing at Baker's. He was appearing at the now-defunct Blue Bird Club as a guest soloist in Billy Mitchell's house band along with Elvin Jones, Donald Byrd, and others. He later dropped into Baker's in a rainstorm, carrying his trumpet like a lucky charm in a paper bag under his coat. Miles walked onto the small bandstand and cut into "Sweet Georgia Brown," being performed by Clifford Brown and Max Roach. However, Miles began playing "My Funny Valentine," one of his favorite calls. Supposedly Miles was so embarrassed about the mix-up, he decided to get clean. The story has bounced around Baker's for years, although Miles disputed it in his 1989 bestselling autobiography.

Scat singer Eddie Jefferson was shot to death in the early morning hours of May 8, 1979, while leaving Baker's. "He had some kind of dispute and walked outside the club," Whitaker said. "I just know the history as it is written. Despite the reputation of Detroit, that's the only incident that happened here. Service people frequent Baker's for lunch, dinner, or entertainment. We constantly have someone that may be in uniform or may not be in uniform."

Between 1953 and 1954 Baker's underwent the renovation that visitors see today. It is mid-century style at its purest form. "That's when the famous piano-shaped bar [with black and white keyboards] came into existence," Whitaker said while nodding at the curved bar that seats eighteen people. Liberace visited Baker's, saw the piano bar, and used the concept for the piano-shaped swimming pool at his Sherman Oaks, California, estate. Whitaker said, "That's when they expanded the club [to its current ninety-nine-seat capacity]. That's when these art renditions on the wall were commissioned by Harry Carew."

Harry Julian Carew painted mid-sized Art Deco murals of European cities and New Orleans. "He was doing work in downtown Detroit," Whitaker said. "Someone suggested he come over here and Clarence had him do the murals."

In the mid-1990s young Detroit entertainment entrepreneur Alan Floyd wanted to buy Baker's. Clarence Baker took him around the club. "At the time the paintings were all covered by mirrors, except for maybe the back one," Floyd said while ordering chicken wings at Baker's. In the summer of 2014 Floyd was still looking to purchase

After Liberace visited Baker's he used the restaurant's piano-key bar as inspiration for his California swimming pool.

a jazz club in Detroit despite having his neck broken in a March 2007 hit-and-run accident. Someone driving a stolen car hit his Monte Carlo while Floyd was stopped at a red light on the Lodge Freeway. Floyd visits Baker's Lounge in a wheelchair accompanied by a caregiver.

Ray Baker has been coming to Baker's Lounge since the club was integrated in the late 1950s. Ray is no relation to Clarence Baker. Ray is African American. Clarence was white. "I used to go to the bar next door," Baker recalled during an interview overlooking the original coolers behind Baker's bar. "It was a 'black and tan' [for predominately black and brown ethnic groups] called the Alamo. We were more welcome there. They had jazz too. It's a catering company now. A lot of people don't know that story. As a kid I used to come out here on my bicycle but I had to leave before dark. If you were black, you would get arrested. Clarence didn't cater to blacks until later years."

Ray Baker was born in 1937. He spent thirty-eight years as a parts manager at the Ford Motor Company.

Clarence's brother Maury operated the Showplace Lounge in Detroit, where soul singer Melvin Davis often headlined. "That catered to blacks," said Baker, who grew up in downtown Detroit. "The only major jazz singer that did not appear here was Nancy Wilson. She appeared at Maury Baker's Grande Ballroom down the street from here.

"But there was nothing like this place. This was strictly name entertainment. In the late 1950s Miles [Davis] would play a set here, then go back to the Blue Bird Inn [where Davis had befriended Detroit boxer Sugar Ray Robinson] and play a set."

Baker's menu offerings include greens, mac and cheese, yams, turkey and dressing, black-eyed peas, pork chops, and ribs. No chitlins.

"It's food for the soul," Whitaker said. "As opposed to soul food. You can still enjoy some of the tastes people have grown to love about soul food, but enjoy it in a healthier manner. With less fat. Certainly a lot less sodium. And we've found different ways to give people the same taste without adding those [fatty] ingredients, especially to the extent of what had been done previously here. If you want to stay in business you not only have to be conscious about their taste, but also their health.

"They're not going keep buying from you if they're not around."

Whitaker and Smith are only the third owners of Baker's. In 1996 Clarence Baker sold the club to John Colbert and Juanita Jackson. Colbert declared bankruptcy in 2010 and Detroiters feared the historic club was going to close. "During the Colbert–Jackson ownership there weren't as many national acts booked here," Whitaker said. "One of my primary goals is to put Baker's back in that prime arena for jazz clubs. My partner does most of the booking. It's a difficult task to meet the financial challenges required of national acts but we are trying."

Whitaker was born in Detroit and grew up in Flint. His father, Grady, was a Detroit brick mason and his mother, Alma Tate, worked for General Motors. Whitaker worked for thirty-five years as an engineer for General Motors before retiring in 2008. "I enjoyed myself for the first three years of retirement and then the opportunity to purchase Baker's came along," he said. "My partner [Smith] was a manager here. We had a bit of an uphill climb with the previous owner, but we've been trying to restore Baker's as one of the premier jazz clubs in the world. Getting into Baker's was a different mode for me: entertainment, food, and alcoholic beverages."

He received a serendipitous nudge from his wife, Jackie Vaughn-Whitaker. Her younger sister, Dolores Grey Reynolds, was a co-owner and manager of Army and Lou's, the most historic soul food restaurant in Chicago. Their mother, Mary, also worked at Army and Lou's while also operating a Chicago beauty supply company. Her late father was a mechanic. Army and Lou's ran from 1945 until 2011 on East Seventy-Fifth Street in Chicago. The Whitakers were married on April 22, 2013. She was born in 1953. He was born in 1955. Dolores died of complications from cancer forty-eight hours before the wedding.

"We were like twins," Vaughn-Whitaker said. "She loved doing things. Picking the tablecloths. Picking the dresses." Whitaker added, "She was not only Jackie's sister and best friend but she was one of my rocks in getting into the restaurant business. She was immensely helpful in knowing what to look out for because she had been involved in Army and Lou's so long."

Dolores gave Whitaker tips on how to manage the kitchen through portion control. Vaughn-Whitaker added, "She told him to never change the recipes. If you have a cook that comes on Wednesday and somebody else on Friday, the mac and cheese is going to taste the same no matter who is cooking. People really love the food here, especially the chicken and catfish."

Baker's serves the Army and Lou's traditional macaroni and cheese blend with sharp cheddar cheese and processed cheese dip. "Today you'll find mac that has seafood and other nontraditional ingredients." Whitaker said. "We'll do nachos, which customers like late at night."

Baker's inherited the short ribs recipe from Army and Lou's. She said, "The only thing Eric didn't take that Army and Lou's was known for is the seafood gumbo. I love making it at home and he loves it. But it is a huge endeavor. We have to make sure we have the customer base to support the expense."

Army and Lou's was the go-to restaurant for late Chicago mayor Harold Washington, the first African American mayor in the city's history. Muhammad Ali, James

Brown, and Smokey Robinson ate at Army and Lou's when they came to Chicago. Dr. Martin Luther King Jr. ate at Army and Lou's in the 1960s.

Many of their pictures lined the walls of the restaurant. "We had 'the Jesse Jackson booth,'" Vaughn-Whitaker said. "You knew he would sit there. A lot of significant decisions and meetings happened there. Because Army and Lou's served breakfast, lunch, and dinner, it gave people a reason to come."

Vaughn-Whitaker looked at her husband, who was listening across a table. "If I were to line up food to food with Baker's and Army and Lou's there is such a similarity. The mac and cheese, the same. The greens? Army and Lou's beats you. The chicken, it's good. It's neck and neck. We never had this discussion. Your pork chops are much bigger, but taste-wise you're on the same level. Now, the peach cobbler. Army and Lou's crust was a complete piece of crust instead of layered, which meant you got a lot of crust. And Army and Lou's had sweet potato pies all the time. We don't have sweet potato pies."

Whitaker took it all in. After a pause he said, "I'd like to hear what we do better."

Vaughn-Whitaker laughed and responded, "Your catfish is better. I'm not trying to change any recipes, but if it is not hitting it you want somebody to say, hey, we need to adjust it. And your ribs are better."

Whitaker said, "I certainly listen to my customers. But more importantly, I listen to my wife. She has good comments and great rapport, especially with our chef. She's gotten in the kitchen with those guys and talked to them. I'm not a cook. If you don't have a passion for cooking, you don't belong in the kitchen."

In 2007 Vaughn-Whitaker was living in a home on the ninth hole of the Shenandoah Golf Course in West Bloomfield, Michigan, when she met her future husband. She was talked into cooking for forty men coming off the golf course. "He was one of the last ones coming in," she said. "He was impressed I saved him a plate. Lamb chops. Asparagus. Grilled potatoes. I really laid it out for the guys. They didn't want to eat in the club house."

Whitaker said, "She made me feel so at home. It was the first time I had come to her place. Some of the other guys I was with had been there for events she hosted. But the fact she got me a special plate had a special meaning to me."

Baker's Lounge co-owner Eric Whitaker and his wife, Jackie Vaughn-Whitaker.

How is soul food evolving?

Vaughn-Whitaker is owner and CEO of White House Services, a health industry organization that assists people with brain and spine injuries. She said, "There's still the core people who appreciate soul food. But there's a lot of people focused on health consciousness. The food industry as a whole has taken a different angle. Restaurants do caloric counts of each dish. The habits of people are changing, especially younger ones. Balance is important. We don't always have to have fried catfish. We now have blackened catfish and we can blacken with less seasoning, too. People are asking for chicken on top of their salad. That wasn't a thing in soul food restaurants. People just ate chicken.

"I go out with this one girl, I love her, she's one of my best buddies, but my goodness, it takes her fifteen minutes to order. 'Can you tell me if there's any MSG?' Things like that. They're trying to go back and forth [to the kitchen] to check on each element. A lot of people have allergies and we're more astute in this area. From a health perspective our world has changed dramatically. Soul food never really had appetizers because soul food was so much. Maybe a salad or coleslaw ahead of time and you were going for it. But we're finding is that because Baker's is a jazz club and some people want to sit at the famous keyboard they want something small. Instead of the catfish filet, now it's catfish nuggets. We're adjusting."

The challenges were abundant when Whitaker and Smith took over Baker's. "Baker's probably had fifteen years of no reinvestment," Whitaker said. "I had leaking ceilings. Plumbing issues. Problems with some of the foundation. We've been reinvesting to get the old girl some lipstick and a new dress. That has been a major hurdle. We make improvements every day, whether it is my staff or the building. Plus, the media put out the notion that we had closed. We never closed."

His wife stepped in to assist with marketing. Vaughn-Whitaker was in Chicago radio and television advertising and marketing before moving to Detroit in 1985 to work at rock 'n' roll station WILF. "Baker's was in foreclosure," she said. "When people think 'foreclosure' they think 'closed.' But they [her husband and Smith] caught it before it was gone. But we're back and we're new."

Deborah Nero is one of the new jazz performers at Baker's. The jazz singer was in rotation at Baker's between 2006 and 2008 and still sings spot gigs at the club. She also sings with the Detroit-based Charles Bowles Quartet.

Nero was a guest at the May 24, 2014, eightieth anniversary celebration at the club–soul food restaurant. Miles Davis would have turned eighty-eight on May 26, 2014.

"It is humbling to sing here," Nero said while sitting at the black-and-white piano-key bar. "I also sang at the Cotton Club in New York. You feel overwhelmed knowing you had all these great individuals who came before you. I'm proud of this and treat it accordingly." At Baker's she will sing the legacy jazz tunes of Ella Fitzgerald, Sarah Vaughan, and others. She does Duke Ellington's "Lush Life."

Nero was born in 1955 on the west side of Detroit. She is not related to conductor-pianist Peter Nero although her late father, Gene Nero, was a popular

Diners get up close and personal with live music at Baker's.

alto sax player around the Motor City. "My father played at the Peabody Hotel [in Memphis] behind a curtain," she said. "In the late 1940s, early 1950s black people could not play in front of an audience. It's odd now because my daughter is the director of room service for the Waldorf-Astoria Boca Raton [Florida] resort. Things have evolved immensely.

"We moved to this neighborhood in 1967 after the [Dr. King] riots. The neighborhood was changing. It went from Jewish to black. It is still a beautiful neighborhood. Wonderful homes. My father had cancer and was not able to play any more so he became a commercial estate salesman. He sold Marvin Gaye's house. It has a sunken living room. The neighborhood has lots of nice brick houses. I had one of them. Then I got laid off from the Ford Motor Company. I was with them thirty years."

Nero was a health and safety administrator for Ford. In 2007 she moved to the east side of the city along the Detroit River.

"Baker's must stay," declared Nero, also a church choir singer. "It has its place in history and it needs to stay where it is, like it is."

Army and Lou's Macaroni and Cheese (Dolores Grey Reynolds)

(Serves 8 to 10)

Ingredients

1 pound dried elbow macaroni (4 cups)

1 8-ounce package shredded sharp cheddar cheese (2 cups)

1 8-ounce package pasteurized prepared cheese product, cut up

¼ cup butter, cut up

3 eggs, lightly beaten

1 12-ounce can evaporated milk

1 cup processed cheese dip or 1 10.75-ounce can condensed cheddar cheese soup

¼ teaspoon ground white pepper

Directions

Cook the macaroni according to package directions. Preheat the oven to 325°F.

Meanwhile, let the cheeses and butter stand at room temperature. Drain the macaroni and transfer it to a very large bowl. Add 1½ cups of the shredded cheddar, the cheese product, and the butter to the hot pasta, stirring well. Set aside.

In a medium bowl, whisk together eggs, milk, cheese dip, and white pepper until combined. Stir the egg mixture into the macaroni mixture. Transfer mixture to a 13-by-9-by-2-inch baking dish (3-quart rectangular), spreading evenly.

Bake, covered, for 25 minutes. Uncover and stir well. Sprinkle with the remaining ½ cup shredded cheddar. Bake, uncovered, 15 to 20 minutes more or until the cheese is melted and mixture is heated through (160°F). Let stand 10 minutes before serving.

Sizzlin' Peach Cobbler

Ingredients

3 cups flour

Pinch of salt

Cold water

1 stick (½ cup) Crisco

2 64-ounce cans sliced peaches in
  heavy syrup

3 cups sugar

1 teaspoon ground cinnamon

½ teaspoon ground nutmeg

2 sticks butter

3 tablespoons cornstarch

Directions

Place the flour in a large bowl with a pinch of salt. Add the stick of Crisco, kneading it continuously, adding tablespoons of cold water until the dough is completely solid. Roll up two balls of dough and set aside while preparing the peaches.

Open the cans of peaches and reserve a small amount of the syrup for later. Place the peaches in a bowl. Add the sugar (more or less depending on your taste). Add the cinnamon and nutmeg and stir until well mixed. Melt the butter and add to the mixture, mixing well.

Place the cornstarch in a small bowl and add water until a consistent texture forms. Add the reserved peach syrup and mix until the mixture is consistent. Combine this mixture with the peaches.

Preheat the oven for 30 minutes at 375°F.

Use a rolling pin with extra flour to roll out the dough, one ball at a time. Grease a casserole dish with butter, place the crust in the pan, and add the peach mixture.

Roll out the second ball for the top crust. Some like the lattice look, which means cutting the dough in strips, while others like the covered look. If you choose to cover, cut a few slits in the dough so it breathes while cooking.

Place extra butter pats on top of the crust, and sprinkle a little cinnamon over the entire cobbler for a final touch.

Bake for 40 to 50 minutes, until the crust has browned. Remove from the oven, let it cool, and serve with ice cream.

(Note: If you're not sure you can manage making the crust from scratch, you can buy ready-made dough.)

NEW BETHEL BAPTIST CHURCH KITCHEN

◆◆◆

8430 Linwood Street, Detroit, Michigan
(313) 894-5789 • www.nbbcdetroit.org

THE MOST OVERLOOKED SOUL FOOD DESTINATION IN AMERICA IS ON THE GROUND FLOOR OF THE NEW BETHEL BAPTIST CHURCH ON THE TIME-RAVAGED WEST SIDE OF DETROIT.

You walk past the large church lobby and turn right into a large kitchen. The empty kitchen is spotless and only a few clean silver pots and pans sit by the sink. Ten gold chandeliers hang from the ceiling but they are dark. Vases of artificial purple lilies adorn a dozen circular tables.

Services are still held every Sunday morning at New Bethel and the kitchen remains in play once or twice a month. From 1963 until the 1980s the kitchen was an incubator for the American civil rights movement. The space is a higher ground. Rev. C. L. Franklin was the electric pastor of the New Bethel Baptist Church between 1946 and 1979. He was the father of gospel-soul singer Aretha Franklin, who remains a member of the church.

"I don't think the civil rights movement could have taken place without this church," present-day Rev. Robert Smith Jr. said on a snowy Saturday afternoon in December 2013. "The kitchen epitomized what New Bethel was about. As one lady said to me, 'Reverend, New Bethel was born in a greasy spoon. New Bethel *is* the kitchen. Reverend Franklin really was the financial arm of much of the movement." In 1982 Smith had the unenviable task of replacing C. L. Franklin. How do you scale a mountain?

In June 1979 someone broke into Franklin's nearby home and shot him. He died July 27, 1984, after spending five years in a coma. The crime remains unsolved.

"Dr. Martin Luther King could come to C. L. Franklin and he could raise whatever amount of money was needed until the support from the NAACP or other organizations kicked in," Rev. Smith said. "If I press people for money they could get offended. But nobody got offended with Reverend Franklin. Of course they put on the great march here in June 1963 that led to the August 1963 March on Washington. People came here to get in on the conversation. They knew politically active people would be in our dining room."

A small history room adjacent to the kitchen features pictures of C. L. Franklin with baseball pioneer Jackie Robinson, Motown's Berry Gordy, and Dr. King. The last known photo of Rev. Franklin hangs on a wall in the kitchen. He is wearing sunglasses as he officiated the February 27, 1976, funeral of the Supremes' Florence Ballard, who died of heart failure at the age of thirty-two. More than five thousand people lined the street in front of New Bethel for her services. Rev. Smith and Minister Louis Farrakhan of the Nation of Islam spoke at the 1991 funeral of Temptations lead singer David Ruffin before more than two thousand mourners at New Bethel.

Rev. Smith walked around the empty dining room. He looked like a man who had missed the last train of the night.

Between 1968 and 1972 New Bethel had a congregation of ten thousand people. On this day it was three hundred, and Rev. Smith was hedging his bets.

"The kitchen seating capacity is forty-five," said the gregarious preacher. "It stayed packed from one end to the other every Sunday. This adjacent room was called 'the Bake Sale Room' [now the history room]. It was famous for soul food. There's a very famous pound cake here. The lady who made pound cakes when I got here was Eliza Butler. The theory was that the recipe came from a lady named Mattie Butts. Anyway, it is a super cake. Congressman John Conyers always got one. [Former Detroit mayor] Coleman Young always got one. People on the city council. On Sundays they bought in thirty to forty pound cake orders."

New Bethel member Lydia Jeanette Barnes Bougard knows the magic of the pound cake. Her great-aunt Eliza Butler made them.

Bougard became a member of New Bethel in 1957—the year she was born. "After I got married I made that pound cake two at a time," Bougard said in a conversation in the historic kitchen. "I was a teenage mom. All I wanted to do was cook. I'll tell you—the recipe is going to cost you. What makes the pound cake unique? The butter. She used a pound of everything. She put a little bit of vanilla and lemon in her pound cake. People loved that. The kitchen? Oh my!

Church member Lydia Jeanette Barnes Bougard.

"The fried chicken. Eliza taught me how to cut chicken. They don't do that anymore. They come cut. We had to cut the wings off, split the breast. We'd go shopping at the Eastern Market [in Detroit] to get a case of chicken. The collard greens. The candied yams would be laying in a pan so beautiful, they looked like little oval boats. Eliza had a special dish called sweet and sour cabbage and it would knock you off your feet. She made little lemon tarts and sold them on Sundays and she made her famous egg custard pies. On special Sundays she had her homemade ice cream."

Because of her popularity, Rev. Franklin gave Butler the shift on the first Sunday of the month when communion was served. Franklin also hosted a popular 9 AM Sunday service remote from the church that drew parishioners from all over the neighborhood. Bougard said, "That dining room was jammed. When I was eight and nine years old I would be in that dining room from 6 AM until midnight. They started cooking on Saturday. I was a bus girl and when I became old enough to wait tables I was a waitress. I made a lot of money on tips."

Her mother, Elizabeth Barnes, typed the menus for the Sunday feast. Deploying carbon paper, she would make five menus at a time. Bougard set tables, placing flowers as a centerpiece along with the menus, ashtrays, salt and pepper shakers, sugar bowls, and creamers. "I would come out with a glass of water and a salad," she said. "A tomato salad with a dab of Miracle Whip on the top. Not mayonnaise. Miracle Whip! We served breakfast with grits, bacon, eggs, and ham every morning. I loved it. Eliza loved it. Everybody followed Miss Butler, remember she came from Hastings [the previous New Bethel location]. It was my beginning at New Bethel Baptist Church."

The New Bethel Baptist Church moved to its current location in 1963.

New Bethel Baptist Church moved to its current location in 1963. The eighteen-hundred-seat church is in the former Oriole Theater (circa 1927) at 8430 C. L. Franklin Boulevard.

Michigan State University maintains the history room. Visitors can see Rev. Franklin's chair he used from his pulpit. The room contains robes and a Plexiglas cross from the original New Bethel, where Aretha Franklin made her singing debut in 1956 at the age of fourteen. That church was razed to make way for I-94, the way in and out of Detroit.

And today's kitchen is no longer used on a regular basis. For special occasions Rev. Smith will cook his "Popeye Potatoes," boiled white potatoes with skins, cut into cubes and cooked in olive oil, butter, and parsley. The potatoes are seasoned with hot pepper.

Aretha Franklin caters annual dinners, generally in the fall or around the holidays. "One time she brought in 286 slabs of ribs," Rev. Smith said. "And all the other stuff that goes with it. It would be a Saturday evening, last time it was a Sunday evening. She loves to cook. She likes to feed the crowd. She brings in nice chinaware. Scoops of ice cream. The kitchen was cooking during her era and her father's era."

"Perhaps that is what she is reflecting on."

Rev. Smith is proud of the kitchen's legacy. "It was equally as famous as a soul food place as it was a church for gospel singing," he said. "I'm going to give you a secret. They used to save grease from their cooking and put it in a mayonnaise jar. They'd have that 'seasoned grease,' I guess you would say, and put it in their food to give it taste. That's why it was one of the top soul food places in Detroit. As you would imagine the people that made the kitchen what it was have all died out.

"Our kitchen died. In the early nineties women were paying seventy-five dollars to get their nails done. You don't want to be cleaning chitlins with seventy-five-dollar fingernails. The older generation would come at four o'clock in the morning and slave over that stove. In January they would sell four hundred pounds of chitterlings on a Sunday. I would make jokes about it and the congregation got upset with me. I'd say, 'Why do chitterlings start with a c? Because they use all the 's's.

Rev. Smith laughed and continued, "Boy, they'd get so mad in that kitchen they'd want to strangle me. But what killed the kitchen is more black women became professionals. And more black women took less pride in being a good cook."

The church nourished the souls of 150,000 people of all colors who marched with Dr. King down Detroit's Woodward Avenue on June 23, 1963. During the March on Detroit, Dr. King also gave his first "I Have a Dream" speech at Cobo Hall in Detroit. Soul was in the new summer's air.

This circa mid-1970s kitchen team at the Rev. C. L. Franklin's New Bethel Baptist Church fed the spirit of the civil rights movement. From left to right: Pam Agee, Ann Byrd, Willie Goodson, Louise Bailey, Joanne Davis, Mattie Butts, Ada Waddell, Maggie Saulsby, and Cedsenall Sharp. *Courtesy of New Bethel Baptist Church*

Just a month before the Detroit appearance Rev. Franklin and Dr. King had joined forces in Chicago for a fundraiser with headliners Mahalia Jackson, Harry Belafonte, and Aretha Franklin. The event was hosted by author–disc jockey Studs Terkel and raised more than $50,000 for the SCLC.

"New Bethel and the kitchen was always open to anybody who wanted to meet and discuss justice," Rev. Smith said. "Everybody wasn't like that. It had to be church related."

The New Bethel history museum near the kitchen includes a church door that was shot out after Rev. Franklin allowed the Republic of New Africa (RNA, established 1968) to meet at the church. "It was a group of radical negroes from Wayne State," Rev. Smith said. "Lawyers and such. They formed their own nation and got their own passports. They had their own 'soldiers' even though they weren't armed." In 1969 Detroit police raided the RNA's first anniversary conference at the church and one police officer was killed during the raid. "People ran from the church and the kitchen into the basement," Rev. Smith said. Three RNA members were acquitted of any crimes.

The Rev. Robert Smith Jr., present-day pastor of New Bethel Baptist Church.

"That shoot-up incident was the opening to black political power in Detroit," Rev. Smith continued. "The balance between black and white jurors would change. Coleman Young would be elected [the city's first African American] mayor four years later [1974]."

Rev. Smith was born in 1951 in the coal-mining town of Pratt City, Alabama. He began preaching in Pratt City at the age of seventeen. He was pastor at Bethel Church in Birmingham, Alabama, where his father was a pastor. "Any black person in Birmingham in the 1950s and '60s was involved in politics," he said. Late Detroit pastor William Holly started bringing Rev. Smith to preach in Detroit when Rev. Smith was just nineteen years old. Rev. Holly helped orchestrate the New Bethel transition while C. L. Franklin was in a coma.

"When I started here the first message I got from Mayor Young was to bring him some golden fried chicken and peach cobbler," Rev. Smith said. "We were going to watch football. I declined the invitation. I told him I didn't want him to get to know me as a caterer. I wanted to invite the mayor of Birmingham up and let him tell [Young] the kind of guy I was so he could use me in proper positions. We did share meals after that in the mansion and different homes. The point is the mayor knew of the church as a place to also get good food.

"Before the [1967] riots there were a lot of restaurants around here. The neighborhood was a main business thoroughfare. This area has been neglected all through the years since then. Enterprise zones, tax zones, tax-free zones, all to encourage business, this neighborhood has never been included in anything for rehabilitation. One street over, which is Rosa Parks Boulevard [formerly Twelfth Street], they put a whole shopping center there. But Lynwood proper itself, nothing."

The 1967 Detroit riot was one of the most destructive riots in United States history with 43 people killed, 1,189 injured, and more than 2,000 buildings destroyed. The riot began at Rosa Parks Boulevard and Clairmount Street, not far from the church.

Rev. Smith still works in the community and conducts voter registration drives, but he also travels to Haiti once a month to guide relief efforts. "They have red beans and rice with rich oils," he said with a satisfied smile. "They take a chicken drumstick and split it into five little pieces. It is so good. Here, I don't want red beans and rice. But when I'm there with their cooking, it is the love that goes in it. That is all they got."

Food is as powerful as the soul of religion for Rev. Smith. He cannot stop talking. "To be soulful is to have emotions that you connect with emotions of others," he said as his baritone echoed about the still kitchen. "It is to be able to emphasize and sympathize.

"To feel what another person is feeling is to have soul."

Audrey Towns's Pound Cake

The New Bethel Baptist Church began preparing food in its main floor kitchen in 1963. The historic pound cake recipe was handed down to Audrey Towns, church member since 1985. Fellow church elder Karla Ross pointed out the basic nature of the recipe. "You know old ladies didn't write down specific amounts of ingredients. I usually add more of the ingredients until it tastes as I remember."

(Serves 10)

Ingredients

8 eggs
1 pound butter, softened
3½ cups sifted flour
8 tablespoons whipping cream

2⅔ cups sugar
1 teaspoon vanilla extract
1 teaspoon lemon extract

Directions

Preheat the oven to 350°F. Separate the eggs. Whip the egg whites and set aside.

In a large bowl, blend all the other ingredients, adding the egg yolks two at a time, and the whipped egg whites last.

Pour into a greased Bundt cake pan and bake for 1 hour.

Part 4

Vegan Soul

ORIGINAL SOUL VEGETARIAN

◆◆◆

203 E. 75th Street, Chicago, Illinois
(773) 224-0104 • www.originalsoulvegetarian.com

DETROIT VEGAN SOUL

◆◆◆

8029 Agnes Street, Detroit, Michigan
(313) 649-2759 • www.detroitvegansoul.com

AROUND EVERY CORNER THERE IS A NEW VIEW ON LIFE. This maxim dictates the swagger of a walk along East Seventy-Fifth Street on the South Side of Chicago: moving from the 50-Yard Line, 69 E. Seventy-Fifth Street, a lounge that is known for the city's historic "Steppers" dance craze, to Original Soul Vegetarian, aka "Soul Veg," located in a former nursery school at 203 E. Seventy-Fifth Street.

Soul Veg opened in 1982 as one of America's first vegan soul food restaurants. Back then there were more Village People than vegans.

In the 1970s Warren Brown was a jukebox operator on the South Side of Chicago and president of his family's Eastern Music Corp. He worked all the South Side soul food hot spots and dance clubs. Eastern Music was the first African American business to install a jukebox in downtown Chicago when the Hyatt Regency opened in 1974 on East Wacker Drive. Brown worked the jukebox in the hotel lounge.

Today he is Prince Asiel Ben-Israel, owner of Soul Veg. His wife was born in 1939 as Patty Brown; she is now Yohanna Ben-Israel. Yohanna is one of his four wives.

Prince Ben-Israel was born in 1941 at Forty-Third and Evans in Chicago. His father, Archie Brown, was a cook on the Santa Fe Railroad. In the 1980s Prince Asiel

The Original Soul Vegetarian in Chicago is a template for the acclaimed Detroit Vegan Soul in Michigan.

Ben-Israel was leader of the Black Hebrew Israelite sect, a group of more than three hundred Chicagoans who believed they were direct descendants of ancient Israelites.

Ben-Israel is no longer involved with that group but in the mid-2000s began his own community development advocacy organization called Better World, which he said is more inclusive of African American and white Jewish people.

Ben-Israel began researching his roots. "I began to identify some of us as African Hebrews, or the Jews of the Bible—the original people," he said in gentle tones. "In the Book of Genesis in the fifteenth chapter, twelfth verse, it said Abraham's people would go into a land that is not theirs and they shall serve and afflict [enslave] them four hundred years. All my life growing up I had heard black people had been in America four hundred years."

Prince Asiel Ben-Israel, longtime owner of Original Soul Vegetarian, in his dining room.

He knew the richness of traditional soul food was killing African American men and women. "God gives you the responsibility for thinking about the choice between life and death. The Book of Genesis said there was a diet that was given for a holistic man and woman. And it was the vegan diet. It is in Genesis 1:29, which was the basis in which this restaurant grew out of: 'And God said, Behold, I have given you every herb bearing seed, which is upon the face of all the earth, and every tree, in the which is the fruit of a tree yielding seed; to you it shall be for meat.'"

Ben-Israel did not stop there.

"And we went to Israel in May 1968, one month after Martin Luther King spoke in Memphis [his final sermon] that God allowed him to go to the mountaintop, look over, and see the promised land," he continued. "My wife and three hundred of us in the African Hebrew Israelite movement made the trip. Can you imagine a kid from the South Side of Chicago realizing that he was part of that vision that Dr. King saw? My wife was a schoolteacher. I was in the family jukebox business. We had to make changes in our life. If we were going to be a healthy people we had to start with diets."

He turned a corner.

When the African Hebrew Israelite group returned to Chicago they began talking to friends on the South Side. Almost all members of the group had become vegans during their pilgrimage. "We realized a lot of people were looking for alternative diets," he said. "We've seen Army and Lou's close. Gladys closed. They were killing all their original clients. They couldn't last with high blood pressure and diabetes. They were eating themselves to death. This food is to bring life. I've never let people cook the food angry or bitter. Because you are what you create.

"This restaurant became known for this new place that doesn't serve any meat. We called it 'Soul Vegetarian' because we created a taste that was palatable for the people. We knew how to make cauliflower taste like chicken. We knew how to make

Former Soul Veg cook Asiah Henderson preparing the restaurant's BBQ Twist.

pancakes without the butter and milk. We have kale every day. It's a high source of iron. When we started no one knew about kale."

Popular lunch and dinner items include the Jerkfu Wrap, made with sautéed onions, bell peppers, and seasoned jerk tofu wrapped in a spinach tortilla, and a hamburger named after Marcus Garvey that is made with TVP (textured vegetable protein), accented with grilled onions and mushrooms and served on a whole wheat bun.

Ben-Israel's son R. L. Brown manages Soul Veg. He is one of Ben-Israel's seventeen children. "When I went back to Israel and Africa I picked up the African culture," explained Ben-Israel, who also operates Soul Vegetarian restaurants in Johannesburg, South Africa, and in the capital city of Accra, Ghana. "Rather than have girlfriends, like most men do, I married the women that said they loved me and that I loved. So out of the four wives, I had another family. R.L. is from my second wife, Havanah. I have four children by her."

In April 2014 Ben-Israel pleaded guilty in federal court to one count of violating federal law by lobbying on behalf of the oppressive regime of Zimbabwe's president despite US economic sanctions. He was attempting to get sanctions lifted while failing to register as an agent for a foreign government. News reports said that Ben-Israel walked into court carrying a polished wood cane from West Africa.

Ben-Israel said his wife Yohanna designed the cuisine and menu. "I started the tasting to make sure it met the standard of somebody who was a meat, fish, and chicken eater. All our recipes came out of our minds." And Soul Veg has even more flavors of ice cream than Ben-Israel has children. The restaurant created its own soy ice cream, which grew into thirty-one flavors including piña colada, coconut, lime, banana, and strawberry.

Photos of former Chicago mayor Richard M. Daley are found throughout the three-room restaurant. Near the front counter there is a signed and framed August 23, 2002, proclamation from Mayor Daley commemorating Soul Vegetarian's twentieth anniversary. Minister Louis Farrakhan and his aides have visited Soul Veg. The late Whitney Houston checked out Soul Veg. Houston and her husband, Bobby Brown, accompanied Ben-Israel to Israel.

"She liked our barbecue," said Ben-Israel while holding a picture of himself with Houston and Brown in Israel. "I was in DC and Whitney and Bobby were in Minister Farrakhan's [October 2000] Million Family March. I was a speaker. She gave me her number and we talked for two years before the trip actually took place. I took her, her husband, her daughter, and her brother who was a basketball player." (Houston's half-brother Gary Garland played for the NBA's Denver Nuggets.)

Just like Houston's music, vegan soul food has crossed over. "Our customers are fifty-five percent white," Ben-Israel said. "They come from all over the country. "

The Great Society is larger than life at Detroit Vegan Soul, a storefront café in the West Village neighborhood of Detroit.

A mid-May 2014 visit to the restaurant coincided with the fiftieth anniversary of President Lyndon Johnson's Great Society speech, his May 22, 1964, commencement address before seventy thousand people at the University of Michigan in nearby Ann Arbor. A fan of Franklin Roosevelt's New Deal, Johnson was capturing the adventure and imagination of the mid-1960s in attempts to eliminate poverty and racial injustice and transform America with a united front.

And now a sign near the front counter of Detroit Vegan Soul reads SOUL FOOD MADE FROM WHOLE FOOD. Owner-operators Kirsten Ussery-Boyd and Erika Boyd would have been unable to open their restaurant in 1964. The African American entrepreneurs are married.

The thirty-seat café's walls are avocado with accents of orange (for sweet potato) and brown, symbolic of the whole earth. The food is a delight ranging from a "catfish" tofu—cornmeal-battered tofu with an awesome secret seasoning accompanied by a broccoli-corn medley and redskin potatoes sautéed in olive oil—to the top seller "Soul Platter"—macaroni and cheese, tenderly smoked collard greens, maple-glazed yams, black-eyed peas, and corn bread muffins. Their menu is 100 percent plant based with zero animal fat.

Erika is the executive chef; Kirsten works the room and handles marketing—a rare function at most small business soul food restaurants.

Kirsten Ussery-Boyd (left) and Erika Boyd, the visionary owners of Detroit Vegan Soul.

"We grew up eating soul food," Kirsten said before a Saturday evening rush at the restaurant. "Erika was veganizing family recipes. Family and friends loved it so we thought 'Why not open a restaurant?' There aren't a lot of vegan options in Detroit. It becomes a good entry point into vegan eating."

The roots of the restaurant emerged in 2010 as a catering business. The physical space debuted in September 2013 in a former bakery and deli. After just a few months, the alternative weekly *Metro Times* named Detroit Vegan Soul as "Best Soul Food" in the city; *Hour Detroit* magazine named it "Best Vegan in the City" in 2013. Notables such as Professor Griff from Public Enemy and spiritual leader Michael Beckwith found their way to Detroit Vegan Soul in its nascent days. The owner-operators live in the West Village, a designated historic district near downtown that contains a blend of apartments and small homes.

Erika and Kirsten became vegans in 2009. "Even traditional soul food restaurants are recognizing soul food needs healthier options because of the alarming rate of diabetes and cancer in the African American community in particular," Kirsten said. "You can still have a comforting, nostalgic experience with soul food here."

Many customers ask how vegan food can actually be soul food.

The "catfish" tofu is as good as and much more tender than any actual catfish soul food I have had. Erika's grandmother Doretha Hall cooked for many prominent Detroit pastors and politicians. "I grew up coming to her house on a Saturday morning," Erika recalled. "She had fried up catfish pieces, grits, and eggs. I was inspired to do something with tofu to mimic the catfish I grew up with. Once I understood how to work with tofu, understanding the different seasonings, how I could use sea vegetables to get that fish flavor, I just started experimenting with it. I finally nailed it one day." The seasoning combination is a secret. Erika creates her own seasoning blends.

She was born in 1973 on the northwest side of Detroit about five miles from the historic Baker's Keyboard Lounge soul food restaurant. Erika related, "My father [Sandy Boyd] went to school with Marvin Gaye and Diana Ross. He passed away of prostate cancer. That spurred me into looking a little more closely at his habits. He didn't smoke. He didn't drink. I thought if I changed my diet I could stop some of these diet-related illnesses from happening to me.

"Our family gatherings always centered around food. My grandmother cooked everything from the main course to the dessert. She made unleavened bread for communion every first Sunday at Hartford Memorial Baptist Church. And I grew up in a church that had over five thousand members. She took it very seriously. She would put on her white clothing and purify herself before she made the communion bread. There was a whole ritual to go along with it."

Kirsten is from the hot barbecue land of Hickory, North Carolina. She was born in 1978. "I grew up on pulled pork," she said. "Huge hams every holiday. Turkey necks. I'm an only child but my mom has eleven brothers and sisters. Whenever there was a holiday we'd all barbecue. It was all about feeding and having a good time."

The wonderful coffee cake, snickerdoodles, and lemon pound cakes at Detroit Vegan Soul are courtesy of Erika and Kirsten's extended family. Kirsten was raised by her mother, Lucy Irene Ussery, who owned and operated Irene's Classic Breads and Cakes in North Carolina before coming to be the baker at Vegan Soul. Lucy Irene formerly operated a textile toe seaming business and became a vegan in 2012. "She was inspired by what we were doing," she said. "She bakes every week and sends the vegan cakes up here."

African American veganism is not a new trend, according to Amy C. Evans at the Southern Foodways Alliance. "There's a community in Greenwood, Mississippi, at Shilo Seventh Day Adventist Church, where veganism is part of their gospel," she said in a phone interview. "It is a century-old congregation. They're part of a church garden program in the Delta. They have church dinners and share their produce with surrounding communities. It is something that is gaining popularity on a national level. It's not necessarily new but since it has gained popularity there is a market for it."

Kirsten agreed. "When we talk about African American history we like to talk about getting the scraps from the table," she said. "But the reality is that a lot of Africans brought plants from Africa, a lot of the staples that we have in our diet. It was plant based. It wasn't the heavy meat-based meals we think about today."

Erika went one step further and added, "The modern-day soul food—heavy pork-based, meat-based diet that African Americans adopted—is just another residual effect of slavery. We didn't come over here with the way we eat food now. This is the effect of the African holocaust, as I call it. We ate what the master did not want. Now we have choices. We've been educated. We don't have to do the same thing over and over again expecting different results."

Erika and Kirsten were mentored by Ben-Israel and Original Soul Vegetarian. "They are pioneers in this vegan soul food movement," Erika said. "You are talking over thirty years on the South Side of Chicago, right in the middle of an African American neighborhood. They have thrived all this time."

When Erika and Kirsten became vegans in the mid-1990s they traveled from Detroit to eat at Soul Veg. "We couldn't believe the flavor profile that was presented to us," Erika said. "We were inspired to look even closer to a vegan diet. Then, after becoming vegans we figured if they can do this business model in the middle of the

South Side and be successful, certainly we can take a chance and see what people think in Detroit.

"We need vegan restaurants in every black neighborhood around the country. Is everybody going to choose this option? No. But some people will. Some people will ask, 'How can you make tofu taste like catfish?' We were totally inspired by Soul Vegetarian's willingness to think outside the box."

Creative genius often doesn't go a long way at the bank. Erika reflected, "Capital was our big challenge. People's fear of the unknown. People's fear of vegan. People in the black community. Customers. Just the perception of women business owners. We had never been in the restaurant business. There were a lot of assumptions."

Erika and Kirsten raised $40,000 with help of family members. Erika's brother Sammie Boyd handcrafted all the maple plywood counters for the restaurant. He also found the photograph of segregated "Ladies," "Men," and "Colored" bathrooms from the pre–Great Society era. He covered the black-and-white photograph with a clear glass frame that was etched with the word "History."

Erika and Kirsten are steadfast in bringing what Kirsten calls "food justice" to the Detroit community. "When you got kids to feed and a little bit of money is only going to go so far, the dollar menu at McDonald's looks really appealing," Kirsten said. "You get fresh food from the market, you can make something that will last much longer and it is not empty calories. It is nutrients. We have to re-educate people how to use fresh food, how to buy it, how to eat it."

Black-Eyed Pea Hummus

(Serves 4–6)

Ingredients

1 15-ounce can black-eyed peas, rinsed
   and drained
2 tablespoons tahini
1 teaspoon minced garlic or 2 cloves
   garlic, crushed

3 tablespoons lemon juice
3 tablespoons olive oil
Salt and pepper to taste
Warm water

Directions

Combine all ingredients in a blender or food processor. Blend for 3 to 5 minutes on low speed until thoroughly mixed and smooth. If hummus is too thick, add warm water, 1 tablespoon at a time, until it reaches desired consistency.

Place hummus in a serving bowl. Create a shallow well in the center of the hummus. Add a small amount (1–2 tablespoons) of olive oil in the well.

Sauteed Collard Greens

(Serves 8)

Ingredients

3 bunches collard greens, stems
    discarded and leaves cut into 1-inch
    strips
½ cup olive oil
3 cloves garlic, thinly sliced
1 teaspoon sea salt

½ teaspoon black pepper
3 tablespoons namashoya
½ medium red bell pepper; ½ medium
    orange bell pepper; ½ medium yellow
    bell pepper, julienne sliced

Directions

Bring a large pot of salted water to a boil. Add the collard greens in batches and cook until just tender, about 10 minutes. Drain the greens in a colander and rinse under cold water to cool; squeeze to remove any excess water.

Heat the oil in a large saucepan over medium heat. Add the garlic and cook, stirring, for 1 minute. Add the greens, sea salt, and pepper. Cook, tossing often, until wilted and tender, 3 to 4 minutes. Place in a serving bowl and toss with the namashoya and peppers to serve.

Black-Eyed Pea and Collard Greens Soup

(Serves 6)

Ingredients

1 tablespoon olive oil
1 medium yellow onion, chopped
3 garlic cloves, minced
2 carrots, cut into rounds
3 red potatoes, chopped
1 yam, chopped
1 bunch collard greens, stems
  removed

3 cups cooked black-eyed peas
1 tablespoon dried basil
1 tablespoon dried oregano
4 cups vegetable stock
1 tablespoon apple cider vinegar
Sea salt and freshly ground black
  pepper

Directions

Place the olive oil in a pot and heat to medium. Add the onions and garlic and sauté until the onions are translucent, about 5 minutes. Add the carrots, potatoes, yam, collards, black-eyed peas, basil, oregano, and vegetable stock. Bring to a boil, cover, reduce heat, and simmer 20 to 25 minutes.

Stir in the apple cider vinegar and season with salt and pepper to taste. Remove from heat and serve.

Acknowledgments

Deep gratitude for pathfinding, research, and support:

Gene Barge, Pat Embry, Amy Evans and the Southern Foodways Alliance, Libby Lloyd and the Little Rock Convention and Visitor's Bureau, Mississippi Senator John Horhn and the Mississippi Civil Rights Museum, Tamika Mallory, the Memphis Convention and Visitors Bureau, Joyce Moore, the Nashville Public Library, Sylvia E. Russell, Tim Sampson of the Stax Museum in Memphis, Angelo Varias, Liz Williams and the Southern Food and Beverage Museum, my photographer Paul Natkin, my empathetic editor Lisa Reardon—and the restaurant owners and voices of the movement who were willing to share their stories.

INDEX

Page numbers in italics indiate photographs and captions.

Aaron, Henry "Hank," 84, 91
Abernathy, Ralph, 82, 114, 127
Adams, Frank, 126
Addams, Jane, 125–126
affirmative action, xi
African Hebrew Israelite, 208
Africanne on Main, 130–137, *130, 135*
Agee, Pam, *199*
Alamo Theatre, 30
Alcenia Healing the Soul (Chester-Tamayo), 53
Alcenia's, 48–56, *49, 51*
Alcenia's Sweet Potato Pudding, 57
Ali, Kamal, 156, 157–158, *159*
Ali, Mahaboob Ben, 149–150, *149,* 151, 152–153, *155,* 156, 157, 158–159
Ali, Muhammad, 165, 187
Ali, Nizam, 157–158
Ali, Virginia, 149, *149,* 150, 151–153, 154, 154–156, 157–158, *157, 159*
Allen, George, 135
Alston, Bettye, 50–51, 53
Amato, Jerry, 16, 18, *19,* 20, 22

Amato, John Dennis "Denny," Jr., 19, *19,* 20, 22
American Civil Liberties Union, 8, 9
Andrews, Helena, 147
Anglin, Helen Maybell, ix, x, xi, xiv, 174, 180
Ansumana, Catherine, 131
Ansumana, Francis, 131, 132
Armstrong, Patricia J., 105–106, 110, 111–112, 113–114, *114, 115,* 116–117
Army and Lou's, 171, 179, 187–188, 208
Army and Lou's Macaroni and Cheese, 192
At the River I Stand (Beifuss), xv
Audrey Town's Pound Cake, 202

Bailey, Loree, xvi
Bailey, Louise, *199*
Bailey, Pearl, 150
Bailey, Walter, xvi
Baker, Chris and Fannie, 183
Baker, Clarence, 183, 184, 186
Baker, Maury, 186
Baker, Ray, 185
Baker's Keyboard Lounge, 182–191, *182, 185, 191,* 212
Baldwin, James, vii, 6, 9

Ballard, Florence, 196
Banks, Art, 87–88
Banks, Homer, 40
Banks, Marguerite, 177
Baraka, Amiri, xi–xii, 146
Barby, William, 114
Barge, Gene, xiii, xiv, 169
Barnes, Elizabeth, 197
Barry, Marion, 112
Bates, Daisy L. Gatson, 94, 98
Bates, Willie Earl, 37–39, 41, 42, 43, 44, 45–46, *46*
Beckwith, Michael, 211
Beifuss, Joan Turner, xv
Belafonte, Harry, 84, 199
Bell, Al, xiii, 40, 42, 97–98
Bell, William, 43
Ben-Israel, Prince Asiel, 205–210, *207,* 213
Ben-Israel, Yohanna, 205, 209
Ben's Chili Bowl, 142, 143, 149–159, *150, 151*
Ben's Chili Bowl: Fifty Years of a Washington, D.C. Landmark, 157–158
Ben's Next Door and Gift Shop, 150
Bertha's Kitchen, 119
Better World, 206
beverages, Georgia Peach Martini, 93
Beyoncé, 20
Biden, Joe, 164
Big Apple Inn, The, 26–35, *27*

Big Apple Inn's Pig Ear Sandwich, 27, 36
Billy Simpson's House of Seafood and Steaks, 147
"Black Broadway," 149–150, 154
Black United Youth (BUY), 100
Black-Eyed Pea and Collard Greens Soup, 217
Black-Eyed Pea Hummus, 215
Bland, Bobby "Blue," 52
Bloody Sunday, 75
Blue Bird Club, 184
Bond, Julian, xiii, 81
Booker T. and the MG's, 37
Booker T. Theatre, 150
Bougard, Lydia Jeanette Barnes, 196–197, *197*
Boyd, Erika, 210–214, *211*
Boyd, Sammie, 214
Bread Pudding, Ruby's, 181
Bridges, Ruby, 100
Brinsfield, Sol, 73
Brixton, 143
Brown, Bobby (activist), 100, 103
Brown, Bobby (singer), 209–210
Brown, Dwight, 100
Brown, Imogene Dix, 102
Brown, James, 9–10, 30, 165, 187–188

Brown, Minnijean, 8, 98–101, 102–103
Brown, Phyllis, 98, *99*, 100–101, 102, 103
Brown, R. Jess, 34
Brown, R. L., 209
Brown, Rudolph, xvi
Brown, Warren, 205
Brown, Willie "Bob," 102
Brown Chapel African Methodist Episcopal (AME) Church, 75
Brown-Wright, Flonzie, 32–35, *32*
Brubeck, Dave, 183
Burroughs, Tyrone, 37, 45–46
Bush, Barbara, 17
Bush, George W., 4, 5, 17
Butler, Eliza, 196–197
Butts, Mattie, 196, *199*
Byrd, Ann, *199*

cake
    Audrey Town's Pound Cake, 202
    Mississippi Tea Cake, 35
    Old-Fashioned Pound Cake, 104
Calderon, Felipe, 4
Campbell, Little Milton, 65–66
Caramel Icing, 104
Carawan, Guy, 126, 127
Carew, Harry Julian, 184
Carmichael, Stokely, 9, 26, 108, 146, 154
Carter, Jason, 79
Carter, Jimmy, 82
Carter, Victoria, 135
Carver projects, 75
Castle, Virgi, 9
Castro, Fidel, 169
catfish, 96–97, 212
Central Grocery, 18–19, 22

Chase, Dooky (II), 8, 9
Chase, Edgar Dooky, III, 9–12, *11*, 13
Chase, Edgar Dooky, Sr., *3*, 4
Chase, Leah, x–xi, *xii*, xii–xiii, 3–9, *3*, *8*, 9, 10, 11–12, 13
Cheeks, Maurice, xv
Chester, H. S., 54
Chester-Tamayo, Betty Joyce "B. J.," 48–50, *51*, *52*, 53–56
Chez Billy, 147
Chicago Housing Authority projects, xv
chicken
    David Swett's Famous Fried Chicken, 118
    hot, 110–111
    Odessa's Baked Chicken, 78
chili, 99–100
chitlin' circuit, xiii, 65–66
Christian, Charlie, 60
Christie, Chris, 15
civil rights movement
    Armstrong on, 111–114, 116–117
    Brown-Wright and, 33–34
    as context, x
    Harlem House and, 52–53
    Paschal's and, 79, *80*
    patronage lost after, 111
    role of soul food restaurants in, xiii
    Ruby's Restaurant and, 171–172
    Saunders and, 127–128
    turning point of, xi
    See also integration; King, Martin Luther, Jr.; segregation; sit-in movement

Clark-Chester, Alcenia, *52*, 54–55
Claudio, James, 145
Cleaver, Eldridge, vii, xvi
Cleaves, Clint and Irene, 41–42
Clinton, Bill, xvi, *79*, 97, 101, 165–166, 167
Clinton, George, 108
Clinton, Hillary, 151
Clinton Foundation, 165
Club Plantation, 60
Colbert, John, 186
Coleslaw, 160
Collard Greens, Sauteed, 216
Collard Greens Soup, Black-Eyed Pea and, 217
Congress of Racial Equality (CORE), 5, 113
Conyers, John, 196
Cook, Sam, 6
Corner Social, 161
Cosby, Bill, 152, 156, 157–158, 159
Cousaert, Freddy, 144
Creole Sausage Stuffed Tomatoes, 13–14
Creole Tomato Sauce, 24–25
Creole tomato sauce, 18
Crockett Stephen A., Jr., 142–143
Crown's, 64
Crump, Edward Hull "Boss," 41
Curve Riot, 38

Daley, Richard M., 174, 209
Daves, J. Herman, xiii
David Swett's Famous Fried Chicken, 118
Davis, Danny, 172, 179
Davis, Joanne, *199*
Davis, Melvin, 186

Davis, Miles, 150, 182–183, 184, 186, 190
Dawit, Fasil, 156
DC riots, *155*
Debris sandwich, 16–17
DeBuys, Larry, 16–17
Dee-Dex snack bar, 122
Demczuk, Bernard, 143–144, 156, 158
DeSaussure, Charles, *123*, 124
desserts
    Alcenia's Sweet Potato Pudding, 57
    Audrey Town's Pound Cake, 202
    Caramel Icing, 104
    Eliza Butler's pound cake, 196–197
    Kathy Watson's Popular Sweet Potato Pie, 47
    lemon icebox pie, 42
    Old-Fashioned Pound Cake, 104
    Ruby's Bread Pudding, 181
    Sizzlin' Peach Cobbler, 193–194
Detroit Vegan Soul, *206*, 210–214
DeVries, Stacia, 76–77
Dexter Parsonage, 71, 72
Diners, Drive-Ins and Dives, 55
Dinkins, David, 166
Dooky Chase's, x, *xii*, xii–xiii, 3–12, *4*, *5*
Dr. John, 58, 65, 66
Dunning, Calshea, 72
Dunning, Calvin, 71, 72–74, *74*, 76–77
Dunning, Calvin, Jr., 72
Dunning, Odessa McCall, 71, 72–74, *74*, 76–77
Duster, Donald, 38

Eastern Music Corps, 205
Edna's, xi, 171–174,
    178. *See also* Ruby's
    Restaurant
Ellington, Duke, 10, 60, 150
Ellzey, Patricia, 15–16, *16*
Emoja Almella, 50–53
entrées
    Army and Lou's
        Macaroni and
        Cheese, 192
    David Swett's Famous
        Fried Chicken, 118
    Keli-Willy (Sweet
        Fried Plantain and
        Vegetable Medley),
        138
    Marvin Dijon Mussels,
        148
    Odessa's Baked
        Chicken, 78
    Salmon Croquettes, 170
    Sweetie Pie's Mac and
        Cheese, 67
Estrada, Brandon, 20
Evans, Amy C., xiv–xv,
    137, 168–169, 213
Evers, Charles, 29–30, 33
Evers, Medgar, 26, 30,
    33–34

Farish, Walter, 29
Farrakhan, Louis, vii–viii,
    196, 209, 210
Ferdi po'boy, 15, 20, *21*
Ferragamo, Vince, 11
Floyd, Alan, 184–185
Floyd, Eddie, 40
Ford, Robert, 128
Four Way, The, 37–46,
    37, 55
Fourway Grill, 37
Fox, 121–122
Franklin, Aretha, x, *xiv*,
    xiv, 37, 44, 86, 195, 198,
    199

Franklin, C. L., xiv, 44, 88,
    89, 195–196, 197, 198,
    199, *199*, 200
Freedom House, 9
Freedom Riders, 5, 8, 9,
    10, 33, 113–114

Gadsden, Martha Lou,
    119, 121–124, *122*, *123*
Gadsden, Ruth "Butter,"
    121, *122*, 124, 125
Garnett, Christopher, *177*
Gay, Marvin, Sr., 144–145
Gaye, Marvin, 141–142,
    143, 144–146, 183, 191,
    212
gentrification, 142–143
Gentry, Howard, 106–107
Gentry, Howard, Jr.,
    106–108, 112
George, Barbara, 15
Georgia Peach Martini, 93
Gillespie, Dizzy, 10, 86
Gladys Luncheonette, 174,
    180, 208
Glover, Danny, 108, 174
Gold Cook Book, The, 71, 73
Goodson, Willie, *199*
Gordy, Berry, 196
Grant, Janet, *21*
Greene, Gael, 165, 167
Griff, Professor, 211
Gullah (Geechee),
    120–121, 125

H and H Cafe, 180
Hager, Jenna Bush, 55
Haley, Oretha Castle, 9
Hall, Carsey, 34
Hall, Doretha, 212
Hamilton, Betty, 21
Harlem House, 52–53
Harper, Stephen, 4
Harris, Neil Patrick, 20
Harvey, Fred, 112–113
Harvey, Fred, Jr., 113

Henderson, Asiah, *208*
Henderson, Gloria, 174,
    177, 178, 179
Henderson, Henry,
    173–174, *173*, 176–179
Highlander Folk School,
    xiii, 125
Hill, Tony, 130, 132, *133*
Hilton, Eric, 141–142,
    142, 143, 145, 146–147
Holly, William, 200
Holyfield, Evander, 74
Hooker, Earl, 58
Horne, Lena, 86
Horton, Myles, xiii,
    125–126
hot chicken, 110–111
Hotel Theresa, 169
housing projects, xv,
    15–16, 61, 63, 64, 75,
    100, 124, 132, 137, 163
Houston, Whitney,
    209–210
Hummus, Black-Eyed Pea,
    215
Hunter-Brown, Irma, 97
Hurricane Katrina, 12, 22
Huskey, Lloyd, 97

integration
    in Biloxi, 34
    effects of, 88, 117
    Farish Street and, 29
    Little Rock Nine and,
        8, 98–99, 100–101,
        101–102
    in Nashville, 106–107
    planning for, 6
    See also civil rights
        movement;
        segregation; sit-in
        movement
International African
    American Museum, 119
Isbell, Albert, 98
Isley, Ron, 65

Jackson, Jesse
    Anglin and, ix
    Army and Lou's and,
        188
    Ben's Chili Bowl and,
        156
    Dooky Chase's and,
        xii–xiii
    Edna's and, xi,
        172–173, 174
    King and, xv–xvi
    Mother's Restaurant
        and, 20
    Odessa's Blessings
        and, 74
    Paschal's Restaurant
        and, 82, 84, 86, 89,
        90
    on role of restaurants,
        x
    Ruby's Restaurant and,
        172, *172*
    Swett's Restaurant
        and, 108
Jackson, Juanita, 186
Jackson, Mahalia, 199
Jackson, Maynard, 84
Jackson Packing Company,
    28
jambalaya, 18, *18*
    Jerry's Jambalaya,
        23–24
James, Elmore, 26
Jay Z, 20
Jefferson, Eddie, 184
Jenkins, Esau, 127
Jerry's Jambalaya, 23–24
Jessie Junior's, 122
Jim Crow laws, xiii, 89.
    See also civil rights
    movement; segregation;
    sit-in movement
Johnson, L. S., 34
Johnson, Lyndon B., xi,
    106, 154, 210
Johnson, Marian, 90

Johnson, Syl, xiv, *178*, 180

Johnson's Luncheonette, 162

Joiner, Lillie, 179

Jones, Booker T., 40

Jungle Fever, 165

Jungle Inn, 150

Kathy Watson's Popular Sweet Potato Pie, 47

Keli-Willy (Sweet Fried Plantain and Vegetable Medley), 138

Kendall, Mae Armster, 82

Kennedy, Robert F., 30–31, 74, 165

Khan, Chaka, vi–viii, 65

King, B. B., 44, 52

King, Coretta Scott, 71, *73*, 83, 124, 128, 172

King, Don, 39

King, Martin Luther, Jr.
    Anglin and, x
    Army and Lou's and, 188
    assassination of, xiv, 83–84
    Chase and, 8
    in Detroit, 199
    Dexter Parsonage and, 71
    Edna's and, 172
    final sermon of, 207
    food and, 128
    Four Way and, 37, 38–41
    Franklin and, 196
    Highlander Folk School and, xiii, 126
    Jackson and, xv–xvi
    MIA and, 71–72
    Odessa's Blessings and, 74
    Paschal's Restaurant and, 81, *85*, 87, 88
    riots after assassination of, 141, 142, 143, 154, 156, 168, 175–176, 191
    Ruby's Restaurant and, 82
    Saunders and, 127
    Scaritt-Bennett and, 117
    SCLC and, 112
    Webb-Christburg and, 75–76
    Wright and, 34–35
    See also civil rights movement

King, Martin Luther, Sr., 6

King, Yolanda ("Yoki"), 71

Kitty Kat Restaurant, 33

Knowledge Quest, 43

Ku Klux Klan, 26, 113

Kyles, Gwen, xv

Kyles, Samuel "Billy," xv

La Carrousel Lounge, 86–87, 90

Ladson House, 122

Lamonica, Daryle, 11

Landry, Eddie and Jack, 21

Landry, Frances, 21

Landry, Simon and Mary, 16–17, 19, 20, 21

Lange, Charles and Hortensia, 7

Lassis Inn, 94–103, *95*

Lassiter, Art, 65

Lawson, James, 105, 112, 113

Lee, Geno, Jr., 27–30, *28*, 32–33, 35

Lee, Geno, Sr., 28–29

Lee, Harold, Jr., 29

Lee, Harold, Sr., 29

Lee, Harry, 12

Lee, Mary, 28–29

Lee, Spike, 165

Leipzig, Arthur, 111

lemon icebox pie, 42

LeMoyne-Owen College, 43

Lewis, Betty Jean, 97

Lewis, John, 105, 112

Lewis, Ramsey, xiv, 87, 90, 183

Liberace, 184, *185*

lima beans, 124, 129

Lincoln, Abbey, *143*

Lincoln Theater, 142, 150, 152

Little, Malcolm, 161–162

Little Jack's, 179

Little Palermo, 12, 18

Little Rock Central High School, 98, 101–102, *101*

Little Rock Nine, 8, 98–99, 100–101, 101–102

Liu, Brian, 141

Lorraine Motel, xiv, xv–xvi, *xvi*, 51

Louis, Joe, 3, *3*, 162

Lowe, Rob, 18

lunch counter sit-ins, 105–106, *106*, 112–113, *115. See also* civil rights movement; integration; segregation

Lupo, Salvatore, 18

Lynn, Teri, 65

Ma Musu, Ida, 130–137, *133*

macaroni and cheese
    Army and Lou's Macaroni and Cheese, 192
    Sweetie Pie's Mac and Cheese, 67

Malcolm X, 156, 162, 165, 169

Mallory, Tamika, 163–164, *164*, 169

Mama Quill, 16

Mandela, Winnie, 165

March on Detroit, 199

March on Washington, 82, 196

Marshall, Thurgood, 6

Martha Lou's Kitchen, 119–128, *120, 123*

Martin, Bernice, 42

Martin, Deana, 11, 12

Martin, Trayvon, 103, 164

Martini, Georgia Peach, 93

Marvin, 141–147, *143*, *146*

Marvin Dijon Mussels, 148

Maselli, Frank, 11, 12

Mayfield, Curtis, 141–142, 151

McDaniel, Dustin, 97

McDuffie, Glenn, 21

Meredith, James, x, 6, 30–32, *31*, 66

Merida, Rita, 97

Midler, Bette, 125

Mingus, Charles, 183

Minnehaha Theater, 150

Mississippi Tea Cake, 35

Mitchell, Samuel, Sr., 171

Montgomery, Andre, 65

Montgomery, James, 61

Montgomery, Janice, 62

Montgomery, Linda, 62, 64

Montgomery, Ora, 61

Montgomery, Robbie, 58–66, *58*

Mora, Juan, 27–28

Morgan, Lloyd, Jr., 164

Morial, Ernest "Dutch," 6

Morris, Jodi, 102

Mother's Restaurant, 15–22, *17*

Motown Records, 144, 145–146, 182

Moultrie, Mary, 128

Mulligan, Gerry, 183
Musselwhite, Charlie, 53
My Life (Clinton), xvi

NAACP, 5, 8, 9, 10, 26, 34,
    94, 98, 196
    Brown-Wright and, 34
Nash, Diane, 112
Nashville Christian
    Leadership Council
    (NCLC), 112
Nation of Islam, 162, 196
National Action Network
    (NAN), 163–164
National Civil Rights
    Museum, *xvi*
Nero, Deborah, 190–191
Nero, Gene, 190–191
New Bethel Baptist
    Church and kitchen, 88,
    195–201, *198, 199*
Norman, Sandra D., 136
Norman, Tim, 59, 62
Nunn, Michelle, *79*

Obadek, Biamani, xv
Obama, Barack, 4, 141,
    150
Odessa's Baked Chicken, 78
Odessa's Blessings, 71–77,
    72, 75
Old-Fashioned Pound
    Cake, 104
Operation Breadbasket
    (later Operation PUSH),
    ix, xiii, 82
Original Soul Vegetarian,
    205–210, *206*, 213–214

Parks, Rosa, xiii, 37, 126
Paschal, James, 81, 82–83,
    83, 85–86, 87, 88, 89, 90
Paschal, Robert, 81, 83,
    83, 85–86, 87–88, 90
Paschal: Living the Dream
    (J. Paschal), 82

Paschal's Motor Hotel,
    86–87
Paschal's Potato Salad, 92
Paschal's Restaurant, 53,
    55, 79–91, *79*
Patterson, Esmond, 89
Peach Cobbler, Sizzlin,'
    193–194
Peach Martini, Georgia, 93
Pearl's Place, xv, xvi
Pelican Brief, The, 151
People's Grocery
    Company, 38
Peters, Mae "Odie Mae,"
    20–21
Pig Ear Sandwich, Big
    Apple Inn's, 27, 36
Pimengel, Nick, 141
Plantain and Vegetable
    Medley, Sweet Fried
    (Keli-Willy), 138
Polite, Jimmy, 97
Potato Salad, Paschal's, 92
Pound Cake, Audrey
    Town's, 202
Presley, Elvis, 44
Prince, Andre, 111
Prince's Hot Chicken
    Shack, 111
Puckett, Kirby, xv
Pyramid Arena, 48, *49*

Quinn, Pat, 174

Rainey, Ma, 52
Rangel, Charles B., 165,
    166
Rebennack, Mac, 65
Rebuilding Together (RT),
    77
Red Rooster, 161
Redding, Otis, 37
Republic of New Afrika
    (RNA), 6, 199–200
Reynolds, Dolores Grey,
    187, 192

Rhodes, Sam, 61
riots
    after King
        assassination, 141,
        142, 143, 154, 156,
        168, 175–176, 191
    in Detroit, 168, 201
    at University of
        Mississippi, 30–31
    in Washington, DC,
        155
Robinson, Jackie, xiv, 196
Robinson, Smokey, 74, 188
Rock, Chris, 90, 165
Rockefeller, Winthrop, 98
Rogers, Ben, 109
Rogers, Joe, Sr., 52
Rollins, Alphonso and
    Esther, 152
Ross, Betsy, vii–viii
Ross, Diana, 165, 212
Rove, Karl, 5
Ruby's Bread Pudding, 181
Ruby's Restaurant, x, 82,
    156, 171–180, *175. See
    also* Edna's
Rudolph, Wilma, 108
Ruffin, David, 196
Rush, Bobby, xiii, 65–66
Russell, Herman J., 89–90
Russell's Concessions
    International, 90
Ruth's Diner, 94

Salmon Croquettes, 170
Sampson, Tim, 55
Samuelsson, Marcus, 161,
    167
sandwiches
    Big Apple Inn's Pig Ear
        Sandwich, 27, 36
    Ferdi po'boy, 15, 20, *21*
Santiago, Pat, 20–21
Saulsby, Maggie, *199*
Saunders, William "Bill,"
    125, 126–128, *126*

Sauteed Collard Greens,
    216
Scahill, Jeremy, 147
Scott, Sheldon, 143, 144,
    147, *147*
seafood
    Marvin Dijon Mussels,
        148
    at Mother's, 19
    Salmon Croquettes, 170
segregation, xiii
    banking and, 4
    Clinton and, xvi
    on interstate
        transportation, 33
    Meredith and, 30–31
    Paschal's Motor Hotel
        and, 86
    See also civil rights
        movement;
        integration; sit-in
        movement
Seigenthaler, John, 116
Shackelford, Lottie, 97
Shapiro, Lucy, 177
Sharp, Cedsenall, *199*
Shaw, Robert, 174
Showplace Lounge, 186
Shuttlesworth, Fred, 82
side dishes
    Black-Eyed Pea
        Hummus, 215
    Coleslaw, 160
    Lima Beans, 129
    Paschal's Potato Salad,
        92
    Sauteed Collard
        Greens, 216
Simpson, Ruth, 166–167
Simpsons (gospel group),
    161, 166
Sirleaf, Ellen Johnson, 135
sit-in movement, x,
    105–106, *106*, 112–113,
    115. See also civil rights
    movement

Sizzlin' Peach Cobbler, 193–194
Slack, Marshall, 79–81, *81*, 83–85, 86–87, 88, 89, 90–91
Slur, Jim, 114
Smith, Ben, 9
Smith, Frederick, 52
Smith, Hugh, 183, 186–187, 190
Smith, Kelly Miller, 112
Smith, Robert, Jr., 88, 89, 195–196, 198–201, *200*
Smith-Simmons, Doratha "Dodie," xii, *xii*, 5, 8, 9, 10
Smithsonian magazine, 151
Snyder, Dan, 135
Solomon's Fisheries, 180
Soul Eatery, 171
soul food, as term, xi–xii
Soul Queen Restaurant, ix, 171, 180
Soul Veg. *See* Original Soul Vegetarian
Soup, Black-Eyed Pea and Collard Greens, 217
Southern Christian Leadership Conference (SCLC), 40, 128, 154
Southern Food and Beverage Museum, x, xii
Southern Foodways Alliance, xv, 137, 168–169, 213
Southern Kitchen, 64
Spencer, Cheryl, *177*
Staple Singers, 37
Stax Records, xiii, xiv, 37, 39–40, 144

Stern, Ferdinand "Ferdi," 20
Stewart, Edna, x, 171–172, 173, 174, 176–177, 178–179
Stewart, Martha, 20
Streisand, Barbra, 183
Student Nonviolent Coordinating Committee, 105, 154, *155*
"swagger-jacking," x, 142–143
Sweet Fried Plantain and Vegetable Medley (Keli-Willy), 138
sweet potatoes
    Alcenia's Sweet Potato Pudding, 57
    Kathy Watson's Popular Sweet Potato Pie, 47
Sweetie Pie's, 58–66, *59*, *60*, *63*
    Mac and Cheese, 67
Swett, David, 106, 108–111, *109*, 116
Swett, Susie, 108, 111
Swett, Walter, 108, 111
Swett's Restaurant, 105–117, *107*
Sylvia's Restaurant, vii, xiii, 161–169, *166*, *168*

Tamayo, Alcenia Altovise Nia, 54
Tamayo, Will A., "Go-Go," III, 54
Tatum, Art, 183
Taylor, Johnnie, 42
tea cakes, 35

Temptations, 196
Terkel, Studs, 199
Tex, Joe, 40
Thievery Corporation, 141
Thomas, Carla, 44–45
Thomas, Lorene, 44
Thomas, Marvell, xiv, 39–41, 42, 44–45
Thomas, Rufus, 39, 44
Thompson, Helen, xv
Toddle House, 52–53
tomatoes
    Creole Sausage Stuffed Tomatoes, 13–14
    Creole Tomato Sauce, 18, 24–25
Towne, Carlie, 121, 125
Townsend, Robert, 174
Turlow, A. P., 6
Turner, Ike, 58–59, 65, 66
Turner, Tina, 42, 58–59, 65, 66
Tyler, Stephen, 20

Upper Crust, 60, 61, 62, *63*
Uptown Bar, 166
Ussery, Lucy Irene, 213
Ussery-Boyd, Kirsten, 210–214, *211*

Vaughn-Whitaker, Jackie, 187, 188–190, *189*
voter registration, 125, 128

Waddell, Ada, *199*
Walton, Shirley, 39, 40
Washington, Denzel, 151
Washington, Elihue, 94–97, 98, *99*, 100, 103

Washington, Harold, 187
Washington, Walter, 154
Watson, Joe, 94
Watson, Kathy, 47
Watson, Molassis, 94
"We Shall Overcome," 126
Webb-Christburg, Sheyann, 75–76
Welcome to Sweetie Pie's, 62
What's Going On (Gaye), 146
Whitaker, Eric, 182–183, 184, 186–187, 188, *189*, 190
White, Barry, 171
Williams, Liz, x–xi, xii
Williamson, Sonny Boy, 26, 29
Winfrey, Oprah, 62, 107, 156, 180
Wings and Things, 59–60
Witt's, 94
Woods, Bedelia, 163
Woods, Crizette, 163
Woods, Herbert, 162
Woods, Kenneth, 163
Woods, Sylvia, 161, 162, *162*, 166, 167–168
Woods, Van, 163
Woods-Black, Tren'ness, 163, 165, 167–168

X, Malcolm, 156, 162, 165, 169

Young, Andrew, 81, 82, 83, 87, 90
Young, Coleman, 196, 200–201
Young, Jack, 34